SACRED HIGH CITY, SACRED LOW CITY

Advance copy from

OXFORD
UNIVERSITY PRESS

198 Madison Avenue, New York, NY 10016-4314

Title: Sacred High City, Sacred Low City: A Tale of Religious Sites in Two Tokyo Neighborhoods

Author: Steven Heine

Publication date: 12/02/11

Cloth ISBN: 9780199861446
Cloth price: 29.95

SACRED HIGH CITY, SACRED LOW CITY

A Tale of Religious Sites in Two Tokyo Neighborhoods

Steven Heine

OXFORD
UNIVERSITY PRESS

OXFORD
UNIVERSITY PRESS

Oxford University Press, Inc., publishes works that further
Oxford University's objective of excellence
in research, scholarship, and education.

Oxford   New York
Auckland   Cape Town   Dar es Salaam   Hong Kong   Karachi
Kuala Lumpur   Madrid   Melbourne   Mexico City   Nairobi
New Delhi   Shanghai   Taipei   Toronto

With offices in
Argentina   Austria   Brazil   Chile   Czech Republic   France   Greece
Guatemala   Hungary   Italy   Japan   Poland   Portugal   Singapore
South Korea   Switzerland   Thailand   Turkey   Ukraine   Vietnam

Published by Oxford University Press, Inc.
198 Madison Avenue, New York, New York 10016

www.oup.com

Oxford is a registered trademark of Oxford University Press

Library of Congress Cataloging-in-Publication Data
Heine, Steven, 1950–
    Sacred high city, sacred low city : a tale of religious sites in two Tokyo neighborhoods / Steven Heine.
        p. cm.
    Includes bibliographical references and index.
    ISBN 978-0-19-538620-2 (hardcover : alk. paper)—ISBN 978-0-19-986144-6 (pbk. : alk. paper)
    1. Tokyo (Japan)—Religious life and customs.   2. Religion and sociology—Japan—Tokyo.
    3. Sacred space—Japan—Tokyo.   I. Title.
    BL2215.T644H45 2011
    294.3'4350952135—dc22
                            2010046679

1 3 5 7 9 8 6 4 2

Printed in the United States of America
on acid-free paper

TABLE OF CONTENTS

ACKNOWLEDGMENTS

My special thanks go to Cynthia Read, editor at Oxford University Press, for believing in this project, as well as the American Academy of Religion, which awarded me a travel grant that helped start up the research at a critical juncture. This book has been a long time coming, and I am grateful to many colleagues over the years for brainstorming sessions about various topics related to the main issues. To name just a few, I thank Theodore Bestor, Victor Forte, Ishii Seijun, Richard Jaffe, Ma Li, Matthew Marr, Matsumoto Shirō, Michaela Mross, Joseph Murphy, Laura Nenzi, Ian Reader, Morten Schlüter, Jacqueline Stone, Sueki Fumihiko, John Allen Tucker, Pamela Winfield, and Dale Wright. I also greatly appreciate the extremely helpful efforts in assisting with editing the text and developing the visuals made by Jennylee Diaz, Maria Sol Echarren, Jennifer Ann Garcia, Wendy Lo, Danielle Nelson, Anna Scharnagl, and Therese Sollien.

SACRED HIGH CITY, SACRED LOW CITY

SACRED AND SECULAR

INTRODUCTION: JAPANESE RELIGIOUS CONTEXT IN TRADITIONAL AND CONTEMPORARY PERSPECTIVES

Introducing the Neighborhoods of Akasaka (High City) and Inarichō (Low City)

Tokyo, one of the major megalopolises in the world, with sprawling commercial complexes and residential developments, is celebrated for its new-wave architecture and unorthodox city planning, which "often strikes the outsider as hardly a city at all in the Western sense, but rather a metamorphic environment perpetually responding and adapting to change and the expediency of the moment."[1] Despite massive rebuilding and urban expansion following a series of devastating twentieth-century conflagrations (e.g., earthquake in the 1920s and war bombing two decades later), Tokyo is also well known for upholding a rich historical legacy that remains evident today in the layout of its neighborhoods and the style of its buildings, which reveal a "layered complexity that seems to go its own way, obeying organic rather than structural codes."[2]

One of the major factors linking the traditional and contemporary dimensions of the city is the pervasiveness of sacred space. As a central part of the labyrinthine maze that is Tokyo, hundreds or perhaps even thousands of religious sites that are frequently mobbed with exuberant patrons on festivals, holidays, and other ritual occasions, yet may also be vacant or underused, are at once everywhere apparent and often hidden in back streets and alleyways. These places range from the spectacular locations of Asakusa's Sensōji temple and the Meiji Jingu shrine in the northeast and southwest corridors of the city, respectively, to a multitude of smaller temples and shrines in nearly every nook and cranny of all the various sectors around town.

How important are the vast number of religious sites in Tokyo? Why and to what extent do they endure and even thrive in the context of modern society, which responds to the push of ancient traditions and the pulls of contemporary secularization? This book examines a carefully selected number of holy sites in order to

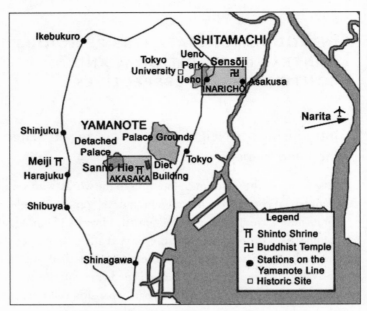

Two Tokyo Neighborhoods:
Akasaka in Yamanote and Inarichō in Shitamachi
MAP 0.1

consider the various ways that traditional notions of sacred space are appropriated and continue to function in Tokyo, as well as in urbanized Japanese
society more generally. It analyzes case studies of temples and shrines drawn
from two representative yet contrasting neighborhoods: Akasaka in the
affluent and influential central district of Yamanote, or the High City, and
Inarichō in the downbeat, yet perpetually creative, peripheral district of
Shitamachi, or the Low City.

These neighborhoods are strategically selected for the study of sacred
space because they reflect distinctive elements of the social landscape and
cultural history of Tokyo derived from early modern history. As indicated by
Map 0.1, each embodies a part of the fundamental division of the city into
two main districts that transpired during the Edo, or Tokugawa, period.
Yamanote (literally "in the hills," or uptown) is located in the area that sur-
rounds the imperial palace, which was formerly the privileged quarter of the
shogun's castle and his retainers and is now the city center, which houses the
capitol and the financial quarter. Shitamachi (literally "lower town," that is,
beneath the hills, or downtown) is found in the stigmatized northeast corner
of the city, which was referred to in Chinese *feng shui* as the "demon's gate"

(*kimon*), where negative spiritual forces tend to intrude upon a town or dwelling place.

Beginning in the early seventeenth century, as patterned on the geomantic requirements of other East Asian capitals—although, unlike Chang'an and Kyoto, Tokyo was deliberately built in a tangled rather than a gridlike pattern for defense purposes—the division reflected the shogun's desire to separate social classes. The autocratic ruler sought to at once protect and keep an eye on powerful warlords and samurai, who maintained an elite lifestyle in the inner circle, while banishing to the outskirts of town expendable or undesirable elements of society involved in inferior occupations, ranging from actors and artists to executioners and migrant workers.

The legacy of early modern Japanese society still very much affects the arrangement and lifestyle of contemporary Tokyo. Although the formal separation and prohibitions that affect the interaction between the Yamanote and the Shitamachi districts no longer apply, the city's primary commuter train system, the Yamanote Line, more or less captures in today's hi-tech world the traditional contour demarcating the distinction between the High and Low cities designated by the shogunate.[3] Originating in 1885 and completed in 1903 with twenty-nine stations connecting to many other rail and subway systems that fan out in every possible direction, the Yamanote Line is a crucial transportation hub for the greater metropolitan area and beyond. The sectors inside the rail line, where blue-suited salarymen populate the streets, continue to be prosperous and imbued with social power, whereas those outside the line generally represent marginalized and working-class, if not necessarily impoverished, parts of society.

Both Akasaka in the Yamanote district and Inarichō in the Shitamachi district contain a diversity of religious sites that offer opportunities for worshipping deities by performing rites and observances, in addition to places of related cultural and historical interest. This highlights the resiliency of Japanese sacred spaces, which have endured multiple challenges, including continuing shifts and pressures regarding the ways that urban sprawl contributes to the degrading of tradition along with the natural environment, which was so crucial for the formation of premodern religiosity. While most temples and shrines are officially sanctioned by national associations or registries as representing either Buddhism or Shinto, others operate as autonomous juridical entities in a way that reveals Japan's enthusiasm for participation in rituals. Although quite a few of the sites seek to uphold traditional ceremonies, many have undergone changes in recent years to facilitate commercial growth by renting out space to tenants or making other accommodations to secularization.

The High and Low cities appear quite different in terms of their respective styles of ritual practice. Akasaka's sacred spaces tend to promote the material gains of well-being, happiness, and good fortune by emphasizing the life-based issues of attaining health and wealth, which are generally affiliated with Shinto. The religious sites of Yamanote, on the other hand, are primarily shrines whose ceremonies revere a local deity that symbolizes the quest for prosperity and protection by conquering evil and overcoming temptation. Akasaka houses several prominent shrines that offer rites for obtaining practical benefits by worshipping the rice-fertility deity, Inari. Inarichō, on the other hand, contains numerous shops that sell memorial altars, or miniature shrines installed in people's homes to venerate the spirits of ancestors, and other paraphernalia for funerary rites. These symbols represent the overcoming of impurity through the elimination of vengeful ghosts and baleful demons by means of instilling a sense of remorse and repentance and by fostering forms of devotion that are mainly affiliated with the Buddhist faith.

The religious sites in these two neighborhoods are analyzed here as specific instances that illumine larger sociohistorical themes because they stand for distinct and divergent, yet overlapping, cultural and conceptual realms in the complex global cityscape of Tokyo. The creative tension between the High and the Low cities serves as a vehicle for observing, as well as a springboard for reflecting on and interpreting a series of polarities intrinsic to Japanese religiosity. This involves assessing the complex nexus of interrelationships that involves the Buddhist and Shinto institutions and the ways they serve the causes of living and dying, practicality and impracticality, and this-worldliness and other-worldliness as seen in connection with the forces of modernization.[4] The juxtaposition of the two locales creates a context of social geography that enables commentary on the nature of sacred space, in addition to more general issues regarding spiritual life—and its linkages to the afterlife—in assessing how Japan adapts and adjusts premodern religious sites.

Akasaka Shrines and Temples

Akasaka is an upscale, primarily commercial area that contains many stylish high-rise hotels, corporate headquarters, and fashionable shops. In pathways running off the main street, it also incorporates an antiquated entertainment center, which has been frequented for years by politicians and other VIPs, in some unfortunate cases leading to high-profile scandals. Here, too, is a very large area of quiet residential streets. Because it is centrally situated near the palace grounds and the Diet building, Akasaka does not stand next to a station on the Yamanote Line, which covers the outer edges of the district; the closest station to Akasaka is Harajuku. Like many Tokyo neighborhoods, its modern political boundaries were drawn in the early Meiji period and reconfigured—in this case, expanded rather than contracted—after WWII.

The main sites in Akasaka include Sannō Hie Jinja, which, over the course of many centuries of transitions, has served as a protector of the government, currently housed in the Diet building in nearby Kasumigaseki; Toyokawa Inari, a Sōtō Zen temple (Myōgonji) that functions more like a shrine in offering rituals and thus represents a full integration of Buddhist and Shinto elements in an intriguing example of syncretism that completely merges—or submerges—the two traditions into one site; Nogi Jinja, a multifaceted compound that celebrates a modern war hero while incorporating a flourishing wedding shrine and gardens; and Hikawa Jinja, which was the tutelary temple of a leading eighteenth-century political figure. In addition, Akasaka includes the ample grounds of the Aoyama Cemetery, which for some visitors serves as a recreational park, as well as numerous small Buddhist temples whose primary function is to provide and sustain family graveyards.

All of the major shrines in the neighborhood are affiliated with Inari, which is usually symbolized by a magical, shape-shifting fox that is also considered efficacious for business and other kinds of postagrarian economic pursuits. Inari was originally a god of rural society because foxes, which live just outside the domain of human activity, were thought to be a good luck charm for rice crops when they lurked near the paddies at twilight. In ancient Japan, Inari represented a supernatural force charged with defending the rice crop against natural disasters, such as flood, drought, and noxious pests, but since the early modern period the deity's power to help achieve profit and economic growth has been taken from its agrarian roots and transferred to an urban setting's concerns with mercantilism and commerce. The magical fox is, therefore, no longer only the guardian god of grain cultivation but also a protector and promoter of modern business.

This auspicious quality of Inari was installed in Edo when countless shrines were built in the Yamanote foothills on the border between the developing city and the countryside beyond, with the aim of transforming chaotic energy at the limits of urban development by means of a beneficial spiritual power. At most Inari shrines, divine foxes are adorned with a red bib to keep them from getting their coat messy while they devouring the vixen's favorite food, known as Inari-zushi, offerings of fried tofu with rice balls, which devotees place at the foot of the icon. During the Edo period, the prominent Iseya company had placed its signs all over Tokyo, and, as an indication of how widespread Inari worship was at this time, "a popular alliterative ditty held that the three most common things in Edo were '…Iseya shops and Inari shrines [which] are as numerous as dog droppings' (*Chōnai Iseya, Inari ni, inu no koso*)."[5]

Today, as shown in Figure 0.1, Inari shrines in Tokyo and elsewhere accommodate a broad-based merchant class, which includes executives, managers, and entrepreneurs, as well as shopkeepers and salespeople, in addition to many other individuals such as politicians, travelers, or performers who are in the process of starting or attempting to complete a new venture. Most stores enshrine a small Inari icon somewhere on the premises, and many of Japan's larger department stores have a small Inari shrine on their roof. The age-old agrarian practice has survived and is now flourishing amid the bustle of Japan's ultramodern cities.[6]

The image of a wild fox is also found in Buddhist temples as a symbol of faith and protector of the Dharma, whose powers of shape shifting normally used to seduce, deceive, and betray have been converted from the demonic and transformed into the beatific. The phenomenon of religious facilities permeating an area that otherwise seems to be highly secularized is by no means unique to Akasaka, as they can be found throughout many neighborhoods in

FIGURE 0.1 Votive Banners at Akasaka Inari Jinja

the Yamanote division. This includes the prestigious financial district of the Ginza, a bastion of modern institutions and shops located to the southwest of the imperial palace grounds which featuresnearly three dozen sacred spaces, including more than a dozen small Inari shrines situated in space-saver fashion on the rooftops of department stores and banks.[7] Some of the sites are believed to contribute to the economic stability of prominent commercial enterprises, while others are important primarily for festivals or for offering the kinds of worldly benefits that participants in traditional rituals tend to pursue.

Inarichō Shops, Temples, and Shrines

Inarichō is home to an extensive row of over fifty shops that sell Buddhist altars, or *butsudan*, along with other mortuary supplies and ritual implements that contribute to the funeral industry and the memorialization of death, yet nearby there is also an impressive array of Shinto shrines that perform rituals for attaining prosperity. The butsudan shops and Buddhist temples with graveyards claim to promote peace of mind by the remembrance of deceased ancestors in a way that mitigates or eliminates the possibility of retribution (*tatari*) stemming from the unappeased spirits during their sojourn, happy or otherwise, in the hereafter.

The neighborhood lies just one subway station on the Ginza Line west of Ueno Station, a gateway to the northeast corridor of Tokyo, where Ueno Park, with its prominent museums and other cultural centers, including the once-revered Kan'eiji temple, are located. Inarichō is also two stations east of Asakusa, home of both Sensōji temple (known for venerating Kannon) and an entertainment district that offers assorted types of enjoyment from theater and literature to prostitution. Both Ueno and Asakusa, which are prime commercial and amusement areas, have long been important religious centers and remain vital areas of worship and sacred tourism.

Inarichō probably became the home of altar shops based on its proximity to Yanaka, which is just to the northwest of Ueno. This area became known as the "temple town" when Buddhist sites were relocated there from central Tokyo following the devastating effects of the Meireki, or "long-sleeves (*furisode*) fire," of 1657. Yanaka and its environs are still graced with numerous temples—there are eighty-eight of these, according to local lore. Inarichō is also interesting because of its proximity to and associations with the Minami Senjū Station, which is in turn near the shogun's former execution grounds of Kotsukappara, where several prominent temples have historically catered to the needs of deceased criminals and the dispossessed. These included young prostitutes who occupied the nearby Yoshiwara licensed quarter, as well as outcasts in the impoverished San'ya day-laborer area. This district still contains several crematoria and remains plagued by poverty and homelessness, although some areas retain a lively atmosphere.

Whereas Akasaka in a sense is not unique in that there are many other Tokyo neighborhoods with diverse sacred sites, Inarichō is the only such center of altar shops—it is to the butsudan industry what Akihabara is to electronics, Shinjuku is to watches, and Jinbochō is to used books. However, stores are springing up in other areas of Tokyo that offer alternative approaches to manufacturing and marketing altars, such as those that feature a more sedate or modern design by using imported wood or exotic features that differ from the old-fashioned styles generally produced in Inarichō. In competition with the Yakigen Company and other newcomers to the industry, Inarichō has recently tried to compete by promoting a "contemporary altar" (*gendai butsudan*) campaign.[8]

In Inarichō, the focus on funerary rites highlights the cultural style of sacred sites in the Shitamachi district. Some of the shops exhibit exotic architecture, such as a butsudan store with a pagoda on the roof that evokes continental religion and recalls a bygone era of premodern Japan even while standing just a block away from another butsudan storefront that is next to a McDonald's. Such a nostalgic atmosphere is not limited to Shitamachi but can also be experienced in the ways that Akasaka's shrines present themselves. For example, Toyokawa Inari features a series of lanterns lit up at night on a thoroughfare that leads up a slope from the New Otani and other fancy modern hotels, which often include gardens, teahouses, and other cultural attractions for the guests and whose appeal is the evocation of a classical tradition.

Connections and Disconnections

Akasaka in Yamanote and Inarichō in Shitamachi as upper-class or prestigious and lower-class or marginal districts, respectively, are somewhat connected by two intriguing wordplays, which often count for a great deal in understanding the significance of Japanese religious sites. For example, a shrine in Kyoto that wards off floods caused by heavy rains, or *ame*, is also believed to protect the eyes, or *me*. Many first-time visitors to Tokyo, as well as those with more experience, easily conflate the names of the cross-town neighborhoods of Akasaka, to the southeast, and Asakusa, to the northwest, and report that they have been to one when it is really the other, extremely different area they visited. "Oh yes," they may say, "I've been there," when I tell them of my research on Akasaka. "There is a big temple," they respond, referring to Sensōji in Asakusa. They may also have visited Akasaka, especially since it is near another famous tourist destination in Roppongi, but were not aware of this since the name of the neighborhood is less well known.[9] Perhaps this is an ironic indicator that the quality of life in both the High and the Low cities of Tokyo is closer than one might imagine.

The other interesting wordplay is that Inarichō literally means "Inari town," thus taking the name of the rice/fox deity, which would seem to make an association with the variety of Inari shrines in Akasaka. Inarichō may have earned this moniker because of its proximity to Ueno, which, throughout the Meiji era, was a large wooded park that trailed off into a rural area where foxes lurked. Foxes are known to dwell on the borderline between the human and the nonhuman, civilized and undeveloped territory, such as rice paddies, as well as the boundary between city and countryside, as in Ōji Inari Jinja, located on what was once the northern outskirts of Edo. This is what gives the fox a mystique as either an auspicious harbinger of good fortune or an intrusion that signals impending threat or misguidance. Nevertheless, a comparison of the neighborhoods may reinforce conventional notions of a division of labor that involve Shinto shrines emphasizing an affirmation of life and Buddhist temples that stress death exclusively. The altar shops in Inarichō cater to the Japanese need to commemorate death, which seems to be very much removed from the Inari cult's focus on fertility rites in Akasaka.

My observations of and reflections on on-the-ground ritual practices in these neighborhoods, however, indicate that there are many exceptions and counterexamples that reveal that the religious context is considerably more complex than the conventional polarity of living versus dying suggests. Both neighborhoods, for instance, are known for their proximity to the largest cemeteries in the city: Aoyama Cemetery is located near Akasaka, and Yanaka Cemetery is near Inarichō. Furthermore, dozens of Buddhist temples contain graveyards in Akasaka, an area associated with life, while Inarichō, an area associated with death, has many shrines and temples that highlight life-oriented rituals. Inarichō also has shops that sell Shinto altars (*kamidana*), which are used to install indigenous deities into the home as part of the memorial process. In addition, they make portable shrines (*omikoshi*) and other ritual implements and related objects that are featured in Shinto festival processions (*matsuri*).

These examples reveal the vast crossover connections between Shinto and Buddhism, as well as the need for exploring anew some of the basic notions used to understand the function of religious institutions, which have assimilated a layer of folk religiosity that undercuts conventional labels. A key aim of this study is to show there may not really be a sharp discrepancy between rites for living and dying in that the sacred sites in both areas of the city honor in various ways the traditional elements of practice covering both realms infused into the contemporary world. Instead of supporting the conventional approach, which sees Shinto and Buddhism as separate though linked traditions that are visited on special ritual occasions (primarily in order to seek practical gains), an examination of sites in the Akasaka and Inarichō neighborhoods helps to reopen and reevaluate basic questions about the status of the religious institutional structure, as well as the ongoing motivational factors that support and sustain Japanese ritual practices. Where do the borders of one religion end and the other begin? Should Shinto be regarded as a repository for all rites and icons that are non-Buddhist, or should it be treated differently from what constitutes a fundamental layer of folk religious practices? Furthermore, what is the significance of the apparently magical, polytheistic worldview that links all forms of practice in both parts of the city?

"In Japan, We Dance"

Analyzing the role of sacred space in contemporary Tokyo serves as a basis for reexamining several main assumptions about Japanese religiosity that stem from the challenge of coming to terms with a fundamental contradiction between the extent of active participation in rituals and limited expressions of enthusiasm for religious belief. As many observers ranging from casual tourists to specialized researchers have noted, the presence of temples and shrines is pervasive in most urban and rural areas, which means that countless examples of festivals and ceremonies are on display, creating a sense of religious vitality and dynamism. This seems to reflect a high degree of interest and near universal involvement in rites that feature icons or symbols of various sorts, which are in abundance in every sector of society.

However, surveys and other indicators suggest a lack of dedication in that most Japanese people seem lukewarm at best when asked about their convictions. It is clear that in most cases the Japanese appear to lack familiarity with or appreciation of some of the basic elements of religious history and doctrine, which are probably known to only a handful of priests, scholars, or other specialists. The contradictory quality is compounded by the fact that institutional membership is nearly twice the population since nearly all of the Japanese consider themselves followers of both Buddhism and Shinto (sometimes in addition to an affiliation with the New Religions movement, although some of these groups tend to be exclusivist in order to bolster a sense of identity and loyalty).

Fueling this conundrum are conversations that lead one to feel that the Japanese have little regard for traditional religiosity. Like many researchers, I have had numerous exchanges during which a companion inquires incredulously as to why I am interested in this field of study when the Japanese themselves do not seem to care much about it. In responding that I admire the beauty of a traditional temple, a typical retort is, "When you've seen one temple, you've seen them all." Perhaps this type of remark is made disingenuously as part of an ingrained cultural reticence in order to conceal a deeper level of concern that is considered different from the typical Western standpoint. A Japanese colleague uneasy about the apparent decline of traditional spirituality once remarked wistfully, "Buddhism is everywhere in Japan...and nowhere at all."

The contradiction involving the strength of ritual practice accompanied by a weakness of commitment to religion is discussed with a reverse emphasis on the popularity of ritual practice by Winston Davis, who cites a study that shows that the "number of Japanese having religious feelings far exceeds the number willing to call themselves believers."[10] According to Andrew Bernstein, the observance of funerary rites in contemporary Japan is the single main role played by temples and their priests. He also notes, however, that "This does not mean that most Japanese today understand the teachings of Buddhist sects or literally believe in their heavens or hells. When surveyed about religious attitudes, most Japanese tend to deny belief in a particular cosmology or doctrine. Nevertheless, the majority of these professed unfaithful regularly participate in religious activities and rituals, making them doers if not necessarily believers."[11]

In a similar vein, Ama Toshimaro comments on the pervasiveness of practice despite the absence of belief: "In short, although Japanese people profess to having no religion, they do not dismiss religion out of hand in the way that atheists do. It is rather the case that people who profess to a lack of religion are often very enthusiastic believers in their own particular form of folk religion."[12] Ama further argues, "There are many Japanese who profess to a lack of religious belief. However, the fact is that there is hardly anyone who completely denies all religion, nor any diehard atheists in Japan.... [A]ll surveys found that roughly 70% of people answered that they were not religious. Yet, 75% of all respondents replied that although they themselves do not follow any particular religious beliefs, a religious sentiment is important."[13]

Inverting Mark Twain's Disconnect

The Japanese outlook appears to invert the thought implied in the famous observation attributed to Mark Twain, who said ironically, "Everyone talks about the weather, but nobody does anything about it." In the case of Japan, there is considerable religious activity on different levels but very little discourse on its meaning and significance or about the degree of belief (or disbelief) in forms of the sacred. In other words, nearly everyone in Japan takes part in rites of one type or another, but very few are willing or able to talk about their reasons for doing so. By contrast, in the West, with its long-standing pattern of the separation of church and state, there tends to be much discussion about the Almighty and whether or not God does or should occupy the public square, but relatively less overt activity is visible. With the exception of Christmas and Easter, the largest communal celebrations in America, such as Independence Day, Thanksgiving, New Year's Eve, or Super Bowl Sunday, are generally secular rather than sacred in nature and fulfill the concerns of patriotism or national loyalty instead of sectarian interests.

Perhaps belief is not much discussed by the Japanese because religion is more a matter of behavioral pattern than thought or of action over intellect or orthopraxy instead of orthodoxy. Joseph Campbell, the renowned scholar of comparative mythology, once remarked that when asked at a conference on world religions why faith in Japan is scarcely articulated in terms of its theological or ideological foundations, a Shinto priest responded, "We don't have theology. We don't have ideology. In Japan, we dance."[14] The term *dance* in this context presumably refers not to a form of diversion but to ritual performance that involves native rites such as *kagura*, which is a style of fertility dance of shamanic origins that is intended to bring the deity into a state of worldly presence. Kagura is based on a myth recorded in the *Kojiki* about the sun goddess, Amaterasu, who was lured from hiding in her cave when she saw the other gods dancing. The Campbell reference highlights the value of practical behavior as a deep-seated habit that does not necessarily require theoretical underpinnings to be effective and in fact may become more compelling for the lack of this.

To reverse the direction of the inquiry, given the apparent paucity of conviction, one wonders how premodern sites and rites remain vibrant in modern society. Japan continues to contain some of the most marvelous sacred spaces in the world, including forested shrines in remote mountain locales and exquisite temples with delicate gardens in ancient cities like Kyoto and Kamakura. In highly developed urban areas like Tokyo, however, where being immersed in nature is anything but common, just about every neighborhood has dozens of sacred spaces, some located down tiny alleys and others in more prominent locations, many of which are vigorously maintained and upgraded. In view of inflated prices and growing demand for a shrinking real-estate market, one might expect that places that house temples and shrines, which could be considered extraneous to modernization, would have given way to speculators. Why is it that sacred sites are so plentiful in cities that highlight commerce and industry and have not gradually faded away or died out along with other remnants of obsolete tradition in the fast-paced world of contemporary Japan?

Many holy places in Tokyo have been able to make an effective though modified transition from premodern to secular society. In figure 0.2, a traditional temple bell tower stands in the midst of an ultramodern apartment complex, and countless other examples of archaic sites like torii gates are situated sidebyside with contemporary structures that may appear to conflict with rather than complement their cultural legacy. Although seemingly out of place at first glance, the sacred spaces create a qualitative impressiveness that reflects the persistence of religiosity in modern Tokyo, thereby showing

FIGURE 0.2 Temple Bell in Akasaka

that, while society is fluid and ever changing, the Japanese still desire to preserve traditional forms of worship.

A further question concerns the ongoing popularity of rituals that continually take place in sacred spaces. In addition to major national holidays and local festivals, which may seem like obligatory, group-based affairs, individual Japanese can be found patronizing diverse religious sites on an individual basis on any given day of the year. Icons of foxes associated with Inari, which strive for prosperity and longevity, are also used, along with flowers for ancestor veneration in ritual iconography typically found all over Tokyo and throughout Japan's urban and rural areas. Another pervasive religious symbol is the small strip of paper taken from an *omikuji*, or small divination scroll, which is purchased for a modest donation at a temple or a shrine. These strips are hung by the hundreds on a nearby tree or post in order to allow the wind to circulate their spiritual energy so that the fortune predicted will be more likely to come to pass. These are among the numerous sorts of talismans and amulets distributed in various venues in every neighborhood.

In addition to widespread shrines, mortuary ceremonies (e.g., the use of butsudan in the home) and other kinds of ritualism that support burials and memorials are adopted by more than 90 percent of the population, although, according to surveys, far fewer than two-thirds of that number say they find the rites meaningful or relevant in today's world.[15] Such practices are maintained despite the exorbitant cost of funerals and accessories, which is often at least three or four times more than comparable expenses in the United States. Observations reveal examples of such an obscurely located cemetery affiliated with a temple in Akasaka that is visited on a dreary summer afternoon by members of a bereaved family. Nearby stands a plaque with an inspirational proverb: "Each person has only one life to live," which may refer to recent debates in Buddhism on the ethics of organ donation.

Mortuary customs have survived the savage lampooning in Itami Juzō's 1980s' film, *The Funeral* (*Osōshiki*), along with *I Have No Grave!* (*Ohaka ga nai!*), produced a decade later. *The Funeral* gained international acclaim for targeting seemingly outdated manners that are driven mainly by clerical greed. Responding to peer pressure, the uninformed congregants acquiesce to their fear of the unknown, such as retribution by their ancestors' spirits. In the film, family members who are not familiar with the required etiquette for funerals watch instructional videos so they can act out the customs according to expected form, while other aspects of family intrigue and scandal go unnoticed or unchecked. Meanwhile, the priest who will bestow a posthumous ordination name (*kaimyō*) on the deceased, which is an expensive item for the family to purchase, arrives at the ceremony in a chauffeur-driven limousine and wearing a robe laced with heavy gold embroidery.[16]

On Overcoming Conventional Notions of Religiosity

Evaluating the contradiction between practice and belief, which has as a corollary the surprising endurance of sacred spaces and rituals, necessitates rethinking and challenging some of the basic conceptions and/or misconceptions about what constitutes religion in Japan, especially involving the relation between Buddhism and Shinto, living and dying, tradition and modernity, and sacrality and secularity. This book revisits favored notions, whether accepted and confirmed or rejected and revised, about the role of syncretism involving the two major religious institutions and the relation of these traditions to a more basic level of religiosity, as well as the drives and intentions that underlie and motivate ritual practices in connection with a pursuit of worldly concerns and the worship of ancestors. These issues are cast in light of the enduring cultural legacy, which is often characterized in modern society as something chimerical because it is vanishing or perhaps was invented in the first place.

My analysis seeks to overcome generalizations and stereotypes that reflect hidden agendas indicative of Orientalism and/or Reverse Orientalism, which tend to apologize for and defend or critique and attack Japan's purportedly vaunted sense of cultural exceptionalism. Conventional notions of religiosity as found in a number of well-known recent studies can be summed up as follows:

> The Japanese choose and are willing to continually shift their primary affiliation with either Buddhism or Shinto based on the required ritual function that aids their pursuit of pragmatic material goals involving the attainment of health or wealth. Therefore, the supposed recollections of an authentic bygone spiritual tradition constitute little more than a collective myth propagated for cynical reasons in order to promote an ideological agenda.

While this summary has much merit and cannot be considered inaccurate in defining Japanese religiosity, it is important to recognize that the approach so encapsulated seems to be based on untested assumptions. It is necessary to examine and deconstruct some of the presuppositions that underlie the conventional view, which reflects a couple of frequently repeated adages that characterize the nature of religion in Japanese society.

I focus on two main interrelated yet provisionally separable issues: One involves institutional structure, or the relationship between the Buddhist and the Shinto traditions, which is usually referred to when describing the Japanese as people who are "Born Shinto…die Buddhist"; the other concerns religious motivation, or the reason so many people participate in rituals that they often profess to disbelieve, as captured by a famous saying that refers to pursuing "practical this-worldly benefits" (*genze riyaku*). Both of these oft-cited adages capture a key aspect of Japanese religiosity, that is, the interconnection of institutions and the drive to attain goals, whether primarily material or spiritual. However, each maxim is also problematic in falling short of conveying the full picture of how the sacred functions in modern Japan, and therefore both are in need of being rethought and recast.

The Question of Institutional Structure

Despite ongoing religious activity in addition to polls that show high levels of institutional affiliation in that both of the major traditions can claim more than three-quarters of the total population as members, researchers often get the impression that neither Buddhism nor Shinto is as spiritually dynamic a tradition as might be expected since the adherents consistently demonstrate a lack of loyalty to a sense of sectarian identity. Most Japanese people do not necessarily know or even care which Buddhist denomination they belong to since this was assigned to families by the authorities in the early modern period for political reasons as part of the parish system (*danka seido*) or the very much related temple registration system (*terauke seido*), required by the shogunate. Before the Meiji era, Shinto shrines were invariably linked to temples and probably did not have a separate membership. Since that custom was changed, most people assume they belong to both religions, but what are their respective roles?

The axiom "Born Shinto…die Buddhist"[17] tries to explain this matter by referring to a specialization of ritual tasks distributed between Shinto, which supports the "land of the kami" (*kami no kuni*), which promotes the forces of life through naming ceremonies for babies and weddings, and Buddhism, which is primarily a mortuary cult generally referred to as "funerary Buddhism" (*sōshiki Bukkyō*) and which appeases the elements of death. The standpoint underlying this motto, which emphasizes the inclusive or combinatory rather than the exclusive or sectarian nature of Japanese religiosity, is valuable in overcoming outdated notions still prevalent today in some quarters, such as those expressed in the "Gotta have faith" section of a recently published tour guide to Tokyo, which unfortunately states, "Though the majority of Japanese people happily embrace both native Shinto and imported Buddhism, these are about as different as two faiths could be. Shinto is unconcerned with matters of afterlife, which is a major concern in Buddhism, for example."[18] Such an extreme dichotomy between traditions, which fails to recognize their common bonds and overlapping framework, is simply untenable.

By tending to presume that Shinto and Buddhism are independent entities, one native and local and the other foreign and universal, which have somehow been synthesized or amalgamated over the centuries, the "Born Shinto...die Buddhist" approach, which emphasizes distinct functions, does not go nearly far enough in stressing the cohesion of an underlying religiosity. The maxim misses a fundamental layer of integration whereby the institutions are connected by virtue of multifaceted linkages that take priority over their degrees of institutional separation. Therefore, I argue that a basic level of popular, primal, or folk religiosity focused on the worship of indigenous gods such as Inari and other crossover deities lies behind diverse aspects of religiosity, so that the axiom should be recast as "Born Shinto...live Inari...die Buddhist."

This revised version does more than show that sectarian identity, which is crucial on some levels, is a relatively insignificant factor in defining institutional structure or that the various rites of passage do not determine allegiance. Rather, it highlights the pervasive status of a rhizomatic network of complex alliances and associations that transcend the dichotomy of traditions and the rituals they perform that are relevant to particular existential situations, such as career advancement and learning, well-being and travel, or marriage and childbearing, as well as communion with ancestral spirits, whose affections and disaffections continue to have an impact on events in this world. In forming this approach, I am indebted to—yet in some important ways I depart from—the emphasis on folk religion in the works of Japanese scholars Hori Ichirō, Miyake Hitoshi, and Ama Toshimaro, in addition to research on Japanese religiosity conducted by a variety of prominent Western scholars, including Winston Davis, Michael Pye, and Ian Reader, among others.[19]

The Question of Religious Motivation

The motivations that underlie the practices of Japanese religiosity are mysterious and difficult to discern. Perhaps they are vague and inexpressible or are not fully understood and acknowledged on a conscious level by the participants, but they must surely be powerful enough to drive the remarkable degree of ritual activity at sacred sites found throughout the country. A commonly used maxim stresses the role of seeking to gain practical benefits, especially for healing and well-being, as the primary factor driving religious behavior and suggests that Japanese people attend ceremonies and participate in devotional exercises mainly to acquire material rewards.

An approach based on practicality is particularly emphasized in a remarkably well-researched and detailed examination of contemporary religiosity by Ian Reader and George J. Tanabe Jr., *Practically Religious: Worldly Benefits and the Common Religion of Japan*, which examines the votive rites of countless practitioners who yearn to attain prosperity, longevity, and protection from hazards, among other similar objectives.[20] According to the cover blurb of this book, which in stressing materiality denies the pursuit of spiritual release or peace of mind (*anshin*) as a motivating factor, "Benefits are both sought and bought, and the authors discuss the economic and commercial aspects of how and why institutions promote practical benefits."

The pragmatic side of worship can indeed be seen in the popularity of rites for safe travels, success in new business ventures, good grades on exams, solutions to infertility, and the conquering of other kinds of blight and illness. However, an exclusive focus on practicality and materiality overlooks a number of other factors that seem to inspire the Japanese who participate regularly in ritual observances. These factors include seeking out sanctuary and finding safe harbor from a hectic, humdrum world, while also having an opportunity to communicate with ancestors and commune with nature by finding pockets of frail beauty and tranquility amid the hustle and bustle of the modern cityscape. The approach based on practical benefits also dismisses notions of legitimate pious longing or the aspiration to transmit cultural legacy. It may lead to a cynical doubting of the sincerity of engagement or a casting of aspersions on the search for spiritual rewards as somehow being only a psychological cover-up that conceals greed and corruption.

Therefore, I agree that the typical motives of practitioners are "worldly" in that even the Japanese preoccupation with death is carried out for the sake of how the afterlife affects the here and now but argue that they are not necessarily "practical" because the impetus also encompasses other factors. These include ruminations on history and memory, as well as the pursuit of consolation and refuge from daily stress and strife through an appreciation of naturalism, in addition to an acceptance of supernaturalism. Based on the interweaving of life-oriented and death-oriented rituals conducted at a wide variety of sites, the factors that propel the Japanese into active involvement with sacred space can be referred to as "impractical this-worldly benefits" (*genze hi-riyaku*), to coin a phrase.

Chapter Overview

I thus argue that the enhanced notions of "Born Shinto...live Inari...die Buddhist" and "im-practical worldly benefits" are designed to resolve the conundrums regarding why the Japanese so extensively practice what they claim to not take seriously as a form of belief. Following this introduction, the book consists of four chapters in two main sections. The first two chapters contained in part I on the "Sacred and Secular" provide a critical overview of the role of sacred space in relation to secular Tokyo (and Japan more broadly conceived) in order to better understand the significance of the fundamental contradiction concerning practice and belief. Chapter 1, "Sacred Space Is Alive and Well and Living in Japan," considers on the basis of my own personal reflections seen in terms of cross-cultural perspectives how contemporary urban sacred sites seek to preserve a deteriorating past that is greatly affected, for better or worse, by the main factors of modernization. These factors include rapid commercial development and an aggressive emphasis on an efficient use of space as an end in itself, accompanied by ecological degradation, which causes a deterioration of the natural landscape. Sacred sites must absorb the ongoing impact of a general trend toward secularity, or unbridled mercantilism and consumerism, which tends to dismiss the past as merely anachronistic and thus deviates from and diminishes traditional religious institutional structures. The first chapter makes use of on-the-ground observations in inquiring as to where the secular leaves off and the sacred begins in comparison with sacred sites typical of Western cities.

The second chapter—"Tokyo, City of...Temples?"—provides an overview of the significance of Akasaka in Yamanote and of Inarichō in Shitamachi in terms of the geocultural landscape of Tokyo, which stems and extends from the social structure of the Edo period in a way that continues to permeate and determine the boundaries of today's urban society. The chapter begins by asking why Tokyo has been selected for this study since other locations in Japan are far more renowned for their sacred sites. By looking at the two neighborhoods in light of the social history of the capital, the chapter shows that neither area is monolithic in its religious context and that both represent a mixture of sacred elements that supports the interplay of Shinto and Buddhism as part of the fundamental level of folk religions.

The historical and theoretical discussions of sacred vis-à-vis secular space in Tokyo in chapters 1 and 2 set the stage for the detailed analysis in part II, which is titled "Living and Dying." There, chapters 3 and 4 focus on religious sites in the two neighborhoods, as well as the implications of understanding their functions for reevaluating conventional notions of Japanese religiosity. The two conceptual issues of structure and motivation, like the religious traditions of Shinto and Buddhism, as well as the existential matters of life and death that each tradition addresses, are inextricably linked but are provisionally separated here for the sake of undertaking a comprehensive analysis of sacred space.

Chapter 3, "Akasaka in the High City: Born Shinto...Live Inari...Die Buddhist," examines the wide variety of shrines in Akasaka, including Sannō Hie Jinja, Toyokawa Inari, Nogi Jinja, and Hikawa Jinja, which are all dedicated to Inari, at least in part, although each has its own distinctive areas of religious and cultural significance. The Yamanote neighborhood of Akasaka also contains the Aoyama Cemetery, as well as dozens of smaller Buddhist temples, shown in Figure 0.3, most of which function as graveyards while tucked away in alleys or streetside openings. When seen collectively as a network of sacred sites and associations in the social context of the High City, an examination of this area at once confirms and calls for a reassessment of the notion that Shinto exclusively represents rites for living and Buddhism represents only rites for dying. This chapter focuses attention on an underlying level of folk religiosity that sustains both institutional structures.

The fourth and final chapter, "Inarichō in the Low City: Im-practical Worldly Benefits," investigates the role played by the butsudan shops that are concentrated on the main street in the Shitamachi neighborhood of Inarichō. This role is considered in relation to other important sacred, historical, and cultural sites of Shitamachi, especially death-oriented temples around the former execution grounds near Minami Senjū Station, as well as life-oriented shrines in the vicinity. Special attention is given to recent modifications in butsudan design that seek to accommodate contemporary lifestyle trends and put more emphasis on the peace of mind of those living than appeasing the ghosts of deceased ancestors. This examination is carried out in order to reconsider the conventional emphasis on "practical this-worldly benefits" as the key motivational factor of Japanese religiosity. The chapter argues a multiplicity of elements supports the religious intentions of the Japanese people, some of which are intended to attain success in a very pragmatic sense, but for the most part the motives are this-worldly

FIGURE 0.3 Small Graveyard at Dōkyōji Temple in Akasaka

yet impractical, including communal obligations, as well as nostalgia and memory, which complement supernatural beliefs in warding off the revenge of untamed spirits. Therefore, an analysis of the roots of sacrality should not be limited to any one particular factor that is seen to be exclusively applicable to a complex situation.

Throughout, I argue that there are more important elements for understanding religious structure than focusing on the division (or union) of Buddhism and Shinto and for understanding motivation than emphasizing the role of pragmatism in a world of vanishing tradition. The aim of my analysis is not so much to argue against conventional notions that have become deeply ingrained in discussions of Japanese religiosity, in large part because these after all are useful and valuable tools for categorizing different aspects of religious behavior. Rather, I seek to clarify and refine and in some ways either to extend or complement the usage of these perspectives by looking at the ways that participants in Japanese religions adapt their approach to the fundamental matters of living and dying and of suffering and redemption in the context of contemporary society as evidenced in the diverse sacred sites of complementary High and Low city neighborhoods.

Japan: Lost or Found?

Much of the discussion and argumentation in this book is framed indirectly by a broader discursive context concerning what can legitimately be said and what perhaps cannot or should not be articulated in regard to understanding and interpreting the historical unfolding and qualitative status of Japanese religiosity as seen in light of a variety of discourses, in both the past and the present, on the issue of cultural identity. The following brief discussion is an attempt to clarify the conceptual framework and its bearing on the issue of sacred space in Tokyo neighborhoods. This analysis is accompanied by a disclaimer in that I seek to avoid direct involvement in or commitment to any particular ideological agenda by striving for a middle-ground standpoint in relation to what I see as four very useful but potentially extreme positions that have dominated the field.

Four Paradigms

One paradigm emphasizes the ongoing integrity and distinctiveness of Japanese tradition, which valorizes indigenous folk customs and practices in a way that highlights the linkages between religious institutions, as well as the common roots of sacred sites and rites in their diverse manifestations. This view shows that a unity and a continuity of ritual practices underlie apparent divisions between native and imported beliefs about living and dying. However, the limitation of this approach is that it may unfortunately emphasize the priority of cultural exceptionalism in a way that could be considered a throwback to ethnocentric agendas regarding the complete, coherent, and unchanging nature of culture that promote Japanese superiority in a classic case of Reverse Orientalism. A view based on developing a make-believe or fantasy realm of enduring, undying tradition may reveal that nativist musings and self-assertions generally referred to as the ideology of *nihonjinron* (literally, "the Japanese thesis") are inseparable from nationalist priorities and, therefore, must be checked and balanced from the standpoint of healthy skepticism and self-doubt.

The paradigm at the other end of the spectrum emphasizes cultural relativism in order to debunk the "myth of Japanese uniqueness"[21] as a construction that requires liberation from the romanticized illusions and idealized nostalgia of traditionalist conceptions. This represents a fabricated confabulation disingenuously designed to legitimate either a particular sociopolitical agenda or to promote the propaganda of the Japanese nation. However, the weakness of this approach, which tends to discredit tradition as mere invention, is that its critique of self-promotional myths may dovetail with Orientalist assumptions about cultural deficiency or decline.[22] Like the emphasis on "practically religious," this standpoint becomes rather cynical at times by cultivating, in a hypercritical, Japan-bashing style, the view that most assumptions about traditional Japan are a concoction that results in diabolical claims about the national polity which contrive the past and, therefore, interfere with an understanding of the present.

Another trope often used in reference to cultural legacy, including the role of religiosity, is the notion of postmodernism, whereby Japan is said to represent a distinctively innovative approach to cultural development. According to the postmodern approach, after a delayed start due to its policy of isolation during the Edo period, once the process of modernization began in the late nineteenth century, Japanese society somehow managed to move rather quickly through the stage of linear progress that is universally characteristic of modernity, while managing to retain a hold on the traditionalist view of cyclicality. In other words, Japan has already transcended the modern but also is not far removed from the premodern, so that it represents the best, in the sense of combining cyclical and linear time, or the worst, in the sense of contradicting traditional complacency with a frantic sense of progress, of both worlds.

A fourth paradigm involves the axioms of the "discourses of the vanishing," or "lost Japan," which refer to the way both Japanese religion and culture are understood as an apparently disappearing legacy, but these maxims are ambiguous enough to cover both sides of the story. In considering the dictums it must be asked, what exactly is it that is lost? Is it the supposedly true Japan that the exceptionalists claim it to be, which can be remembered but cannot be fully recovered and appropriated in the modern world? Or is it Japan itself that has lost its way, according to the relativists, because it fantasizes with nostalgic longing about an authentic Japanese culture that is a simulacrum, or the resemblance to an image of something that never existed in such a form in which it is imagined in the first place?[23] Table 0.1 sums up the relationship between the four paradigms, with two supporting and two skeptical of claims about Japanese cultural identity.

Given the disconnect between practice and belief, perhaps nothing is what it seems to be in regard to Japanese religiosity, so that trying to nail down the cause and effect of people's actions is like chasing after a mirage that gives rise to countless false claims and misguided assumptions. Is Japan an enigmatic realm, a wonderland where myth making or constructing expedient "realities" has replaced really real reality (assuming there ever is such a thing)?[24] For

Table 0.1 Contrasting Paradigms of Japanese Culture

Promoting Japan	Critiquing Japan
Reverse Orientalist	Orientalist
valorizing tradition	myth of uniqueness
postmodernism	lost Japan

example, Tokyo seems to be susceptible to the charge of having become a virtual reproduction of itself because it is a city of replicas. So many structures have been rebuilt after the effect of fires, many times in different locations and with flourishes that vary from yet are closely identified with or labeled as the original. In recent years, tourist creations abound, such as the Oedo Onsen Monogatari, which is a theme park remake of an Edo-period town that is called the "Disneyland of hot springs" and praised (or scorned) as an ideal place to get "a taste of Japan."[25] At the same time, officially sponsored campaigns have tried to transform mere sightseeing excursions into opportunities for subjective encounters with cultural heritage as a part of the rediscovery of the self with the geo-ritual landscape, whether urban or rural based, which can serve as the setting for moments of revelatory insight.[26] Of course, the culture that spawned the multiperspectivism of Kurosawa's *Rashōmon* might be forgiven for indulging in the kind of unreality the film seeks to expose and deconstruct.

Middle Way

A constructive compromise between cultural exceptionalism and relativism, or remembrance and erasure, or continuity and discontinuity—both sides of which greatly contribute to the conversation but become problematic when taken to an extreme—can be reached by adapting a standpoint based on impartial, objective observation and analysis of the multiple functions of sacred space in terms of ethnographic and statistical studies, as well as a textual examination of relevant documents such as religious writings and gazetteers. Such an approach begins by recognizing that Edo-cum-Tokyo was fundamentally a political environment, a great castle town (*jōkamachi*) at the center of Japanese society founded on the fortress that protected the city where the political apparatus that established the shogun at the peak of his power was subsequently located.

The spatial structure of the city that encompasses the Yamanote and Shitamachi districts was basically designed as an extension of the castle's defenses, with a maze of walls and imposing constructions laid out to create a spiraling labyrinth of dead ends, T-junctions, and narrow twisting lanes to befuddle intruders and maintain an elite ruling class. The distribution of residential areas was used to help promote lines of authority and modes of defense, with the castle surrounded by daimyō estates in the High City forming a buffer between the shogun and the townspeople, as well as marginalized population sectors located in the Low City. Political and administrative information emanated from the shogunate, and the staff in every daimyō's Edo mansion collected the information and transmitted it to their own domain.

However, understanding and drawing from this background in no way implies that sacred space was not viable as a religious entity in that temples and shrines throughout the early modern and modern periods, which may have played a protective function for the regime, have also served as places of refuge and sanctuary continually and enthusiastically supported by devout pilgrims, as well as locations for more casual, idle getaways. Seeing the sacred functioning in a multiplicity of roles and settings that encompass political and practical, yet by no means exclude spiritual and emotional, factors is the primary goal of a thoroughgoing, impartial analysis of religious sites.

What is needed is to strive for a self-critical, decentralizing, and deconstructive methodology based not on judging or preferring any one particular approach but on positing a constellation of juxtaposed discourses by interpreting the centerless centers of diverse sacred spaces. In this sense, the multiperspectival free play of shifting and continually yet purposefully displaced methodologies constitutes the method or is a kind of nonmethod (or an ever-varying outlook) that allows various approaches to be pursued alternatively and critically. From such an ever-flexible standpoint, the main discourses are neither left to stand in polarity nor prompted into an artificial synthesis but are allowed to play off of, bisect, undermine, or reorient each other in ongoing hermeneutic interaction. In exposing the weakness of each viewpoint relative to the locus, the mutual displacement of perspectives simultaneously allows the strengths or positive contributions of exceptionalism and relativism to come into sharper focus and to be evaluated in terms of an objective and neutral yet subjectively engaged standpoint.

I Beg Your Garden, I Never Promised You a Pardon

One can ask whether pure neutrality or objectivity is at all possible in the context of the heated ideological debates generated by the main arguments concerning the nature of Japanese culture.[27] To highlight the dilemma, I offer a personal anecdote regarding my visit one fine summer day while doing research for this book to Rikugien Garden, a Tokyo metropolitan park located in Bunkyō Ward that I mention again in chapter 1, where I discuss the cultural significance of secular space in relation to sacred sites. A short walk from Komagome Station on both the Yamanote Line and the Tokyo Metro Namboku Line in an area of the city that is, like Akasaka, dominated by commercial and residential high-rise buildings yet with other historical sites, the garden was created and designed by the noted poet and loyal retainer Yanagisawa Yoshiyasu in 1695 by permission of the fifth shōgun, Tokugawa Tsunayoshi, and completed in 1702. In 1938, the park was donated to the Tokyo city government, and it was specified as a special place of scenic beauty (*tokubetsu meishō*) by the Japanese government in 1953.

Rikugien is a spacious area that features a central pond, islands, forested areas, artificial hills, and several teahouses. The traditional Japanese garden within the park, which includes manicured grass, craftily twisted pine trees, curved rustic bridges over gurgling brooks, a lagoon filled with carp and small turtles, and many rare birds, takes about an hour to stroll through at a leisurely pace. The name Rikugien, which literally means "six verses garden" comes from the idea of the six main elements (rikugi) in medieval thirty-one-syllable *waka* poetry (*en* means "garden" or "park") that highlight natural and seasonal imagery as symbolic of human emotions and sentiment. Yoshiyasu shaped this landscape in order to express the eighty-eight scenes described in a series of classic linked (*renga*) waka verses.

During my visit that day, I sat on a bench and, after gazing at the remarkable setting, fell into a reverie while reading a tourist account of the value of the gardens, which in the final passage evokes famous Kamakura-era expressions regarding the rotation of the seasons by Buddhist literary figures Chōmei in *Hōjōki* and Kenkō in *Tsurezuregusa*:

> It's not like listening to a poem or going through it, sitting on the green landscape. But it's like experiencing a poem while taking a stroll.... Secreted behind lofty walls, this 18th-century aristocrat's personal field is now a public retreat of tranquility amidst the hubbub of the modern city. Ranging from maples and conifers to flowering camellias and magnolias, there are over 6,000 trees, both evergreen and deciduous. There is something to see here at all seasons of the year. Is it a winter time? The hills are alive with blossoming azaleas. In summer the spreading boughs of venerable trees provide welcome

shade as you walk along the zigzag ways. Approach the entrance gate, and see the famous "weeping" cherry tree. In spring, it flourishes with gorgeous cherry blossoms. At night, the tree is lit with elegant lighting and looks extraordinary![28]

As I sat quite still, my contemplative mind flashed to an imaginary conversation involving a *deshi*, or disciple, who commented to his *sensei*, or teacher, on the beauty of the park but was rebuffed by the remark, "Beauty? What beauty? You just think it's attractive because you've been reading too many books that refer to Japanese gardens as 'beautiful.'" When the deshi replied that the garden must at least have historical significance, the sensei's retort was, "Historical significance? But this is not the real thing; it's just a replica of what someone imagines it may have once been." After a pause, the deshi with a greater sense of hesitation, if not necessarily trepidation, started to say something about the importance of gardens in the era of the shogun, to which the sensei remarked, "Shogun? What shogun?"

In the context of this kind of reductio ad absurdum, my overall feeling is that one-sided approaches on the topic of Japanese religiosity as a cultural construction can be useful for interpreting certain contexts but must be carefully examined and criticized when they fail to appreciate the diversity of roles played in modern society by various aspects of traditional sacred space. By reflecting on the pervasive presence of religious sites in Japan today, I rethink the emphasis on discourses of the vanishing as a way of demystifying Japanese cultural traditions, which are seen as a fabricated collective myth rather than a historical reality. I maintain that discussions of disappearing, dissolving, or lost Japan, which can go to the extent of arguing that Japanese traditions were once pure but are now tainted or—from the opposite extreme—never really existed because they are essentially a mental construct may fail to observe phenomena in an agenda-free way.

In seeking to moderate the imbalance between criticism and romanticization of Japanese religiosity by creating a middle-way approach, I suggest that an evaluation of sacred space is helpful in finding a creative compromise between apparently polarized views of how the notion of tradition has been lost or has vanished and the idea that it represents a myth that never actually existed. In contrast to the views of Japan lost or found, I argue for an alternative approach of "rediscovering (vanishing) Japanese culture" or "finding (lost) Japan," including the religious sites therein, as a phenomenon that is alive and well. This outlook is based on the view that the so-called disappearing or mythical Japan is actually ever present in the sacred sites of

Tokyo neighborhoods but is often suppressed or at least unrecognized, depending on what the interested party is looking for or, seen from yet another angle, is prepared to discern and acknowledge.

NOTES

1. Stephen Mansfield, *Tokyo: A Cultural History* (New York: Oxford University Press, 2009), p. 247; see also Julian Worrall, Erez Golani Solomdon, and Joshua Lieberman, *21st Century Tokyo: A Guide to Contemporary Architecture* (New York: Kodansha, 2010).
2. Mansfield, *Tokyo*, p. 249; see also Hiroshi Watanabe, *The Architecture of Tokyo* (London: Menges, 2001).
3. The train route is a de facto way of dividing the two districts even though some parts of Shitamachi, including the more culturally refined neighborhoods of Yanaka and Nezu, fall inside the Yamanote Line and are part of the Bunkyō Ward, near the University of Tokyo's main campus in Hongo. There are other cases where the Yamanote Line of today does not necessarily match the *gofunai* (within the shogun's city limits) area of the Edo period.
4. As Jan Swyngedouw notes, "[W]hen applied to religion, [secularization is the] awareness that religious beliefs, actions, and institutions find themselves challenged in an unprecedented way by contemporary sociocultural changes, here understood primarily in terms of the differentiation process. Divergence of opinion arises when it comes to evaluating the nature, importance, and influence of religion's response to this challenge to society as a whole," in "Secularization in a Japanese Context," *Japanese Journal of Religious Studies* 3(4) (1976): 291. As I discuss in chapter 1, secularism in Japan, when compared to the West, means something parallel, yet has its own distinctive flavor, which must be taken into account in analyzing the role of sacred spaces. Also, terms commonly used in Japanese for the secular include *sezoku* and *seken*.
5. Akira Naito, *Edo, the City That Became Tokyo: An Illustrated History* (Tokyo: Kodansha International, 2003), p. 83; see also Karen A. Smyers, *The Fox and the Jewel: Shared and Private Meanings in Contemporary Japanese Inari Worship* (Honolulu: University of Hawaii Press, 1999), p. 19.
6. Jan Swyngedouw, "Religion in Contemporary Japanese Society," in *Religion and Society in Modern Japan*, ed. Mark R. Mullins, Shimazono Susumu, and Paul Swanson (Berkeley: Asian Humanities Press, 1993), p. 57.
7. Kenji Ishii, "The Secularization of Religion in the City," *Japanese Journal of Religious Studies* 13(2–3) (1986): 193–209. Ishii notes that three of four major department stores in the area have roof shrines: One from the Shingon sect at Matsuya is at Ryūkō Fudōzon; one connected with Fushimi Inari at Matsuzakaya is at Kakuō Inari; and one associated with Mimeguri Inari on Mukojima at Mitsukoshi is at

Shusse Jizō. Although the Tokyu Department Store does not have one, there are shrines in many other smaller and larger commercial buildings and streets, including several Inari shrines at or near the Kabukiza Theater near Higashi Ginza Station.

8. John K. Nelson, "Household Altars in Contemporary Japan: Rectifying Buddhist 'Ancestor Worship' with Home Décor and Consumer Choice," *Japanese Journal of Religious Studies* 35(2) (2008): 305–330.

9. It is interesting that in Naito, *Edo: The City That Became Tokyo*, p. 81, there is an error in citing a haiku by Bashō that is also cited but rendered differently in chapter 2, "Clouds of blossoms—Is that bell Ueno's? Akasaka's?" The actual poem states "Asakusa" and not "Akasaka," showing that even an expert can make a slip of the pen.

10. Winston Davis, *Japanese Religion and Society: Paradigms of Structure and Change* (Albany: State University of New York Press, 1996), p. 236.

11. Andrew Bernstein, *Modern Passings: Death Rites, Politics, and Social Change in Imperial Japan* (Honolulu: University of Hawaii Press, 2006), p. 21.

12. Toshimaro Ama, "Interview with Hisashi Kondo," *Japan Plus: Asia-Pacific Perspectives* 4(3) (2006), p. 37.

13. Ibid. According to Ama, "Interview with Hisashi Kondo," p. 38: "What it may mean is that when Japanese people say they have no religion, they are stating that they are not believers in one specific sect, not that they are denying the existence of a god."

14. Bill Moyers cites this anecdote in the opening segment of the six-part television production of interviews with Campbell, which was accompanied by the publication of Joseph Campbell, *The Power of Myth* (New York: Anchor, 1985).

15. Examples of such surveys are cited in chapter 4.

16. In an intriguing cultural contrast discussed in chapter 4, several films give a very positive image of funerary rites, including Kurosawa's *Ikiru* (1952) and *Departures* (2008).

17. Ian Reader, *Religion in Contemporary Japan* (Honolulu: University of Hawaii Press, 1991).

18. From the passage "Gotta have faith," in *Time Out Tokyo* (London: Time Out Guides, 2007), pp. 80–81.

19. Ichirō Hori, *Folk Religion in Japan: Continuity and Change*, ed. and trans. Joseph M. Kitigawa and Alan Miller (Chicago: University of Chicago Press, 1968); Miyake Hitoshi, *Shugendō: Essays on the Structure of Japanese Folk Religion*, ed. H. Byron Earhart (Ann Arbor: Center for Japanese Studies, University of Michigan, 2001).

20. Ian Reader and George F. Tanabe, *Practically Religious: Worldly Benefits and the Common Religion of Japan* (Honolulu: University of Hawaii Press, 1999).

21. Peter N. Dale, *The Myth of Japanese Uniqueness* (New York: Routledge, 1986).

22. Stephen Vlastos, ed., *Mirror of Modernity: Invented Traditions of Modern Japan* (Berkeley: University of California Press, 1998), p. 15, comments as follows in the introductory essay: "Judo, harmony, industrial paternalism, folklore studies, 'home': these and other new cultural practices of the prewar period either actively collaborated with militarism and imperialism or were severely compromised by not resisting." The same formula for criticism could be applied to notions such as *bushidō* and *sakoku*, but interestingly enough, this book does not include a chapter on religion or the sacred.

23. Marilyn Ivy, *Discourses of the Vanishing: Modernity Phantasm Japan* (Chicago: University of Chicago Press, 1995); and Alex Kerr, *Lost Japan* (Melbourne: Lonely Planet, 1996). For related discussions on very different yet comparable topics regarding cultural construction, see Eric Hobsbawm and Terence Younger, eds., *The Invention of Tradition* (New York: Cambridge University Press, 1992); and Stephen Greenblatt, *Will in the World: How Shakespeare Became Shakespeare* (New York: Norton, 2005).

24. Karel van Wolferen, *The Enigma of Power* (New York: Vintage, 1989), pp. 230–31.

25. http://www.tripadvisor.com/Attraction_Review-g1066449-d532056-Reviews-Oedo_Onsen_Monogatari-Koto_Tokyo_Tokyo_Prefecture_Kanto.html (accessed July 5, 2009). Also, since the Edo period there have been many replicas of Mount Fuji in Tokyo and other places.

26. See Ivy, *Discourses of the Vanishing*, pp. 44–45, on the "Discover Japan" campaign of the 1970s in response to Kawabata Yasunari's famous Nobel Prize acceptance speech, "Japan, the Beautiful, and Myself" ("Utsukushii Nihon to Watakushi"), which is characterized by "deadvertisement" in seeking to stress the authenticity of self-discovery through the Japanese environment over concerns driven by commercialism. Ivy argues that, in overreaching, the campaign revealed its disingenuousness and becomes its own version of inauthenticity.

27. See Steven Heine, "Ie-Ism ('Sacred Familism') and the Discourse of Postmodernism in Relation to Nativism/Nationalism/Nihonism," in *Japan in Traditional and Postmodern Perspectives*, ed. Charles Wei-hsun Fu and Steven Heine (Albany: State University of New York Press, 1995), pp. 26–27.

28. http://www.asiarooms.com/travel-guide/japan/tokyo/tokyo-parks-&-gardens/rikugien-garden.html (accessed April 20, 2010).

1 SACRED SPACE IS ALIVE AND WELL AND LIVING IN JAPAN

On Tradition and Modernity

One of the leading issues in this examination of the role of sacred space is the apparent contradiction between Japanese behavior or ritual practice, which embraces traditional religiosity through festivals and other rites, and discourse regarding belief, which seems to avoid, deny, or at least downgrade the role of faith. Because this disconnect seems to be directly linked to the decline of religious conviction in the modern era, an important corollary question is whether and to what extent secular society has lost touch with the traditional elements of religion or, conversely, in what ways does Japan carry on and adapt its traditions in a contemporary setting? Is there an underlying conflict or opposition involving the sacred and secular, as in many Western countries, where remnants of traditional religiosity tend to be suppressed, ignored, or compartmentalized by the forces of modernization that emphasize divisiveness rather than collectivism, materialism over spiritualism, and movement toward the future instead of remembrance of the past?

Or, does the case of Japanese religion reflect another, possibly postmodern, alternative beyond the conventional dichotomy of clinging to the traditional seen in contrast to advancing toward the modern? According to this standpoint, apparent differences between Buddhism and Shinto, as well as a seemingly widespread indifference to traditional beliefs despite examples of pervasive ritualism, have not caused the sacred to dissolve and disappear or to exist in a state of incompatibility with the secular. Rather, diverse factors of religious structure and motivation are encompassed and transformed as part of the current urban lifestyle, which seems able to integrate conflicting elements of sacrality and secularity.

To clarify the inconsistency between practice and discourse, this chapter examines the function of traditional religiosity and sacred space in contemporary Japan in relation to the secular, which refers to the body, the physical, the temporal, and the mundane as opposed to the soul, the spirit, the eternal, and the transcendent.

"An idea is a greater monument than a cathedral," said Henry Drummond (the fictitious character who represented lawyer Clarence Darrow) at the climax of *Inherit the Wind* in a moving soliloquy at the so-called monkey trial regarding freedom of speech and the legal issue of teaching evolution in schools. But it is also the case that a cathedral or even a more modest religious site can be considered greater than the sum of the ideas that helped to produce it; or, to put it another way, ideas are conveyed—sometimes subtly and on other occasions in a more direct fashion—through the formal construction and configuration of any and all spaces, whether sacred or secular.

As with the realm of the sacred, secularity as experienced in worldwide cultures is by no means limited to being a modern phenomenon; rather, it is an age-old concept based on the fact that, throughout history, however observant of rituals or devout a society may have been, there invariably existed a segment of group behavior that was essentially nonreligious or profane. According to the original Latin sense, the term *profane* referred to whoever or whatever existed "pro-fanus," or stood outside the temple grounds as the primary religious site. At first it was a neutral term that indicated a basic division between realms, and only in later usage did it come to take on a pejorative sense of disrespecting or desecrating the sacred in combination with terms such as *pagan,* or "paganus" in the original Latin,[1] which initially referred in neutral fashion to the ex-urban or rural community far removed from the religious center. Later it became synonymous with the anti- or at least the nonreligious.

The sacred and the secular, or profane, remain relative terms in that each can be defined only in regards to its sense of opposition to the other. However, unlike the case of cutting a pie into portions, the functional relation between sacrality and secularity should not be characterized as a one-to-one, zero-sum game in the sense that one of the realms begins only where the other leaves off, as there are profound connections, similarities, and disguises that link these spheres of influence. Their relationship is more dynamic and integrative than zero-sum in that key aspects of the sacred are created, diminished, or reallocated by means of the ways in which they intersect with the secular and vice versa. Any of the conditions of emerging and declining or coexisting in overlapping fashion may create a net gain or loss for one or the other or even for both of the realms at the same time.

Contemporary sacred sites in Tokyo, like those in America and other developed (or "first-world") countries in the West, must seek to preserve the elements of a deteriorating past that are affected by rapid economic growth and an ongoing emphasis on achieving a pragmatic use of space as an end in itself. In addition, locations traditionally considered sacred inevitably feel the impact of a general trend toward secularity, or unfettered materialism and consumerism, which tends to deviate from and segregate traditional religious institutional structures and either diminish the motivation to participate in sacred rites or lead to a commercialization of ritual. Traditional religiosity is challenged and even threatened by the continuing rise of the profane to the point where there becomes a slow but steady progression of secularization. Just as it is said that rust never sleeps, ongoing secularization is a subtle practice that gradually, often without quite being perceived—in part because members of a community tend to look the other way—eats away at the texture of the sacred. At any given moment, minor changes that indicate decline may not be so noticeable, but over the course of time the seemingly irreversible corrosion of sacrality becomes quite evident.

In order to survive or possibly thrive amid the rise of secularity in both Eastern and Western societies, traditional forms of the sacred need to find ways of adapting or making accord with the forces of modernity. Many of the cultural differences regarding the way this process is handled are often unrecognized or misrepresented because observers tend to look at the Japanese context through a Western lens, and, therefore, the structural and motivating factors that continue to sustain sacred sites in Tokyo remain obscure. A basic feature of research in comparative studies is that scholars who originated from or were trained in Western methodology examine and comment on religion in Japan far more than the reverse. Japan as Other is turned into a "field" of study.[2] This unfortunately means that in the final analysis the findings of researchers may reflect a bias because they react on the basis of discovering or not discovering (or failing to notice) patterns typical of Western society played out in the Japanese context rather than clearly observing phenomena in the native locale. An alternative is to take a *genba* approach based on the actual reality (*gen*) of the concrete here-and-now place (*ba*) of participant observation.

Some of the cultural differences are vividly demonstrated by two tableaux from contemporary Tokyo. The first is a view inside the gates of a public garden located in Akasaka, which conveys traditional values regarding the aesthetics of nature and how it can be cultivated through human effort. This particular garden is located on the grounds of a shrine dedicated to war hero Admiral Tōgō, although many similar examples are not specifically affiliated with a particular sacred space. Is this site to be thought of as sacred, or can it be compared to the peaceful beauty of gardens in the West, which may also bear historical and cultural value but would likely be regarded as secular? A key element that lends a sense of sacrality to the Japanese garden, regardless of whether it is freestanding or situated in the grounds of a temple or shrine, is the presence of a "nine-turn bridge," found in nearly all landscape gardens in Japan, which was inherited from Chinese patch design. This type of bridge contains both folk religious and metaphysical significance. On the level of folk beliefs, the zigzag structure of the bridge is said to ward off demons, which are confused and thrown off course by asymmetry; seen in terms of philosophy, the twists and turns represent a *Rashōmon*-like multiperspectival approach to viewing reality from all possible angles with utmost flexibility yet without attachment to any particular standpoint.

Another interesting scene is of homemade icons being stored amid flowers and garden tools in the garage of a craftsman's home in the Shitamachi artist's lair, which is the neighborhood of Nezu, across town from where this garden is located but close to other comparable landscaped spaces. The garage contains several examples of Hotei, or Laughing Buddha, as well as the auspicious symbol of the Maneki Neko, or Beckoning Cat, in addition to flowers, lanterns, and other ritual objects. Like Inari, both the Hotei and the Maneki Neko are used throughout Japan in both sacred and secular spaces in order to bring luck to business ventures based on a popular faith in their power to attract good fortune and ward off evil. These icons and implements are probably designed for sale to individuals for use in their home garden or as an object they might want to donate to a temple.

FIGURE 1.1 Nine-Turn Bridge in a Tokyo Garden

It is, of course, quite possible to find similar motifs in the West involving serene gardens and propitious symbols, whereby some aspect of the sacred either overlaps with or occupies space that is otherwise secular, but the distinctive aspect in Japan is how readily sacrality intersects with and/or symbiotically coexists with secularity. I refer to the paradigm in Japan as one of "embeddedness," in which there is an ongoing give-and-take or a freewheeling interplay of realms, so that the sacred appears to be far less overwhelmed or defensive and instead much more readily adapted to the secular. The Western, especially American, paradigm is referred to as "indebtedness," in that a greater degree of separation exists between realms and a sense of deference toward the sacred, which either stands as an autonomous entity distanced from the secular or instead tends to get replaced by the symbols of civil religion.

The notion of civil religion as it applies to American society celebrates secular society as the folk religiosity of the nation-state, with collective celebrations like Memorial Day and Labor Day, monuments like the Washington Monument and Mount Rushmore, scriptures like the Constitution and the Gettysburg Address, and festival foods ranging from turkey and sweet potatoes to the venerable grilled hot dog. These customs reflect the separation of church and state, whereby the affairs and symbols of the nation should not be mixed with, but may end up becoming a kind of substitute for, the religious.

This separation is not relevant to the historical situation of Japan, however, where there are almost no rituals or icons that are fully detached from a sacred context mixed with national history. Using the paradigm of embeddedness to characterize the relationship between sacred and secular in Japan goes a long way toward tilting the balance of the basic contradiction, in that nearly everyone takes part in religion, but there is not much talk about its significance. The apparent lack of discourse about traditional religiosity is thereby no longer seen as a deficiency or loss. Rather, it reflects distinctive conditions of the Japanese sociohistorical context whereby participants in ritual practice may not feel a need to comment on what they take for granted or do as a kind of reflexive action interfused with the secular.

My Tokyo *Mairi* (Pilgrimage)

When planning to write this book, I decided to turn what started out a number of years ago as a kind of hobby of visiting shrines and temples in Tokyo—at first related, albeit somewhat distantly, to my major field of research on the medieval origins of Japanese Zen Buddhism (I often say that I would like to be reborn into thirteenth-century Japan)—into a sustained and hope-fully nuanced study of the significance of sacred sites in Akasaka and Inarichō. Are these sites indicative of a vibrant form of religiosity, or do they represent antiques or museum pieces, that is, remainders or reminders of a bygone era that has not quite gone away but probably will soon enough? I retrace the steps of how I more or less wandered serendipitously into this topic by first discussing personal considerations regarding fieldwork visits to Japan and then moving on to a more sustained comparison of Tokyo with urban spaces that are typical, or in some cases atypical, of modern American society as part of investigating where the secular leaves off and the sacred begins in Japan.

The reason for offering personal comments as a springboard for discussing the paradigm of the embeddedness of sacrality and secularity is that much of my thinking in preparing this study has been based on experiences, impres-sions, and memories gained over the course of well over thirty years of obser-vations that at once confirm and help to break through various stereotypes and received ideas about Tokyo's religious sites. Because quantitative results from surveys about religious structure and motivation seem to be ambiguous or confusing, a qualitative investigation is necessary, but it must be developed and polished over time. To limit the discussion, I use a "bookends" approach that is primarily aimed at capturing two periods in my investigative adven-tures at the beginning and the culmination of the process.

The first period covers one of my earliest stages of travel during a yearlong stint in Japan that took place well before I had any idea that I would ever be writing on a topic such as sacred space since at the time I considered myself strictly a textual studies scholar. The second is a much more recent interlude involving a single kaleidoscopic day of touring a variety of Tokyo neighbor-hoods that proved to be a capstone experience when I was accompanied by a junior colleague while I was trying to wrap up my research and realized that new epiphanies could occur around any given corner. In addition, I comment on the prolonged midway period, when there was a dramatic turning point that unfolded in my perceptions of the relation between sacred and secular space based on turning years of textual studies into opportunities to observe the details of the locations, sizes, and accommodations of various Tokyo sites.

In summing up my access and approach to this study, I refer, in part seri-ously but also in somewhat tongue-in-cheek fashion, to the three-decade cycle that encompassed dozens of visits, some with an emphasis on this area of study, although in most cases the topic was far from my mind, as my "Tokyo *mairi*," or "Tokyo pilgrimage." The term *mairi* can indicate travel to a sacred site in order to observe a rite or study with a teacher; it can also convey a narrower sense of an individual's practice or an expanded notion of pilgrimage involving a group of people, such as a collective of monks or a club or community association. Examples of communal pilgrimage include the Edo period's cyclical Ise mairi, which consisted of trips to Ise Jingu, the earthly abode of Amaterasu, when, about every sixty-five years, thousands of people left behind their daily, rather oppressive lives in Tokyo and Osaka in order to descend en masse on the remote shrine; the ritual visits to gravesites to honor ancestors, or *hakamairi*, of a particular family or clan; or travels to the multiple sacred sites of Shikoku or Chichubu, for example, or annual visits to Mount Fuji carried out by confraternal orders that collaboratively sponsor and organize the activity months in advance. Applied to individual journeys, the term *mairi* can refer to the meditative walking exercises of the Marathon Monks of Mount Hiei, as well as treks of renunciation in a land well known for its solitary poets and reclusive ascetics, who leave behind civilization and enter a hermitage so as to attain a state of contemplation by communing with nature in deep mountain forests.

My case is quite different from these examples because it is largely based on scholarly endeavors about—rather than active participation in—spiritual activities. For most of the time there was no real planning or staging of the process and procedures, and it was only in retrospect that I came to realize that years of frequently unpredictable travel experiences had created a kind of fabric of knowledge about sacred space that could be recast as an ongoing pilgrimage. I had started the journey with no real purpose other than a sightseeing diversion from my main research. As the years went by, scholarly goals and teaching methods led me to take up this area of inquiry in a persistent and dedicated fashion, although keeping my schedule unplanned and flexible was generally conducive to the process of stumbling across new and fascinating sites.

My odyssey began in pursuit of a research specialty that deals primarily with thirteenth-century Japanese religions, especially the advent of the sects of so-called New Kamakura Buddhism, which broke away from the central Tendai church at the end of the Heian era and led to reforms, including the formation and spread of the Zen, Pure Land, and Nichiren schools, among other movements that have dominated the religious landscape ever since. The main topic of my studies since graduate school has been the life and thought of master Dōgen (1200–1253), the founder of the Sōtō Zen sect. In the 1220s Dōgen studied in China for four years and returned to Kyoto, his birthplace, but eventually left the capital in 1243 to take up residence in the lofty and secluded mountains of Fukui (traditional name: Echizen) Province.[3]

For many years, my main idea of what constituted sacred space in Japan was based on the image of Eiheiji, the temple Dōgen established in remote mountains, which is now less than an hour to the east of the current Fukui City, far removed from and seemingly antithetical to the hustle and bustle of the cityscape of modern Tokyo with its labyrinthine transportation system, hodgepodge of above-street power lines, and high-rise apartments where residents hang their clothes and futon bedding out to dry on the balcony. The construction of Eiheiji was patterned on the Song-dynasty style of Chan/Zen architecture and temple layout and was largely inspired by the admonition of Dōgen's Chinese mentor, Rujing, that on returning to his native country, he should stay free of secular attachments and distractions in the capital of Kyoto while cultivating a path of solitude and reclusion.

Today, the temple remains a magnificent set of buildings surrounded by the natural beauty of some of Japan's highest mountains, including the cultic *yamabushi* center of Buddhist asceticism on snow-covered Mount Hakusan. The basic layout of the temple compound, set on a peak that affords stunning vistas, adheres to the simple, functional seven-hall style (*shichidō garan*) prescribed by Zen texts, which lends a sense of minimalism and simplicity that blends seamlessly and in no way interferes or intrudes upon the natural landscape. Like many visitors, I quickly learned that secularization has affected Eiheiji and not only because of the presence of souvenir shops (*omiyage*) in the small town at the foot of the mountain or the modern concrete building designed to house foreign guests. A number of the structures were rebuilt in the past century, and none is actually more than a century and a half old. Furthermore, the compound is currently located some meters away from the original site in a spot that was chosen, in part, because it is relatively easy to control the endless flow of tourists, including members of the parishes (*danka*) of the Sōtō sect, whose donations help to support temple activities.

A House Is a Home

As much as I enjoyed escaping to Eiheiji and other exotic sites in the countryside, my studies were primarily conducted at Komazawa University in downtown Tokyo, in the largest department of Buddhist studies in the country. Koma-dai, as many call it, is located a little to the southwest of Shibuya Station, which is a major stop on the Yamanote Line in an area that was extensively used for the 1964 Olympics. When I first went to the university for an extended research stay, I lived in the small suburban town of Mabashi (literally, horse bridge) in Chiba Prefecture, which lies to the northeast of Shitamachi, and commuted to Koma-dai on a perpetually overcrowded subway car on the Chiyoda Line for almost two hours each way. As luck would have it, the Chiyoda Line was built in the 1970s, just in time for my arrival, as it was able to accommodate the long distance between home and work.

One of the interesting things about the commute is that the subway line covered the full range of the city's districts, from exurban Chiba to the northeast through the Shitamachi section, with a stop at Nezu Station, and then moving on to the Yamanote district and Akasaka before heading to Shibuya Station and back. This was especially interesting on days when I had some leisure time to get off the beaten track and stop at one of the stations on the route in order to stroll and get to know various neighborhoods. As time went by, as noted in Map 1.1, I realized that the Ginza Line was another transportation network that connected seemingly remote parts of Tokyo, and this would prove especially important because it could be taken from Akasaka area (either Akasaka-mitsuke or Aoyama-itchōme stations), where I often stayed on shorter research visits, directly to Inarichō without needing to

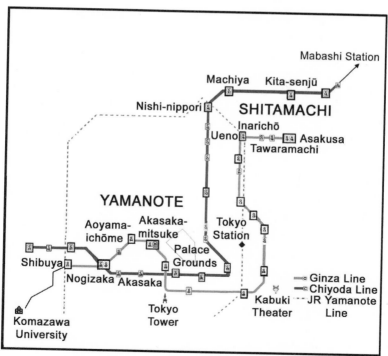

Ginza and Chiyoda Metro Lines

MAP 1.1

transfer. The Ginza Line, the first subway system in Tokyo, was originally designed in 1914 by a businessman who patterned it after the London Underground, and construction of the transit system was completed in the 1930s. At first it extended from Asakusa, to the east, toward Ueno, to the west, with Inarichō as one of several stops; it was later greatly expanded to include the southwest corridor of the city.

As noted by Jean Pearce, the outstanding commentator on Tokyo city life, taking the Chiyoda or the Ginza Line gives a panoramic sense of the full range of Tokyo, in which "[t]he variety is very great. Harajuku along the western sweep and Nippori at the northeast are at the extremes of today's Japan, the one with its boutiques and sports cars and flaming youth and the other with its temples and cemeteries and craftsmen devoted still to the ancient ways."[4] For me, the lines offered a remarkable opportunity to sharpen my sense of contrast between Yamanote and Shitamachi, sometimes on multiple trips during a short period of study in the field.

The part of Chiba where I lived was, at the time, an old-fashioned area still based on a rural economy and where many traditional customs were upheld, such as the profusion of local bathhouses (sentō) and drinking establishments (izakaya). My sense of Mabashi as a throwback neighborhood was reinforced by renting a traditional one-story Japanese dwelling with tatami floors, sliding shoji screens, and amado, or outside interlocking wood doors, as well as a rather large traditional garden. This building, owned by a member of the foreign ministry and frequently inhabited by gaijin over the years, mainly because native Japanese wanted to live somewhere more suitable to the times, was knocked down in the late 1980s and replaced by a garish contemporary structure. Although the home lacked many modern conveniences (despite the fact that it had Western toilets) and featured the unwanted "ventilation" of knotty pine floors that were stilted so as to prevent flooding, which made the house a veritable ice cube in winter months, this dwelling place with its grounds turned out to be an excellent cultural teacher, one from which I gained a firsthand appreciation of Japanese manners.

Just behind my home, which was on the main drag of the town to the east of the station, stood the local Buddhist temple – Shinto shrine complex, which was typical of the amalgamation of the two traditions and has characterized much of Japanese religious history. In the wee morning hours, sometime between the crowing of the roosters at the first hint of dawn and a "proper" hour for waking up, accompanied by the blaring of advertisements through loudspeakers from the shops across the street, came the sounds of chanting at the temple, which was a center for mizuko kuyō (repentance rites for abortion), and of drums beating at the shrine. By the time I walked over to the temple-shrine area after breakfast, however, what I generally found was not the signs of vibrant ritualism but people simply walking their dogs, milling around, heading off for shopping, hurrying by to catch the train on their way to work, or putting trash into nearby bins at these empty, seemingly lonely sites. In other words, the temple-shrine complex appeared more noteworthy for a variety of secular rather than sacred activities. Did the locals, I wondered, consider the sites a necessary nuisance, or did they somehow find spiritual solace in their presence? Or were they simply indifferent? Were the sites thought of as being any more imbued with religious spirit than other traditional cultural spaces, such as the public bathhouse or nearby forested area?

These casual experiences tended to reinforce the impression I had gained from informal readings about modern religion that told of a disinterest in or gradual disintegration of meaningful traditions of the sacred. This feeling was contraindicated, however, when I would go into the city to see some of the major sacred spaces and found evidence of a tradition apparently alive and well at sites such as Meiji Jingu, with its parading rows of priests, or Ueno Park, with its classical five-story pagoda, located near Sensōji temple in Asakusa, which also houses a large pagoda that survived the destruction of wartime bombing while all else in the area was decimated. These two sites, visited by millions of natives and foreigners every year, provide a sacred anchor, so to speak, for the southwest/Yamanote and northeast/Shitamachi corridors of Tokyo, respectively.

Several multifaceted cultural and natural elements contribute to the beauty of Meiji Jingu, which is characterized by "magnificent simplicity," with its "huge trees and wandering paths that effectively mask its center-of-the-city location. The huge torii is made of cypress trees from Taiwan which are claimed to have been more than 1,500 years old."[5] As an indicator of cultural significance, the gardens bear religious as well as important secular meanings: "Since [the irises (*shobu*)] are shaped like swords, they are supposed to impart strength; they are also credited with preventing illness. Once samurai would have a cup of saké mixed with fragrant, finely chopped iris leaves before going into battle. Then the symbolism was slightly different. *Shobu* as a spoken word also has the meaning of victory."[6] Ueno Park, near one of the main shopping districts in Tokyo, is a complex area of historical and artistic sites containing temples, museums, exhibits, and graveyards, as well as various forms of entertainment, including an amusement park, a lake for boating, and a zoo. In spending an afternoon at Ueno Park, one can get lost for hours or enraptured by sacred as well as secular activities.

As I spent more time around Tokyo, the thought crossed my mind that maybe it was not necessary to go all the way to Eiheiji to experience the serenity and majesty of Japanese sacred space. However, Meiji Jingu was a twentieth-century invention that helped to restore veneration of the emperor and Ueno Park was developed first in the 1870s on the grounds of Ken'eiji temple and rebuilt following the devastation of WWII. Thus, I wondered somewhat cynically along with many observers—while also trying to hold on to my innocent reception of the sites—whether these were examples of a kind of commercial presentation or a commoditization with slick packaging of tradition for the sake of attracting tourists rather than an authentic transmission of the past. Maybe visitors participated in traditional religious institutions without a compelling or convincing sense of sincere motivation and commitment. Or, perhaps we should recognize that the notion of an authentic past, along with a sense of loss or of distance from it, as well as an apparent inability to reclaim it, reflects a modern preoccupation with the representation and recovery of what is fading from view yet perhaps never really existed as such.

Inside the Gates

About fifteen years later, my research underwent a crucial turning point as I started to develop a new focus on contemporary religion and society, particularly because studying the origins of Zen Buddhism during the medieval period can require an understanding of current scholarly trends, as well as institutional manifestations, which are often inseparable from the intertwining of Buddhist rites with assimilated indigenous folk religious elements. In researching the famous "Fox Kōan," included in the *Mumonkan* (Gateless Gate) collection of kōan case records and commented on from a primarily philosophical perspective in two fascicles of Dōgen's *Shōbōgenzō*, "Daishūgyō" and "Jinshin inga," it became very important for me to visit Zen temples that incorporate worship of the magical, shape-shifting fox, the primary symbol of Inari, especially at Toyokawa Inari, located in the heart of modern Akasaka, which appears to be a Shinto shrine but is actually a Sōtō Zen temple.

We must recognize that while Eiheiji remains an important meditation center for training monks, many other Sōtō sacred spaces throughout Japan are interfused with folk religious beliefs, such as the worship of a Buddhist or native deity, like another sacred animal (monkey, dog, badger), or a mythical spirit such as a *tengu* (mountain goblin), considered to be endowed with supernatural protective or healing powers. Of the fourteen thousand plus officially listed Sōtō temples, far fewer than a hundred are monastic training sites, which leaves the rest to serve as prayer temples (*kitō jiin*) of one sort or another. Many of the devotional temples, which are often serviced by monks trained at Eiheiji, who perform chants and rituals, as well as chores for cleaning and maintenance, but without including meditation in the daily routine, are located in the countryside, but this trend is also an important factor in appreciating the role of sacred sites in the city. In addition to the Toyokawa Inari shrine in Akasaka dedicated to the fox, which the average devotee might assume was of Shinto derivation, some of the most prosperous Zen temples include a small compound that specializes in purification rites for Kannon. There, believers bathe a statue that is said to help cure the ailments of older women, and a temple dedicated to the memory of a legendary tengu that was said to have protected the site from demons during its founding period in medieval times.[7] What is the basis of the appeal of these icons, I wondered? Is it a belief in supernaturalism, the pursuit of worldly benefits, or a combination of spiritual and material factors that makes the matter more complex and not reducible to a single element?

As time passed and I visited numerous sites in additional neighborhoods all over the city and saw that the integration of folklore beliefs was not an isolated or atypical phenomenon or one linked only to the Sōtō sect but was crucial to the role of contemporary Buddhism and Japanese religiosity more generally, I realized that I was no longer interested in sacred spaces just to serve as a window to the past or as a corollary to textual studies. During the course of the years, I became fascinated by and started trying to reckon with the basic contradiction between Japanese religious practice and discourse by formulating a paradigm of embeddedness. Conversations with various colleagues, as well as conference and lecture opportunities, in addition to external funding and publication prospects reinforced a sense of commitment to the value of the topic. Furthermore, pursuing this research often made what might have otherwise been just another ordinary day in Tokyo particularly edifying and intellectually gratifying. All I needed to do to pass the time in a meaningful and productive way was to pick a new spot on a detailed map—many resources, such as guidebooks and gazetteers, are readily available at newsstands throughout the city—and then wander around looking for or allowing myself to chance upon sacred sites in an otherwise secular area. At this stage of my ongoing Tokyo mairi, several impressions particularly stuck with me.

1. Serendipity

It was serendipity rather than preparation or calculation that often worked best in finding intriguing sites, as occurred one summer afternoon when I happened to get off the Mita Line at Sengoku Station in Bunkyō Ward by mistake (I was traveling between a temple at Sugamo Station and a shrine at Hakusan Station, and this is located midway). There, I discovered Rikugien, which, as mentioned in the introduction, is a beautiful and spacious landscape garden (*tsukiyama*) that was built around 1700 and now consists of a pond, islands, forested areas, machine-made hills, and teahouses. The way I found this gem of a throwback to the Edo period was by getting off at the wrong station and following the signs amid block after block of homogenous, anonymous high-rise buildings until I turned a corner and stepped onto this remarkable terrain.

This garden, located about a fifteen-minute walk from another famous landscape, the Kyū Furukawa Teien, is by no means a unique site as it is one of many such gardens throughout the city. The accumulated feeling I had from this and related experiences was that, in Tokyo, you could be in one kind of space that seems very modernistic and secularized, but then you could walk down an alley, cast your gaze in a different direction, or simply stay attuned to possibilities in your surroundings, and as if through the looking glass a new world opens up before your very eyes. Gardens are significant because temples and shrines in modern cities, especially in Tokyo, with its historical legacy, have a unique situation. Where the sites were once surrounded with forests, the natural environment has been eaten away and taken over by concrete streets. Nevertheless, these spaces continue to function as meaningful gateways that serve as a luminal, intermediating connector between everyday reality and the spiritual world in order to convey concerns and desires to the gods.

2. Spirited Away

Most sacred sites in Japan, including Buddhist temples, feature a torii gate at the entranceway that demarcates a sense of entry into another realm. Throughout world cultures, "Gateways, thresholds and openings mark the transition between one kind of space and another. Crossing them can mark an individual's transition between different kinds of sacred or social space."[8] The torii gate was originally made of two posts set in the ground and a straw rope that was stretched between them, and this was later replaced by one wooden crosspiece that extended past the posts and a second crosspiece that connected the posts below. According to a commentator, "sometimes [the torii] stands alone in the landscape, denoting a sacred place such as a mountain to which it may lead. Passing through a *torii*, the devotee crosses the threshold separating the secular from the sacred world and enters the precinct of the shrine. There, preparing to enter the presence of the gods, the worshipper cleanses him- or herself with a scoop of pure water from a stone trough."⁹ Throughout Japan, torii, which are often painted or lacquered in bright vermilion but are also sometimes made of gray stone, can be an elaborate architectural form in its own right that complements other structures in the compound.

The powerful attraction and inspiration that can be accompanied by fear or trepidation of the sacred—either extreme can create physical signs of high anxiety—are symbolized in an early scene in Miyazaki Hayao's Academy Award-winning, feature-length, and highest-grossing anime film, *Spirited Away* (*Sen to Chihiro no Kamikakushi*), which shows a torii gate standing in the landscape while a family drives by a deserted road as a way of signaling the viewer that the main characters are about to enter a realm of mystery and mysticism. In this magical, mythical arena, emotions are displaced, conventional values are inverted, inhibitions are cast aside, and physical and mental states are altered as the risks and rewards of the spiritual world become manifest. This illustrates what it means for the Japanese to experience the transformative nature of sacrality interconnected with secularity. The popularity of *Spirited Away* also helps explain why so many of Japan's pop cultural products have become exportable to a world full of buyers who are eager for a taste of what lies inside the mystical gates. It seems that Japanese filmmakers, animators, and video-game designers have a knack for preserving and packaging this worldview effectively for global consumption, which speaks volumes about the legacy of Japanese cultural traditions and views of sacred space.

3. Size Doesn't Matter

What does it take for a site to exude a powerful spiritual presence or hold a transformational capacity in the way *Spirited Away* indicates? There are sacred sites of all sizes and shapes depending on the layout and availability of space, and Meiji Jingu is among the largest in the city. However, in the compressed, congested urban context of Tokyo, it can be the small, seemingly innocuous sites that have the most impact because of their staying power. For example, in an alleyway in Akasaka, just minutes away from corporate and government buildings, I came across what seemed like the "world's smallest Inari shrine" in the tiny backyard of a home, which made as big an impression on me as some of the grander sacred sites.

Over the years I have often been struck in finding an intriguing juxtaposition, which occurs by happenstance in the way Tokyo has been developed, between a religious symbol or an example of a secular legacy, such as a garden and a modern building, which may overpower and yet somehow remains integrated with the sacred. I realized that this type of phenomenon—that is, sites that are highly condensed or squashed into the modern cityscape—which easily could have disappeared altogether, especially considering the inflated value of Tokyo real estate, was by no means anomalous.

Rather, the existence of a clear pattern began to emerge. After encountering enough instances in many different neighborhoods, I felt that these apparent oddities must be considered appropriate and, indeed, crucial for interpreting the role of traditional religiosity in contemporary Japanese society. Although such locales might be seen to represent a diminishing of the sacred because the space itself appears to be reduced significantly in both size and importance, from another perspective it appears from the persistence of highly compressed sacred sites that the Japanese are reluctant to give up or are perhaps eager to hold on to these places. There must be a priority and a preference for maintaining their status that abides in people's collective consciousness.

4. The End of the World

A fourth impression of sacred sites came from my experience of finding the "end of the world," Tokyo-shrine style. According to a shtick by Lewis Black, the comedian told the audience that he had been searching for and had finally discovered the place that was located at the end of the world—it was an intersection somewhere in Houston, he said, with a Starbucks on one corner, and, when you went outside and looked across the street, lo and behold, there was yet another Starbucks on that corner as well. Perhaps, Black commented, forgetful people would emerge from one coffee outlet and then, looking up to see the sign, go right over to the other one for their next cup of joe.

My version of finding the end of the world occurred when I discovered two shrines right across from one another on a backstreet in the Yotsuya Sanchōme neighborhood of downtown Tokyo, not far from Akasaka. This was an area with dozens of Buddhist temples located down alleys and on side streets, not far removed from the impressive modern structures of the headquarters of Sōka Gakkai, the largest of the New Religions, on the main thoroughfare. The two shrines, while small, were somewhat larger than the world's smallest Inari shrine, but only one was included on the detailed neighborhood map I was using. Both shrines were dedicated to Inari, but one was actually a Nichiren temple, with a focus on performing mizuko kuyō rites. Like Toyokawa Inari, this was a Buddhist site posing as a Shinto shrine. These sites offer diverse opportunities for purification and prayer, and each creates an atmosphere of quiet reprieve with water and flowers, as well as comfort and consolation in the midst of an otherwise hectic environment.

Tokyo Trifecta

Turning the calendar ahead a few years, during the course of my Tokyo mairi the emphasis of my developing research on the influence of contemporary folk religions led me to spend a considerable amount of time visiting syncretistic sacred sites during many an afternoon strolling through various neighborhoods. One day I was accompanied on a jaunt around town by a junior colleague researching Japanese Buddhist rituals, with whom I began brainstorming about this project. In plotting a long day, I picked out several sites for us to visit in different Tokyo locations, while allowing time to wander about and discover new places without prior planning or set schedule. This was a hot summer weekend, and I was not expecting anything more than a routine visit to a handful of sites mixed with conversations and meals when, in the course of this daylong, dizzying journey, we hit the trifecta, so to speak, of Tokyo sacred spaces—a Shinto wedding in Akasaka, a Zen Buddhist funeral near Roppongi (also in Yamanote), and a Shingon Buddhist *goma*, or votive fire ceremony in Fukugawa (one of Shitamachi's oldest areas). All of this took place in three very different parts of town within the span of a few short hours.

We met in the early morning, and, after visiting the Toyokawa Inari temple-shrine complex in Akasaka, where Zen monks were sweeping the grounds amid a multitude of fox icons, our next stop was an Inari shrine in the area particularly known as a site for marriage ceremonies, with a hotel next door that catered to the wedding party and guests. Sure enough, just as we entered the gate by walking off a busy commercial street, a late-morning wedding procession started moving toward the shrine through a walkway leading from the hotel. A beautiful ceremony was about to unfold, replete with a Shinto priest carrying a parasol to shield the bride from the elements and the beating of drums, along with all the accoutrements of a traditional festive occasion.

This shrine, known as Akasaka Inari Jinja, is a subsection of a larger compound situated on multiple levels of a slight hill near the Nogizaka stop of the Chiyoda Line. As we walked up the steps, we found Nogi Jinja, dedicated to the memory of General Nogi, a hero during the Russo-Japanese War who committed ritual suicide, or *seppuku*, in honor of the death of the Meiji emperor, which represented an interesting mixture of sacrality and secularity. From this vantage point at the top of the hill, we would not have been aware of the wedding taking place below, which was provided a sense of privacy and mystery in the midst of a very open public space (Figure 1.2).

FIGURE 1.2 Wedding at Akasaka Inari Shrine

A couple of hours later in the early afternoon, we stopped by Chōkokuji, located in the Nishi-Azabu neighborhood of Tokyo near Roppongi. Chōkokuji is a funerary branch temple of the main Sōtō Zen temple at Eiheiji. Like many Buddhist temples, the main function of this site is to provide mortuary and memorial services for family members of the sect residing in the Kantō region. The grounds, just a stone's throw away from the hustle and bustle of one of the most popular commercial neighborhoods, offer a serene, Zen-like setting with rock garden and refined, minimalist landscaping, while one of the halls also includes a very large statue of the bodhisattva Kannon. Just as we entered the gates, we saw a funeral ceremony that was wrapping up, with the hearse and limos about to pick up the family and whisk them away from the temple grounds.

By late afternoon, we were in Fukugawa, on the east side of the Sumida River, which was part of the early Shitamachi district dating back to the seventeenth century. This was the neighborhood where the haiku poet Bashō lived before he set out on the northern journey that resulted in the book *Oku no hosomichi* (*Narrow Road to the Interior*), when his first stop was at Senjū, which remains an important section at the northern end of Shitamachi. In Fukugawa, there is a museum of Bashō's works, as well as a memorial statue adjacent to a small Inari shrine in honor of the poet. In looking at these historic sites mixed with religiosity, we stumbled upon the final day of a designer exhibit staged by Amy Katoh, a long-time foreign resident of Tokyo who has published several books on Japanese fashion and folklore.

Amy alerted us to the goma service that was being held at a local Shingon temple dedicated to the deity Fudō Myōō, which is a branch of Naritasan, a large temple compound to the east of Tokyo near the airport of the same name. We ran over to catch the end of the ceremony, which is very dramatic as petitioners seek to cleanse their transgressions and pray for future rewards by tossing petitions into a raging fire while priests chant esoteric spells and beat taiko drums. Not all of the participants were involved in worship, and after the ceremony one of the priests gave a basic evangelical sermon on the history and virtues of the Nichiren sect for newcomers to the temple.

In between the three portions of the trifecta, we observed many other interesting sites, including the expansive grounds of the Aoyama Cemetery district, which houses thousands of graves, numerous Inari shrines, and Fudō temples of various proportions in different locations, in addition to a modernistic Christian church in the heart of Akasaka. We also saw people crossing a pond on a traditional nine-turn bridge in a stunning landscape garden, as well as a home garden filled with popular religious icons. The day ended with dinner in Shibuya near the statue of the famous icon of faithful dog Hachiko at a trendy Zen-like natural-food restaurant situated close to pop culture havens for those dressing up as Harajuku girls.

All of the day's sites and the impressions they made confirmed a feeling that the participants had taken a genuine interest in their religious activities, and nothing seemed to call into question the sincerity of the believers, whether celebrating or grieving, feeling the pain of repentance or the joy of redemption. Although there may be complaints about the high cost of the rituals and questions about the heavy weight of trying to follow traditions and whether they should be strictly upheld or refashioned, it was not evident to me that the Japanese are either seeking radical alternatives or only staying involved because of their pursuit of practical worldly benefits.

A comparable trifecta in an American city would likely include aspects of civil religion with cultural significance, such as a theater, museum, gallery, or restaurant, since the number of sacred sites that one might stumble upon would no doubt be quite limited. If a ritual were being held, the ceremony would be a private affair unless it happened to be taking place on a Sabbath day or a major religious holiday, and access to the site would probably be restricted to dues-paying congregants.

Plethora of Sites, Blights, and Sound Bites

So far I have described embeddedness in largely qualitative rather than quantitative terms. The question that needs to be considered is, what do the numbers indicate? At the same time, however, one can also ask, just how telling are facts and Figures when it comes to assessing the experiential dimension of the sacred in relation to the secular? To a large extent, a quantitative approach simply reinforces the fact that a basic contradiction exists between practice and belief, thereby pointing once again to the need for continuing a qualitative investigation in trying to come to terms with and resolve the matter.

At first, counting sites and the number of people that visit them appears to strongly support a view of the importance of traditional religiosity. It is said of the greater metropolitan Tokyo area, for example, that a matsuri that features the parading of omikoshi takes place in one neighborhood or another every single day of the year. According to an account of the throngs of worshippers and the enthusiasm of the bearers of portable shrines, "The god-presence embodied in the *mikoshi* is carried about the village or urban neighborhood on the shoulders of young men of the community, although women are increasingly permitted to join, with ritual purification beforehand and much drinking of *saké*. A common practice is to jounce the mikoshi to express the exuberance of the god; the amount of *saké* drunk, too, is a manifestation of the god in a kind of holy madness."[10] Furthermore, dozens of different deities and icons are worshipped at diverse religious sites throughout the city and elsewhere. Worshippers may choose from a cornucopia of gods, and rather than offering a devotee only one option, various sacred spaces strongly promote a multiplicity of diverse objects of worship.

It is hard for anyone casually observing these occasions, let alone the local residents, who often join in the yearlong preparations, not to get swept up in the lively (*nigiyaka*), even passionate, quality of the spectacle. The preparations involve ritually installing the god, or *kami*, into the float before the procession takes place. In recent years I have seen that this activity almost always includes younger people, not only children but also teens and young adults, some with dyed hair, pierced body parts, punk clothes, and other indicators that might suggest they would be susceptible to a high level of disbelief and disinterest. Nonetheless, every indication is that the youth are just as comfortable and enthusiastically engaged as both their elders and their juniors or even younger children, who are not yet jaded by modern society. In fact, a quiet sense of joy exudes from the premises of just about every ritual procession I have attended.

Another quantitative factor that seems to support the idea that the Japanese are preoccupied with religion is that the official sectarian membership rate is close to double the population. Of the nearly 130 million people, more than 90 million (nearly three-quarters) report that they are adherents of Buddhism, and about the same number say that they have a Shinto affiliation. This seems to reveal an excited interest in annual ceremonies for observing ancestor worship, such as *Obon*, or Ghost Festival, and *Ohigan*, or the fall and spring equinoxes (all originally based on the lunar calendar but now regularized according to dates on the solar calendar), as well as life-cycle rituals, such as those for childbirth, coming of age, marriage, and death. The Japanese readily partake of both the Buddhist and the Shinto traditions for ceremonies depending on the circumstance of local history and familial affiliation.

In addition to rites of passage, participation in seasonal and daily ceremonies is also strong. Stopping by a Buddhist temple at midnight on New Year's Eve (*Oshogatsu*) to hear the 108 peals of the bell, which symbolically erase transgressions and purify the congregation based on an auspicious number (according to Buddhist tradition, the number of defilements is the same; once shed, these contribute to enlightenment), one observes an atmosphere of religious intensity mixed with a feeling of secular celebration. Similarly, watching the Shinto-oriented rite of purification by shopowners, who throw water or salt in front of the steps to the store, as do sumo wrestlers in the arena, conveys a powerful impression that traditional religion continues to guide daily life even in the world of commerce.

Despite what seems like an affirmation of religion on various levels, however, a visitor may feel that the fifteen-hundred-year history of Shinto and Buddhist interaction is more of a cross to bear than a powerful legacy. Going to a temple or shrine on an ordinary day when no special event is taking place can lead, as I found near my Chiba home, to a sense that these are out-of-date and even abandoned locations. Apathy looms large. Conversations with Japanese ensconced in modern secular society reveal that they have little interest in or zeal for traditional religiosity and in many cases profess to attend ceremonial rites, maintain familial connections to a parish temple, or venerate an altar in the home as a kind of perfunctory display of respect (or guilt) for an abstract sense of propriety toward their ancestors. They generally lack curiosity about some of the basic elements of tradition and may even deny its significance.

This is reinforced by the fact that foreign scholars consistently receive puzzled looks in Japan regarding their research goals. This happened to me more than once while riding the bullet train or stopping by a café and telling a

Japanese acquaintance that I was visiting the country to study Buddhism (rather than, say, for "business" purposes). As mentioned in the introduction, in trying to explain the topic of religious sites, which I thought might have a greater resonance than medieval religion, I have frequently heard dismissive remarks. However, it was also clear to me that some of this was meant to elicit further comments by checking and testing the sincerity of my interest. Some of the best advice about what sacred spaces I should see came from those who at first were all too eager to proclaim their lack of concern.

In a different context, when teaching courses back home, I have had experiences that similarly highlight the idea of Japanese disinterest and disbelief. I have had exchange students from Japan, invited by an American friend attending the course, come in and tell my class that their compatriots "do not care about religion," thereby almost defeating the aim of my lecture on the richness and diversity of Japanese sacrality. I have also often been asked by American students who have traveled abroad why the Japanese value their traditions so little and whether this would make a good topic for a term paper. My answer to this inquiry is: Yes, but also no, not unless the student is able to put this into the appropriate cultural context.

These accounts are impressionistic but are reinforced by the results of numerous surveys on the impact and importance of religiosity, which are complicated and varied depending on the setting in which they are conducted and, therefore, filled with contradictions that make them difficult to interpret. If Japan is included in worldwide surveys that compare its beliefs with those of other countries, the outcome indicates that, in contrast to many groups, the Japanese have a relatively low, perhaps even minimal, level of belief in God or conviction regarding theology. Both India and the United States—undoubtedly for very different reasons—rank highest on this list. In those countries, decisive majorities express strong religious commitment, including more than 90 percent on the question of belief in God, while northern European countries occupy the middle ground.[11] In Japan, less than 15 percent say they believe in God.

Like many other researchers, I have responded to the surveys, as well as to the remarks of Japanese and American students, by pointing out some of the factors of the intricate sociohistorical background out of which current Japanese attitudes become manifest. One approach is to put the situation of weakened religious loyalty in perspective by recounting the modern history of Japan, in which Buddhism entered into a decline from the beginning of the Meiji era, when it was seen as a foreign cult that stifled the emerging desire to assert a nationalist/nativist agenda. Buddhism suffered greatly from official

Sacred Space Is Alive and Well and Living in Japan • 55

campaigns against its standing in the period leading up to the fanatical nationalism of WWII, when its priests were required to negate their vows by marrying and eating meat. Then, Shinto, which had promoted emperor worship in the prewar phase, was somewhat in disgrace during the period following the war for being associated with defeat and loss of face.

Another response to contextualizing Japanese skepticism is to highlight a more extensive view of cultural history since the time of the Jesuit missionaries in the sixteenth century, who were evicted by the Tokugawa shogunate's policies of exclusion and withdrawal. The parish system, which required all citizens to register with a local temple, was established in large part so that priests could help oversee and suppress any possible subversive activity, including an association with Christianity, which had been expelled from the land at the beginning of the Edo period. Since the time they were told that they had to choose between the "two Js"—their native country and Jesus—the Japanese do not necessarily respond well to Western-based surveys about belief in God and observance of religious ceremonies. Either their polytheism causes them to fail to understand fully questions that presuppose a monotheistic orientation—although this does not seem to be the case in India—or they deliberately thumb their noses at queries that appear to be imposed by foreign interests.

Furthermore, one of the limitations of quantitative surveys is that the Japanese, who express disdain for a conception of religion they do not understand or accept, also do not wish to reveal any belief in the world of spirits, which might seem embarrassing from a contemporary comparative perspective, because of the risk of being labeled superstitious or uncivilized. Another shortcoming is that surveys generally focus on the question of belief and do not give an opportunity for informants to discuss or to reveal the high level of participation in rituals. This is due to the fact that, mixed with a strict sense of obligation, there lingers a sentimental or nostalgic sense of continuity and a longing for a rapidly evaporating past.

However, offering these comments does not necessarily reduce the unsettling feeling that Japanese religiosity remains mysterious and hard to decipher. In acknowledging that the results of surveys that target only the Japanese are equally confounding, Winston Davis reviews the findings of a government-sponsored case study (also cited in the beginning of the introduction) and concludes that a point of departure different from the one customarily taken is needed to evaluate the measurements. According to Davis, "The findings of this government survey incline one to wonder whether belief should be the measure of Japanese religiousness and secularity at all."[12] Moreover,

Davis argues, "[a survey by] Basabe found that even among believers there is a low level of commitment to specific beliefs. On the other hand, he found that those calling themselves 'unbelievers' or 'indifferent' to religion *continue to do religious things.*"

Therefore, the basic contradiction of Japanese religiosity regarding the relation between practice and belief seems to remain an irresolvable conundrum, but this should instigate further investigation that is sensitive to the issue of practice rather than exasperation or misleading conclusions about the matter of belief. According to Davis, the key point to consider is that, in Japan, practice itself equals—rather than is the product of—the underlying motivation to participate in traditional religiosity:

> What these findings indicate is that in Japan, the criterion of "believer" and "non-believer" does not suffice to make an adequate distinction between those souls that are truly religious and those which are irreligious or indifferent. While belief naturally seems to be an appropriate index of religiousness to the westerner (and to the Japanese sociologist trained in western sociology), by itself it tells us only part of the story. The reason for this is that religious praxis (*shugyō*) and feelings (*kimochi*) and not belief per se form the core of Japanese religion. The best way to understand the real genius of this religion (and its putative decline) is to turn from what the Japanese believe or think about religion to what they feel and do. This, of course, takes us from statistics to a more humanistic examination of religious behavior.

Davis's standpoint is reinforced by the following comment made by Ian Reader and George Tanabe: "Indeed, Japanese religion is less a matter of belief than it is of activity, ritual, and custom."[13] Davis goes on to suggest that a way out of the conundrum is to understand that, in Japan, religion functions as an integral part of daily life from cradle to grave, so much so that it is probably understood on a subconscious level. Therefore, high levels of apparent disinterest mask a fundamental commitment to participating regularly in diverse and diffused ritual practices.

Japanese Embeddedness versus American Indebtedness

I wholeheartedly agree with Davis that the ambivalence expressed by Japanese people about religious convictions, as indicated by surveys, as well as on-the-ground observations and anecdotal evidence, calls into question the value of quantitative results and demands that we look at Japanese society qualitatively and in a cross-cultural context in order to clarify the issue of how and why practice is preferred to belief. Whereas Davis's fieldwork primarily deals with examples of New Religions such as Mahikari and Ittōen, along with pre-modern millennial cults, which are movements that occupy the margins, my focus is on examples of traditional institutional religions that reveal the contemporary function of sacred space.

The Japanese outlook of embeddedness regarding the relation between sacrality and secularity stands in contrast to most other societies in which interest in religion is either particularly high or low. Village life in India displays an elevated level of both belief and ritual activity, whereas northern Europe represents the nearly opposite instance of neither practicing nor believing to any great extent. In Lutheran Scandinavia, as well as Anglican England, regular church attendance in most areas has dwindled to less than 20 percent, and society has evolved so that people are reprimanded for showing poor taste when publicly using innocuous expressions such as "God bless you," as this might offend nonbelievers.

Surveys indicate that Americans remain as strong in their religious convictions and commitment to belief as any country in the world except India, but while these poll numbers are often trumpeted, contradictory evidence is also apparent. While more than two-thirds of American respondents say they believe in God and the power of prayer, more than half report that they rarely attend worship services, and a quarter say they fall into a rapidly growing category of being "spiritual but not religious."[14] Participation in ritual activities does not necessarily match the rhetoric of belief and shows far fewer signs of vibrancy as a daily occurrence, especially in increasingly secularized urban areas, than is the case in Japan. In many American communities, on Sundays the pews are nearly bare as people feel they have better things to do with their time by engaging in secular activities, such as shopping or recreation.[15] As opposed to Japanese society, the United States appears to be in accord with the spirit of Mark Twain's dictum, referred to in the introduction, in that everyone speaks but nobody does much about religion.

Yet, Japan and the United States may at first glance appear quite similar because of shared pluralism. In both countries, numerous religions coexist, compete for attention, and are allowed to express themselves freely even if this condition stands amid a high degree of apathy and indifference toward traditional forms of religiosity. Due to an apparent lack of interest in belief in the case of Japan or in practice in the case of America, the role of sacred space tends to be downgraded relative to secular preoccupations with fashion, tourism, sports, and commercial development, except where this is mitigated by a concern for historical preservation, which may reflect the practicalities of the real-estate market rather than spiritual concerns.

However, a close look at the respective cultural contexts of Japan and the United States indicates crucial differences between the Japanese approach to pluralism, based on the paradigm of embeddedness between sacred and secular, and the typical attitude in America, based on the approach of indebtedness. Concealing or obfuscating these discrepancies, especially when Asian inclusivism is seen through a Western exclusivist lens, may lead to misunderstandings about the role of sacred space. American pluralism was founded more than two centuries ago on the principle of the separation of church and state. Each religion enjoys freedom of worship but prohibits participation in another sect or denomination and must defer to the laws of civil society when any question of conflict of interest exists. Crossing over from one religious institution to another is due only to conversion, which is generally caused by a major, life-altering event, such as marriage or personal crisis. Japan, on the other hand, has had a separation of church and state for only about sixty years (since the end of WWII), and based on a lengthy history of interactions and crossovers, ongoing combinations and amalgamations continue to flow between the major traditions.

In earlier periods in Japan, the secular was not considered a distraction from the sacred, and the lines of division between these realms were not sharply drawn. The Jesuit missionaries who first arrived in the sixteenth century were greatly impressed with the extent of devotion and discipline they found in Zen Buddhist temples but were soon disturbed and disappointed when they saw things such as visitors climbing into the back-side opening of the Great Buddha (Daibutsu) statue in Kamakura.[16] This simple, unassuming act on the part of the Japanese struck Western clerics as the height of irreverence or blasphemy and highlighted a sharp contrast in views about the relation between sacrality and secularity.

With the rise of mercantilism in early modern Japan, secular endeavors came to play an important role in relation to the sacred, as shopkeepers sold their wares during festival processions, which often included nonreligious, circuslike exhibitions involving freaks, exotic animals, new kinds of crafts, and inventive storytelling, while the selling of talismans and amulets at temples and shrines was common and unquestioned. During the Meiji period, there were examples not only of the sacred being secularized, such as legislation that required Buddhist priests to marry and eat meat, but also of the secular becoming more sacred, as in the growth of ritualism surrounding sumo contests.

Today, colorful festivals continue to integrate sacred and secular dimensions. Examples of embeddedness include the role played by temples at New Year's and other holidays, ritually performed Shinto purification ceremonies for official occasions, and national rites held at Yasukuni Jinja. On street corners in Tokyo, folk religious practitioners offer the services of divination by reading hands and faces. Furthermore, sacrality is by no means limited to traditional religious sites but infuses diverse aspects of Japanese popular culture and may account for its expanding worldwide impact. Many mythic themes evoked by premodern beliefs in supernatural phenomena, such as the intrusion of spirits and rites of exorcism, are regularly incorporated into contemporary pop expressions, including anime and manga. These products have become remarkably appealing and influential around the globe, along with a host of other Japanese cultural exports like sushi and green tea, which tend to recall the glories of the past, in addition to automobiles and electronics, which invite possibilities for the future.

Furthermore, New Religion cults and eclectic movements that started to emerge near the end of the shogunate (*bakumatsu*) period during the nineteenth century, although many of the current groups originated in the turmoil following WWII, when both Buddhism and Shinto were in a state of weakness, often represent a repackaging of premodern rites in contemporary guise, such as purification practices (*oharai*) that promote healing, safety, and prosperity. A New Religion such as Mahikari, for example, is based on exorcising devious foxes, which was a rite long practiced in the Inari cult, while Agonshū uses a fire ceremony borrowed from the Shingon sect.

Mall Effect versus Cluster Effect

To sum up, whereas the American paradigm of indebtedness implies that the sacred generally stands in contrast to or conflict with the secular, the Japanese paradigm of embeddedness means that the sacred is for the most part seamlessly interfused with the secular. In the United States, traditional forms of sacrality are displaced and segregated from the flow of everyday activity and are often treated with separate yet (un)equal status. In order to fill the void that is opened up by the vanishing of the sacred, secular imagery disguises itself as or replaces forms of traditional religion. The tendency toward civil religion can be seen in ethnic holidays like Saint Patrick's Day for the Irish, Columbus Day for the Italians, or Chinese New Year's, which all feature parades and special seasonal food, music, and other forms of rejoicing. It is interesting to note that even Thanksgiving is rooted in nationalism but resembles a traditional harvest festival yet may be considered to exude a greater sense of reverence than Christmas, which has become highly commercialized.

Similarly, public structures tend to replace the role of inspiring awe that might otherwise be played by traditional religious sites. For example, prominent secular spaces like the Philadelphia Art Museum, with its majestic Greek columns overlooking the Schuylkill River, or the iconic, oversized Figures from the "American Gothic" displayed in a Chicago public square, take on the aura of the sacred. Although American cities have many impressive cathedrals, synagogues, and mosques, these sites are generally not as well integrated into the contemporary urban landscape as they are in Tokyo.[17] Rather, they are districted and set aside in segregated "religion row" areas, wherein several houses of worship are lined up on a thoroughfare so that traffic and parking are convenient, while zoning rules restrict other kinds of activities. Just as the mom-and-pop grocery store has died out as American cities continue to be challenged and changed by postwar suburban sprawl,

FIGURE 1.3 Church in Theater in U.S.

so, too, have many of the smaller local worship centers that were once embedded in neighborhoods.

While mainstream religious groups get relocated to the periphery of the city because of recent demographic and lifestyle changes, America's fringe movements seeking to gain a foothold often protrude or impose themselves into society in order to make their presence felt in an otherwise inhospitable urban setting. For example, a Sephardic Jewish synagogue situated in a bank building, a Baptist church located in an abandoned movie theater, and a meditation room at an airport fight for recognition by trying to merge with their surroundings (Figure 1.3). Despite the exercise in blending as a means of survival in a hostile cultural environment, these sites seek to remain separate from the secular realm that they inhabit.[18]

The trend of separation is not apparent in Tokyo, however, where the presence of temples and shrines, large and small, remains strong in nearly every nook and cranny of the city. In contrast to the mall effect, whereby the sacred is more or less expelled from the neighborhoods of American cities, there is a cluster effect in having a multitude of sites situated side by side in any given area. In the Yotsuya Sanchōme Station neighborhood (Map 1.2), referred to previously in the discussion of the "end of the world," dozens of temples and shrines stand in a compressed area.

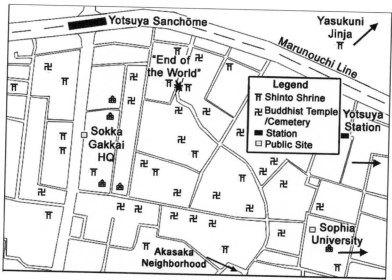

Sacred Sites in Yotsuya Sanchōme

MAP 1.2

Difference and Indifference

In Japan, sacrality is such a strong cultural force that its effects spill naturally over their boundaries and fit comfortably and uncompromisingly into the secular realm. As an example of the intertwining between realms, the sacred pattern becomes part of commerce when the style of traditional votive banners in bright vermillion and white colors typical of an Inari shrine gets appropriated through hangings with the same color scheme that are used for a modern advertising campaign in the commercial neighborhood of Roppongi near Akasaka or as ads at the entrance to a parking garage. To gain luster the secular deliberately presents itself in a way that could be mistaken for the sacred.

In a complementary example, a noodle shop's sign featuring a grimacing Buddhist priest that stands in the heart of Inarichō creates a lighthearted mood that helps soften feelings of morbidity or gloom lurking beneath the surface amid the area's linkages with death and dying (Figure 1.4). In a similar instance taken from the Yamanote neighborhood of Yotsuya Sanchōme, with its multitude of small temples in the backstreets, the image of a winking priest carrying his staff helps advertise a local shop that sells name stamps (*hanko*) and business cards (*meishi*). In all of these examples, the sacred and the secular are intertwined to the point of inseparability, and yet it is important to realize that the priority of sacrality remains strong as secularity seems to capture or emulate its aura of authenticity. Because of the easy interaction between the

FIGURE 1.4 Inarichō Soba Shop Sign

religious and the secular, sacred space in Tokyo is not necessarily a managed site that is clearly defined and distinct from commercial or residential areas.

One way of highlighting the significance of this is to compare Tokyo with another global city much better known for its religious sites—Jerusalem. One of the prayer requirements for all visitors to the Western Wall in the Old City, according to Jewish tradition, is to wear a head covering. Although it is possible to arrive at the wall unprepared and get equipped with a napkinlike paper strip to place on one's head at the last moment before entering the holy area, what happens, in fact, is that most people, both men and women, young and old, and worshippers and tourists alike are out looking for attractive alternatives. Thus, hat shops like the one in Figure 1.5, located at a bus stop that leads travelers to the Old City, have sprung up along the sidewalks of the hectic, modern streets of the New City. This phenomenon represents an element of traditional sacrality that injects itself into contemporary secularity with a mixture of reverence and commercialism in a way that at once tends to overcome religious differences and underscore a casual indifference or even a deep reluctance toward traditional religiosity on the part of the general populace.

In parallel fashion, while Tokyo appears highly secularized and antithetical to tradition, it retains a vibrant ritual life that must be sought out amid the evidences of modernity, yet need not be either romanticized or reduced to pragmatism. For example, a restaurant owner of a noodle shop near Ōji Inari Jinja

FIGURE 1.5 Hat Stall near Bus Stop to Old City, Jerusalem

particularly famed for its veneration of Inari because of its location at what once was the very edge of the city limits, where foxes were said to lurk and congregate for mythical wedding processions with a stolen human known as *kitsune-yomeiri*, shows off his collection of icons gathered from all parts of Japan.

NOTES

1. Peter Brown, *The Cult of the Saints: Its Rise and Function in Latin Christianity* (Chicago: University of Chicago Press, 1982).
2. Theodore C. Bestor, Patricia G. Steinhoff, and Victoria Lyon Bestor, eds., *Doing Fieldwork in Japan* (Honolulu: University of Hawaii Press, 2003).
3. See Steven Heine, *Did Dōgen Go to China? What He Wrote and When He Wrote It* (New York: Oxford University Press, 2006).
4. Jean Pearce, *Foot-Loose in Tokyo: The Curious Traveler's Guide to the 29 Stages of the Yamanote Line* (New York: Weatherhill, 1976), pp. 8–9.
5. Ibid., p. 141.
6. Ibid.
7. See Steven Heine, *Zen Skin, Zen Marrow: Will the Real Zen Buddhism Please Stand Up?* (New York: Oxford University Press, 2008), especially the chapter titled "Zen Rites."
8. Caroline Humphrey and Piers Vitebsky, *Sacred Architecture: Symbolic Form and Ornament Traditions of East and West Models of the Cosmos* (London: Baird, 2003), p. 132.
9. Ibid., pp. 92–93. Furthermore, "Gateways make the most elaborate and explicit statements about controlling who may or may not enter a sacred space," p. 133.
10. Francis Dorai, ed., *Insight City Guide Tokyo* (Singapore: APA, 2007), p. 36.
11. See Hans Joas and Laus Wiegandt, eds., *Secularization and the World Religions*, trans. Alex Skinner (Liverpool: Liverpool University Press, 2009). There is much evidence that attitudes in America are changing since in a 2010 survey of young adults who called themselves Christians, two-thirds said they rarely or never prayed with others, rarely or never attended worship services, or did not read the Bible or other sacred texts, while also saying they were more spiritual than religious; see also Cathy Lynn Grossman, "Survey: 72% of Millennials 'More Spiritual than Religious,'" *USA Today* (Apr. 26, 2010).
12. Winston Davis, *Japanese Religion and Society: Paradigms of Structure and Change* (Albany: State University of New York Press, 1992), p. 236: According to a study of younger men living in urban Japan:

    14 percent said they believed in some religion; 22.1 percent said they did not believe; 59 percent were indifferent.... Still more revealing was the finding that of those styling themselves "unbelievers," 32.5 percent have Buddhist and Shintō altars in their homes, 57.6 percent participate in festivals and pilgrimages, and 27

percent carry an amulet. Of those "indifferent" to religion, 59.3 percent have Buddhist and Shintō altars and 34.5 percent offer prayers before these altars. Six percent do so daily, while 28.4 percent do so occasionally. Sixty-one percent now and then participate in pilgrimages to shrines or temples and 43.1 percent carry amulets. (p. 235)

13. Ian Reader and George J. Tanabe Jr., *Practically Religious: Worldly Benefits and the Common Religion of Japan* (Honolulu: University of Hawaii Press, 1998), p. 7.

14. Christine Wicker, "How Spiritual Are We? Surprising Results from an Exclusive *Parade* Poll," *Parade* (Oct. 4, 2009), pp. 4–5.

15. There are notable exceptions on major religious holidays or in communities that preserve their traditional ethnic character or represent a revival of premodern forms of biblical piety among orthodox Jews, devout Catholics, and fundamental Christians.

16. See Giles Milton, *Samurai William: The Englishman Who Opened Japan* (New York: Penguin, 2002), for a discussion of the shocks that the Jesuits underwent in observing the Zen monks' sexual predilections.

17. Holland Cotter, "Urban Uplift: Sanctuaries for the Spirit," *New York Times* (Dec. 25, 2009). It is interesting to note that a book featuring walking tours of New York City that is part of the series "On Foot Guides" barely mentions a single example of sacred space; see June Egginton and Nick O'Donnell, *New York Walks* (London: Petersen, 2006).

18. Some other examples include an Islamic center next to a donut shop in an inner-city area of Philadelphia and a santeria botanica store that sells ritual supplies in a strip mall in a Cuban-American section of Miami.

2 TOKYO, CITY OF . . . TEMPLES?

Why Tokyo?

The initial question a reader may raise about this book is, why Tokyo? Is it appropriate to begin a reflection on the meaning and significance of sacred space in Japan by focusing on the major city, which is marked nearly everywhere by modernism? It would seem that almost any other location might be more fitting than the capital, a sprawling megalopolis that represents the center of national political and financial power and is a veritable bastion of secularism and consumerism. Western commentators have often referred to Tokyo as an "ugly city" because of its pervasive power lines, train lines, overpasses, tall buildings, and other modern structures that block one's view and prevent access to nature or a sense of mystery and awe for much of anything other than the Almighty Yen, as well as current electronic and fashion trends and antitrends. If characterized in a nutshell, Tokyo might seem to be a "secular altarpiece"[1]—the city of *depaato* (department stores) and skyscrapers or of *konbini* (convenience stores) and transportation networks or of neon signs and maid bars... but surely not temples.

From a cultural standpoint, Tokyo is a storehouse of early history, especially in the aftermath of the four-hundredth anniversary of Edo festivities, which took place in 2003. However, these would seem to represent decidedly worldly rather than sacred designations. At first, it might appear that the closest one might come to religiosity is that there are a number of spots known as Fujigaoka, or "slope for viewing Mount Fuji," and on a clear day from an upper floor of a high-rise office building or hotel this may even be possible. Tokyo appears to be anything but religious, and so one must ask, to what extent does the sacrality of space at temples and shrines play a role in today's urban society?

Further casting doubt on the value of studying sacred space in Tokyo is the fact that Japan is a country well known for its multitude of sublime religious sites, especially in nonurban areas, perched on mountain peaks, secluded in remote forests, straddling waterways, or occupying lush territory, which are attended by regular devotees, inspired pilgrims, and streams of tourists; examples are the shrine that overlooks the spectacular Nachi waterfalls in Wakayama Prefecture, south of Osaka, which is also the home of the magnificent Mount Kōyasan; the main temple of the Shingon sect, founded by Kūkai in the ninth century; and the massive torii at Miyajime, which appears either in the water or on dry land depending on the tides.[2] A key to the beauty and utility of these sites, which makes them so attractive to ritual participants and casual observers alike, is a mystical communion with nature, either by blending in with the environment or by using wood and other elements to construct buildings that are at once aesthetic and efficient in embracing the qualities of minimalism and simplicity of design.

With regard to cities, no doubt Kyoto, with its verdant geographical location in a valley surrounded by mountains on three sides amid the flow of pristine rivers, canals, and hillside streams, would seem to be the city of wondrous religious sites, which are everywhere apparent and epitomize the meaning of sacred space in an urban setting. Kyoto could be considered one of the world's premier "sacred cities," along with Rome, Mecca, Jerusalem, and Benares, where religious institutions are at the core of the urban center's raison d'être.[3] In each of these locales, visitors can easily seek out and find the institutional centers at the heart of the respective traditions and also realize that they cannot avoid seeing at least some sign of the sacred, such as shops that sell amulets, in nearly every area of the city, including the seemingly secular. Kyoto is smaller than Tokyo and easier to get around, and its environs on Mount Hieizan and at Lake Biwa are also replete with some of the most impressive examples of Buddhist temples and Shinto shrines.[4]

Returning to the case of Tokyo, several sites located in the countryside that are accessible yet far removed from the city center stand out for exhibiting a mystical quality in the midst of beautiful natural surroundings, including the esoteric temples at Mount Takao to the west of Shinjuku, Mount Narita in Chiba Prefecture, to the east of Ueno Station near the airport, and Saijōji temple outside of Odawara, a little to the west of Yokohama on the Shinkansen train route. However, discussing these places in no way captures the full picture and should not dissuade us from acknowledging the profusion of sacred spaces within the heart of Tokyo. As indicated by the Map 2.1, in addition to the renowned and frequently visited Sensōji or Asakusa Kannon and Meiji Jingu at the northeast and southwest gateways to the city, respectively, numerous notable sites appear throughout the metropolitan area.

Some of the main examples of Tokyo's sacred sites to the north of the palace grounds include the following:

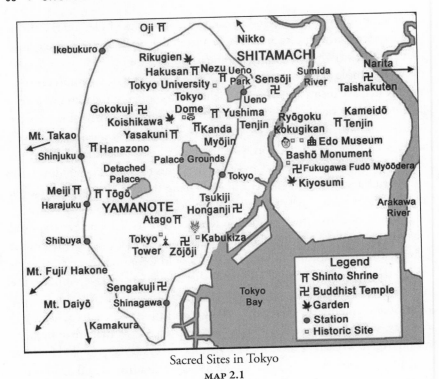

Sacred Sites in Tokyo

MAP 2.1

- Gokokuji, the oldest surviving temple in Tokyo, dating from the seventeenth century
- Hakusan Jinja, which commemorates the deity of Mount Hakusan, a snow-covered peak in northwestern Japan whose beliefs have spread throughout the nation
- Kanda Myōjin, the original protector of the northeast corridor
- Nezu Jinja, an Inari shrine with Buddhist syncretism known for its azalea festival held every summer
- Ōji Inari Jinja, which commemorates the area of "fox weddings" depicted in a famous *ukiyo-e* print by Hiroshige
- Yasukuni Jinja, which houses the war dead and is known for hosting controversial visits from various prime ministers that ignite protests from former opponents China and Korea
- Yushima Tenjin, near Yushima Seidō, a former Confucian academy located in the northeast. High school and university students come here to pray for good grades during the crucial "exam hell" period.

To the south of the palace stand the following sites:

- Atago Jinja, with its tall slope and steep steps to a high summit in the middle of town
- Sengakuji, which memorializes the famed forty-seven rōnin who committed suicide to avenge their warlord's assassination in the Edo period
- Tōgō Jinja, a shrine near Harajuku Station dedicated to Adm. Tōgō Heihachirō, a war hero celebrated as a Shinto kami
- Tsukiji Honganji, a Pure Land temple rebuilt in the 1930s with continental Buddhist influence
- Zōjōji temple, which contains the Tokugawa clan mausoleums and stands in the shadow of the Tokyo Tower in Shiba Park, a pastiche of the Eiffel Tower; constructed in 1958, the temple houses a Shinto shrine on the second floor of the main observatory.

In addition, to the east of the Sumida River the following are found:

- Fukugawa Fudō Myōō, an aged Shingon temple affiliated with Narita temple and famous for its fire ceremony
- Kameidō Tenjin, one of the largest and most active shrines west of the Sumida River
- Taishakuten temple in Shibamata, home of the beloved movie character Tora-san.

Some other important sites that are not necessarily sacred but contribute greatly to the appreciation of traditional culture and spirituality include the landscape gardens of Kiyosumi, Koishikawa Korakuen, and Rikugien, all of which stem from the Tokugawa era and stand immaculately preserved in the shadow of modern buildings or, in the case of Kiyosumi, a Bashō monument near the area where he lived before setting off on the poetic journey that led to the creation of *Oku no hosomichi*; the area near Ryōgoku Station, which houses the Edo Historical Museum along with the Kokugikan sumo stadium; and Kabuki theaters, including the national theater at Higashi Ginza Station and smaller stages in the area of Ningyōcho, near the original locale of the performances held during the Edo period.

Does all of this make Tokyo a city of temples? The challenge underlying this question brings us face to face with the polarities of sacrality and secularity and of tradition and modernity, which occupy the urban setting. As Paul Waley comments on the role of Sensōji, unlike the case of Kyoto, where many of the temples are rarified sites in the peripheral hillside away from and not really affecting the flow of everyday activity, Asakusa and other Tokyo shrines and temples are very much an integrated part of the fabric of ordinary life and yet are also able to stand out as something special and interesting.[5] This minor comment in Waley's lengthy account of the capital city's neighborhoods is crucial for understanding the role of sacred space in Tokyo and the importance of examining religious locations that reflect seemingly commonplace, everyday concerns and habits.

One indication of the significance of the kinds of sacred sites being considered here is the popularity of guide books such as *Tokyo no otera/jinja: Nozo toki sanpo* [*Tokyo Temples and Shrines: A Stroll through the Mysteries*][6] and *Tokyo Goriryaku Sanpo* [Tokyo Strolls to Temples/Shrines for Gaining Practical Worldly Benefits],[7] which, as the titles suggest, highlight the idea of strolling or ambling about (*sanpo*) various areas of the city to find an appropriate place of worship. Although the title of the first book mentioned does not refer specifically to seeking worldly benefits (*riyaku*), as does the second work, the material gains that are supposed to be provided by each site are listed for the several dozen places discussed. These are just two of the many such works available at local bookstores.

Another indicator of the pervasive effects of sacred space in Tokyo is the prevalence in many areas of the city of signs that point out for pedestrians "Scenic Spots and Places of Historical Interest Information," which include local shrines and temples, as well as other notable cultural sites, such as gardens, museums, and memorials. The presence and availability of so many kinds of books and street signs show that many neighborhoods contain clusters of sites, and the experience of touring them is highly valued. While the sites chosen for this work are but a very small sampling of what takes place throughout the city and are not necessarily the most important examples, and even though other neighborhoods could have been used, these are very much representative of Tokyo's complex socioreligious fabric.

The Shogun's City: Planned or Unplanned?

The juxtaposition and comparison of the Akasaka and Inarichō neighborhoods highlight connections and disconnections between two distinct parts of the city, whose origins in the Tokugawa or Edo period as discussed by Edward Seidensticker in *Low City, High City: Tokyo from Edo to the Earthquake*, greatly affect the nature of urban life, as well as the role of the sacred sites contained therein. These neighborhoods adapt city planning initially established by the shogunate for the purposes of maintaining military control and social-political supervision over the general population in the early modern period to the economic realities and lifestyle conditions of the world today. Where much has changed, a great deal has not yet been significantly affected. This ongoing process of preservation tinged with a considerable degree of alteration helps to keep alive the vitality and utility of traditional sacred spaces.

Tokyo can appear to be a confusing and chaotic city, an impenetrable swirl of streets and train lines that is so obtuse that even the Japanese, let alone foreign visitors, must frequently stop by a *koban* (police booth) to ask for directions to a particular address from a policeman who will probably need to draw a map. However, a surface impression that the city is disorderly is misleading because the shogun's meticulous planning has served multiple purposes in creating political authority and military presence, as well as fostering economic ties and commercial exchanges. The shogunate was able to take advantage of the local environment and transmute its apparent weakness as a swampy backwater region into an opportunity to develop complex waterways with landfills that furthered the basic aims of defending the fortress and accommodating the residency of both allies and rivals.

The fundamental division in the city's social landscape is rooted in the political economy and geography of the Tokugawa era, when the shogunate established its main base in Edo in the early seventeenth century, long before the advent of modernization and westernization two and a half centuries later. As the city of Edo was first being formed in the seventeenth century, according to Hidenobu Jinnai, it:

> was built among a particular set of natural conditions that included frontage on the sea and a plethora of hills and rivers—a topography replete with variety. The Shitamachi, Downtown, area that developed along the shores of Edo Bay and the Sumida River was a "city of water" laced with a network of canals. On the other hand, Yamanote, the Upland, which emerged among the plateaus and valleys of the Musahino hills, could be called a "city of fields and gardens" wrapped in green. This dual structure, which developed in close collaboration with nature, is the major characteristic of Edo's urban space, and what makes this Japanese pattern distinctive.[8]

Thus, the shogun made a deliberate decision to construct an inner territory within the seven Musashino hilly sectors, barely discernible in the Tokyo of

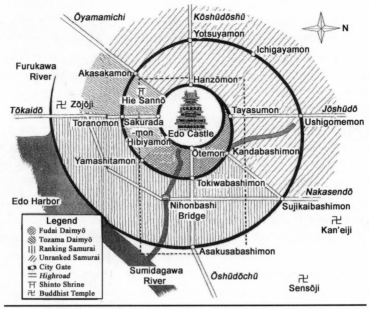

Geomantic Design of Edo/Tokyo

MAP 2.2

today, of Ueno, Hongō, Koishikawa-Mejiro, Ushigome, Yotsuya-Kōjimachi, Akasaka-Azabu, and Shiba-Shirogane, which were separated by a maze of ridges and valleys.[9] Within this area, as seen in Map 2.2, he built up the shogun's castle, which was encircled by a spiral system of canals marked by thirty-six massive checkpoints (the actual figure was thirty-two, but thirty-six was considered an auspicious number), each with an outpost or lookout (*mitsuke*) tower and fortified by a complex series of moats and protected bridges. One of these was Akasaka-mitsuke, the name of the subway station that serves today as the main point of entry into the Akasaka neighborhood.

Paul Waley's explanation is useful in clarifying the illustration of the original structure of early Edo:[10]

> The scheme [the shogun] and his advisers hatched was the "*no*" plan,
> so named because it involved the construction of canals and moats and
> the use of existing rivers to form a continuous web of water like the

whorls of a fingerprint, or like the Japanese character *"no"* (ō). Improvised and sinuous, so different from the stately, square Chinese grand plan, these whorls were crossed by bridges, many of which still exist, and guarded by fortified gates. The two inner whorls of water enclosed the castle itself and its dependent buildings, which included the palaces of family members and the residences of collateral families and senior administrators.[11]

Jinnai further explains that "Edo lacked the walls that typically surrounded European cities and within its precincts, water, hills, and forests blended with city streets to create a special urban environment."[12]

Beginning with the swirling, geomantically based design of the city in 1603, the central feature of Edo/Tokyo's cultural legacy has been that the shogun surrounded himself with powerful warlords and other samurai who were situated inside the precincts of the hills of Yamanote near the castle's central area. The more marginal citizens, along with various sorts of outsiders and outcasts, were assigned to the Shitamachi area, especially to the northeast corridor below the hills. In this way, the shogunate controlled all aspects of commercial and social interaction between classes and ensured that key civic functions were regulated in their appropriate districts.

The shogun placed the prominent *fudai daimyō*, or those provincial warlords who had demonstrated their allegiance and support, immediately to the east of the castle. The *tozama daimyō*, whose commitment to the shogun's leadership was suspect, were situated to the south. To ensure their loyalty and make certain that they would not plot against him, all of the daimyō were rewarded with large mansions near the source of power. As required by the policy of *sankin kōtai* (literally, "alternate attendance"), all of the daimyō were forced to make annual visits to the capital from their respective locales so that the shogun's troops could oversee their activities. The leading members of the samurai class were located farther east and south than the daimyō and enjoyed much of the finery of their superiors, while the rank-and-file warriors occupied the western and northern sectors of the High City in more cramped and inconvenient housing. It was the association with success and prosperity that apparently led to the formation, beginning in the Edo period, of Inari shrines in this part of the city, where upward social mobility gained through good fortune could be seen to prove the efficacy of prayer and demonstrate the rewards that the sacred sites offered to ritual participants.

The lowest-ranking members of the warrior class, who were not even allowed to own a horse and were known as the *kachigumi* (literally, "those who walked"), were situated to the east of the castle and south of Ueno, right on the border between Yamanote and Shitamachi. This eventually gave rise to the name of the Okachimachi train station, located today near the electronics shops of Akihabara.[13] The rest of society was distributed by the shogun into the outlying area east of the hills that was literally "below the [main part of] town" (*shitamachi*), referring to a flat, plains area downward from the hilly territory.

Shitamachi is sometimes translated as "downtown," which is not inaccurate, but the term means something nearly opposite to the way the word is usually evoked in the West to refer to a city center with its confluence of banks, company offices, and civil or government buildings in addition to museums and cathedrals. In Tokyo, this meaning of the term *downtown* would apply best to the High City rather than the Low City. Shitamachi, however, refers to downtown Tokyo along the lines of the way the expression is used to indicate the fringe districts of Manhattan, which contain Greenwich Village and Chinatown. In other words, it is a locale somewhat off the beaten path that provides a desirable reprieve from the humdrum of daily life and has been able to establish its own brand of cultural vitality and social identity, albeit mixed with a sense of the melancholy of those who are dispossessed. Even though it retains a distinctive artistic flair and festive atmosphere, the Low City is distinguished from the classy uptown area in being occupied by a demographic sector that is poorer economically and weaker politically.

Japan underwent a prolonged phase of 250 years of isolation, while having little contact with the outside world other than in the port towns of Nagasaki and Osaka, which received some visitors from China in addition to Holland, who occasionally brought the latest advances from Europe. Once modernization was introduced at the end of the nineteenth century, even though the samurai tended to misunderstand and resist this development and even wore metal helmets to protect themselves from the deleterious effects of telegraph or electric wires overhead, technology was quickly adapted and perfected by Japanese entrepreneurs. For example, railways were not known to the Japanese until the 1860s, and then, within a decade of the opening of the first short line between Shimbashi Station in Tokyo and Yokohama in 1872, Japan had produced an efficient and comprehensive train system that was the rival of any in the world. The development of extensive rail networks had an enormous impact on the spread of urban neighborhoods, which became organized around a station as the center of economic activity, although for many reasons the fabric of traditional lifestyles remained more or less intact.

Empty Center

The layout of the High City, with the secluded castle at its core, is somewhat similar to the structure of Beijing, which harbors the Forbidden City at its center, as established by the Ming dynasty rulers, who wished to isolate themselves from contact with their minions and potential enemies. In an interesting contrast with major Western metropolises, the hub of financial advancement and political authority in Tokyo revolves around what modern French philosopher Roland Barthes calls an "empty center" in his trend-setting semiotic study of Japanese culture, *The Empire of Signs*, which was written after he returned to Europe from a lecture tour in Japan.[14] Barthes envisions the vacant core as a kind of metaphysical void or living symbol of the Zen Buddhist notion of nothingness, which is often represented in calligraphy by a vacant circle (*ensō*).

As the maps in Figure 2.1 indicate—one from the Edo period and the other a contemporary subway locator—there has been and continues to be an empty city center, which reflects where once the shogun's castle stood and

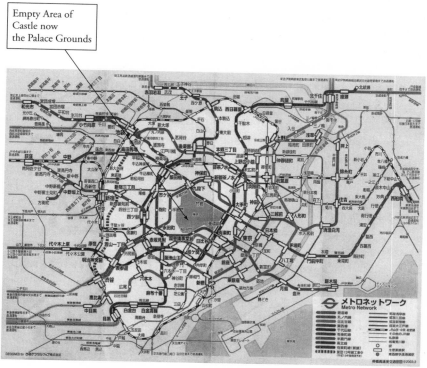

Empty Area of Castle now the Palace Grounds

FIGURE 2.1 Modern Transport Map Revealing the City's "Empty Center"

today the imperial palace stands. Barthes is correct that the empty center remains the key element of urban geography, prime real estate that has been left undeveloped and hidden from view in that it is open to public visits only on special ceremonial occasions. Because of this urban structure, the main buildings of governance and commerce are kept on the sidelines, and the largest temples and pagodas, such as Ueno/Asakusa and Meiji Jingu, are located on the periphery of the city in the northeast and southwest, respectively.

Barthes' approach has been criticized as an Orientalist fantasy or a romanticization of tradition that contributes to masking the essentially political origins of the phenomenon since the empty space at the core of Tokyo has been the source of political power and authority. Nevertheless, Jinnai tends to agree with Barthes' contrast between Tokyo and the West by suggesting, "This pattern illustrates the motif of the interior (*oku*) that the architect Maki Fumihiko has identified as characteristic of Japanese urban and architectural spaces."[15] Jinnai further remarks, "This manner of situating religious facilities in Edo was the exact opposite of the European pattern. In Europe a cathedral, as the religious center of a city, was located at the most prominent place on the square."[16] Although Edo-period castles are an important exception, another striking contrast with the West is that the main buildings in Tokyo traditionally were low and caused the viewer to gaze downward to appreciate functionality and aesthetics rather than upward to admire majestic height.

As a way of further exploring a comparison between Tokyo and major cities in the West, it is notable that Joseph Campbell has commented that in medieval Europe the center of a city featured a cathedral as the most prominent architectural triumph, as with the Notre Dame, one of the first of the great Gothic churches built in Paris during the late twelfth century. The East Asian version of this would no doubt be the pagoda, which, for example, dominated the urban landscape of Kaifeng, capital of Northern Song China. The Ueno and Asakusa pagodas were no doubt the tallest structures of Tokyo, although these were located on the periphery of town. In early modern times in Europe and the United States, the function of the central urban area was no longer based on a religious building but on the pinnacle of secular—especially civil—authority, as with the Eiffel Tower, which was opened in 1889 for the Universal Exhibition and Centennial of the French Revolution.[17]

An interesting case of civil authority being manifest in a central structure is the City Hall of Philadelphia, which was founded in the seventeenth century by William Penn, who strictly followed a grid plan of urban design. Standing right at the central intersection of the grid at Broad and Market streets, City Hall is an edifice that was constructed over the course of thirty

City Hall, 1901

Newer 1980s Office High-rise

PSFS Building, 1932

FIGURE 2.2 Center City in Downtown Philadelphia

years and was hailed as the tallest building in the world when it was completed in 1901, with a statue of Penn adorning its summit. After its height was surpassed by other buildings around the globe, by local custom City Hall remained Philadelphia's tallest structure (Figure 2.2), even dwarfing the major PSFS bank building (now converted to a hotel), which was opened in the 1930s as a symbol of economic power. This situation lasted until the 1980s, when City Hall was finally eclipsed by a new series of office buildings commissioned by the mayor, who was very eager to develop the town's commercial resources and felt it was high time that the unwritten law restricting development be broken.

On the Periphery

A distinction from the typical Western pattern is that the planning of Tokyo, based on the principles of Chinese feng shui, highlighted the importance of the corners of the city just as much as its hidden center. Jinnai comments:

As the city expanded, the cultural and amusement areas were uprooted, not only from the political and economic center but also from the daily life spaces of the city dwellers, and moved to the outskirts, where nature was plentiful and an atmosphere of freedom flourished. In contrast to the centripetal structure of European cities, which were integrated around a walled, symbolic center, Edo developed centrifugally so that the concentrations of energy, where residents gathered, drifted toward the fringes. To some extent, of course, *bakufu* policy was responsible for this, but it might be regarded as a tendency, intrinsic to

Japanese urban culture, to differentiate spatially between the everyday and the extraordinary.[18]

The northeast corridor of Tokyo was established with Buddhist temples in order to subdue the vulnerable demon's gate, where, according to the principles of feng shui, incorporated into Japanese yin-yang practices (*onmyōdō*), intrusion, malady, and misfortune would likely enter into an environment through the power of malevolent spirits, thus requiring a sacred site to provide purification. Kyoto was purposefully situated by its original city planners in a valley with the auspicious natural sites of Mount Hiei and Lake Biwa, located to the northeast, in order to offer spiritual protection. Mount Hiei became the site of Enryakuji and other temples and shrines primarily of the Tendai sect, which guarded the capital city and its rulers. In Edo, hilly Ueno with Lake Shinobazu and the Tendai temple of Kan'eiji, along with Asakusa's large Tendai site, Sensōji, performed a comparable protective function.

The shogun decided to use the demon's gate area as the location for all elements of society he considered unworthy of abiding in the inner domain of the High City, ranging from the commerce and trade of merchants to entertainment and prostitution, as well as execution grounds and burial mounds. In spite—or perhaps because—of the pervasive presence of various kinds of impurity in this area, hundreds of temples were built to provide mortuary rites. These sites represented an opportunity for relief and release, creating a unique ambience that was in part secular, in that the sites represented a place to congregate and mingle as a refuge from daily activity, and in part sacred because of the ritual functions they undertook in an effort to cleanse defilement.

Another example of the interfusion of sacrality and secularity in the northeast sector is Kaminarimon, or Thunder Gate, which stands at the entrance to the expansive Sensōji compound. Even though it has been rebuilt in recent decades, Kaminarimon still exhibits a dramatic, other-worldly façade in addition to serving as an entry to the temple and its holy environs, where devotees stand next to a huge incense burner and try to coat themselves with its smoke and aroma, as well as to leisure, commercial, and sensual pursuits in Asakusa, where pornographic theaters today stand next to shops that make handcrafted omikoshi shrines. This atmosphere inspired a famous haiku verse by Bashō, who, while listening from his abode in Fukugawa, a more southerly segment of Shitamachi, was intrigued by the sound of temple bells. The pealing of the bells served not only as ritual objects signaling ceremonial occasions but also as clocks by announcing the time of the day for general citizens.

In 1666 the poet wrote: "Cloud of blossoms—| Is that the bell from Ueno | or Asakusa? (*hana no kumo | kane wa Ueno ka | Asakusa ka*)."[19]

The residents of Edo-period Shitamachi included members of the three lower castes, or the peasants, artisans, and merchants. In the increasingly developed urban setting, as farmlands on the periphery quickly began to disappear, peasants who moved to the city often tried to go beneath their class status in order to gain social mobility. The shogunate considered farmers, who worked the land, more prestigious than artisans and merchants, who handled currency, but it was these groups that thrived economically and became collectively known as townsmen (*chōnin*). The skilled workers or craftsmen, who produced objects desired by the samurai, and entrepreneurial businessmen, who opened shops and other distribution networks, continued to gain financial strength and, thereby, social status during the course of the Edo period. Although their Low City homes were smaller and less spread apart than the estates of the daimyō in the High City, the townsmen were able to master new levels of economic growth and exhibit a significant degree of upward social movement.

Floating World

During the Edo period, the samurai were ever seeking pleasures that were forbidden in Yamanote by sumptuary laws and therefore offered only, sometimes legally and sometimes surreptitiously, in the off-limits district of the "floating world" (*ukiyo*), or the demimonde of Shitamachi. In addition to townsmen, the Low City was districted by authorities to contain other kinds of professional and social activities considered by the shogunate to be outside of the mainstream and alien to the interests and welfare of the general populace, yet necessary for society to endure. This included performers offering illicit gratification ranging from the occupants in the licensed quarters of the Yoshiwara to itinerant entertainers and Kabuki actors. Their ongoing nighttime activities marked Shitamachi as a wicked place (*akubasho*), or a taboo realm of impurity that was especially attractive to the samurai, who, no longer allowed to engage in swordsmanship or other forms of fighting in the peaceful days enforced by the velvet tyranny of the shogunate, had leisure time on their hands and an insatiable appetite for enjoyment.

An endless flow of samurai disguised their identity in the demimonde by wearing masks and hiding their topknots and swords. However, the warriors, who collected rice as payment from peasants working on their manors, were prohibited from handling cash, which was needed to acquire pleasures, because it was considered impure and beneath their status. Many members of the samurai class became increasingly indebted to innovative members of the so-called underclass of merchants, who not only produced goods and products but also in many cases lent the warriors huge sums of funds that enabled them to complete the acquisitions of what they desired. Because they offered forbidden pleasures patronized by warriors, the townsmen "were well placed to take advantage of this samurai taste for luxuries.... Buoyed by the support of wealthy chōnin [who managed the city's financial institutions and growing markets], both the Yoshiwara prostitution and the theater district—allowed to exist because the shogun recognized that people needed emotional release through artistry and sensuality—and reached their zenith as the two great central fixtures of Edo culture."[20]

The history of the Tokugawa era leading up to the rise of modernization was to a large extent marked by the extended decline of the overly refined samurai, who expended their resources unproductively while relying on an obsolete sense of elitism and privilege. Over the decades, the samurai were often cut off from resources and support and for various reasons drifted into the no-man's-land status of the leaderless warrior, or *rōnin*, which literally means "wave person." The era was also marked by the ascent of the merchants, who became the dominant power in society and in the Meiji era eagerly embraced modernity because it confirmed and greatly enhanced their approach to commercial growth. The eventual demise of the samurai class within a couple of decades after the arrival of Commodore Perry's black ships in the early 1860s was inevitable, although many warriors managed to retool and reinvent themselves successfully in the new social conditions of industrialization by joining forces with the entrepreneurs. A prime example of the transition of warriors to merchants originating in the Edo period is the case of the Mitsui Company, originally a samurai clan that became one of the giant *zaibatsu*, or corporate conglomerates that dominated the Japanese economy before WWII.

At the same time that it offered excitement and appealed to sensual desires, Shitamachi was a melancholy place where the downtrodden and dispossessed dwelled, whether it be geisha who died in their teens of venereal disease or members of the outcast community, condemned to victimization and poverty through a life of social exclusion and invisibility. This group, once referred to by the derogative *eta-hinin* (filthy and nonhuman), was designated *burakumin* (literally, "village people") in the Meiji era, when legislation outlawing discrimination was passed in the 1870s. Marginal and exacerbated people were treated inequitably by the harsh shogunal authoritarian regime, not particularly known for practicing human rights, although the *bakufu* (shogunate) acknowledged the need to allow some behavioral leeway since repression could foster rebellion. Furthermore, in Shitamachi the elements of death and dying were prominent. Situated there were the official execution grounds and the notorious Bridge of Tears (Namidabashi), which prisoners were forced to cross en route to their capital punishment while well wishers were left behind to bid farewell and grieve; the district also contained crematoria and cemeteries for disposing of the bodies of the deceased, considered impure and taboo.

Many Buddhist temples were located in Shitamachi. These were populated with priests who performed rites of passage for the spirits of the dead. Priests were considered irregular members of what was an essentially Confucian-oriented society that stressed family values, as well as the power and refinement of class status based on education in language and the fine or literary arts; these key factors sustained the social hierarchy.[21] The clerics of the Low City served in the midst of the realm of impurity to help purify and preserve the spiritual status of the departed by providing a proper Buddhist funeral, which was delivered on behalf of the soul of the deceased regardless of social status or the cause of death. Itinerant preachers often engaged in oral storytelling or streetside dramatic recitations of morality tales as a persuasive way of evangelizing. These recitations tended to blame a person's problems not on personal flaws but on the ability of demons to possess and corrupt those who were vulnerable to seduction or betrayal due to ethical lapses, such as considering a path of disloyalty to one's wife or warlord.

Priests also claimed to be able to produce the magical effect of exorcism in order to rid one's spirit, even after death, of spiritual intrusion and restore purity to the soul, which sought to reside in the realm of the ancestors. This approach resonates with the Japanese worldview shown in Noh theater and other cultural expressions, which indicates that one must experience the depths and agonies of hell so as to claim the heights and benefits of heavenly reward. According to this perspective, wickedness or evil itself is not spiritually lethal but can paradoxically serve as the gateway to nirvana (*aku soku nehan*). According to a famous dictum by celebrated iconoclastic Zen poet Ikkyū, who regularly and purposefully bypassed the Buddhist precepts to pursue enlightenment through a life of transgressions, including illicit love affairs, "Entering into the realm of the buddhas is easy, but entering into the realm of the demons is difficult."

Therefore, funerary rituals were necessary to create an avenue toward redemption for those who struggled mightily with temptation and sin but were condemned to a life of suffering due to an unjust and corrupt social system. In the Low City, long-standing associations with misfortune and death, which involved karmic retribution and were accompanied by cleansing and spiritual attainment through Buddhist rites offered by the multitude of Shitamachi priests, helped to cause the multitude of butsudan shops to be located in Inarichō. The altars and implements provided by these stores served as a vehicle for facilitating rites of repentance offered by the living, who hoped to attain spiritual release and redemption for the deceased next of kin.

Disorderly Order versus Orderly Disorder

Based on a complex social history, a twofold level of approach/attraction and avoidance/repulsion functioning both within the Shitamachi and Yamanote districts, respectively, and in terms of the interrelations has long existed between the two main districts of the shogun's city. Inside the world of the Low City, which housed hundreds of temples alongside the Yoshiwara district, which originally was walled off to disallow traffic, a creative tension prevailed between the sacred and the secular, "religion and the sensual,"[22] or "prayer and play," to cite Nam-lin Hur's work on the role of the Sensōji temple dedicated to Kannon in Asakusa, where these oppositions were interwoven in multifaceted ways.[23] As Hur says of its contradictory aspects of purity and impurity:

> Sensōji developed into a remarkably large, diversified temple ground which became a place for *taberu* (eating), *kau* (buying), *miru* (watching), and, eventually, *asobu* (playing). Visitors to Sensōji were fascinated by the abundant choices of pastimes, which ranged from street markets, noodle shops, restaurants, storytelling halls, theaters, circuses and other street arts, and archery halls to the attractions of toothpick shops and teahouses.[24]

As a complement to secular delights, Sensōji's Buddhist halls provided a cornucopia of religious offerings, and a towering pagoda enabled one to worship all kinds of Buddhist deities, including Jizō, Fudō, Yakushi, Fugen, Benzaiten, Enma, and Seishi, in addition to Kannon. Sensōji also hosted Shintō branch deities invited from the Fushimi Inari, Kumano, Atago, and Tenmangu shrines and became a center of local pilgrimage for the cult of Shichifukujin (Seven Gods of Happiness).[25] Despite its festive, celebratory atmosphere, Sensōji, in addition to other temples in Shitamachi, was also very much involved in catering to the mortuary needs of geishas, outcasts, criminals, and the executed, whose spirits would otherwise have been neglected and might have been able to haunt those who had caused their suffering This created a melancholy atmosphere of resignation toward inevitable decline and decay, which was somehow tempered by a sense of compassion and an appreciation of the value of the souls of the downtrodden.

In the Low City the basic polarity between the forces of sensual and artistic pleasure, or Eros and aestheticism, in creating a carnivalesque atmosphere that sometimes led to gluttony and spectacle, and the forces of regret and repentance, or Thanatos and asceticism, in fostering a heightened sense of remorse that sometimes led to disillusion, reclusion and shame, was mirrored by comparable conceptual polarities taking place inside the High City. The main polarity in Yamanote involved the tension between success and failure, or the prosperity, prestige, power, and the finer things of an elitist life and the price that had to be paid for regulating social hierarchy, which was an overly strict and frequently harsh sense of order and control enforced by the authoritarian Tokugawa regime.

To a large extent, the Edo period's sense of the High City's being held under a powerful command has endured in the modern era due to the power exerted throughout the twentieth century by the successive forces of Meiji nationalism, prewar militarism, and postwar corporatism. However, even during the early modern period, a sense of social order frequently broke down precisely because the regime simply could not prevent its elite members from succumbing to the appeal that the illicit gratification of Shitamachi offered. For the samurai, whom philosophers encouraged to develop a refined sense of self-cultivation but nonetheless felt constrained and unfulfilled in their daily existence, the anxiety caused by the polarity between order and disorder often led to an unchecked impulse for self-destructive pursuits in seeking out the contradictory, forbidden interplay of Eros and Thanatos in the pleasure quarters.

Structure and Antistructure

Therefore, the polarization between activities in Yamanote and Shitamachi involved a conflict between forces of structure and antistructure, authority and irregularity, or rectitude and transgression. In Japanese culture, these sorts of divergences are generally encompassed by the terms *tatemae* (face) and *honne* (true feeling), or *ura* (front) and *omote* (back), which imply that every coin has two sides, Janus-like, and that the face that one shows to the world may be at odds with inner feelings that remain hidden from view but consume a person's heart and mind. Depending on the particular situation and parties involved, one may experience either an overwhelming feeling of fundamental contradiction between outer expression and inner feelings or a joyous sense of harmonious complementarity reconciling these dimensions.

In this sociocultural context, Yamanote represented a realm of disorderly order in that it was basically a place of structure yet harbored inherent anti-structure for those who tried to break free of its confinement despite all of the restrictions and precautions taken by the regime to prevent disorderliness from breaking out. Shitamachi, on the other hand, was exemplary of orderly disorder in that it was at heart a place of antistructure that held its own brand of organization for those who tried to take advantage of either spiritual or sensual offerings found within its confines. People who thrived on their cultivation of *en*, relations or substantial social connections and associations, which primarily benefited the citizens of the High City, suffered (or in some cases were redeemed) when they entered the perplexing domain of *muen*, a state without relations or the arena of tragic disconnections, which primarily took place in and around the Low City.

In other words, while the behavioral trends in each of the two main urban realms encompassed their opposite side or inversion of attitudes, in considering the relation between High and Low cities, there was also a basic contradiction. Yamanote served primarily as the domain of *giri* (duty, obligation, or responsibility) in terms of upholding a fundamental commitment to obeying and preserving social hierarchy and class distinctions. People knew their place and acted in accordance with expectations and requirements. Shitamachi, on the other hand, represented the realm of *ninjō* (human emotions, love, or passion), where people often visited from Yamanote in the pursuit of freedom and fulfillment. This reflected a deep longing that often led to transgressing the societal order by trying to override class and resulted in punishment or retribution.

As Table 2.1 indicates, when viewing the relation between the two districts of Tokyo in terms of their respective emphases on particular social classes and religious worldviews, we find that a sense of the mutual attraction-repulsion of mirror-opposite behavioral ideals functions at each and every discursive level. Contradictory elements continually interact at the cultural crossroads, where the upstanding citizens of Yamanote seek to enter the so-called wicked place of the floating world, for which Sensōji's Kaminarimon has long functioned as the symbolic gateway, in order to find sensual pleasure, as well as sacred respite from the constraints and restrictions of life in the High City.

Table 2.1 High City vs. Low City

Yamanote	Shitamachi
Tatemae/Ura	Honne/Omote
Society	
shogun	chōnin
daimyō	entertainers
samurai	itinerant priests
rōnin	Eta-hinin
Religion	
Shinto	Buddhism
giri	ninjō
life	death
en	muen

The polarity leading to a somewhat hopeless sense of contradiction and conflict between ninjō and giri is epitomized by double suicide or love suicide (*shinjū*, literally, "within the heart") theatrical dramas, in which a samurai who has fallen in love with an outcast geisha must choose between his responsibilities to family and society and his passion for a forbidden lover. Such samurai often suffered the humiliation of being unable to afford to buy out their romantic partner's contract from a merchant, who was their wealthy "inferior" on the social ladder; in that polygamy was not necessarily restricted, the transgression was more a matter of loss of face than immorality. According to the *bunraku*, or puppet theater, Romeo and Juliet-like tragedies written and staged in the early eighteenth century by famed playwright Chikamatsu, who is considered Japan's Shakespeare because he also penned historical epochs, taking one's life with honor in the hope of attaining eternal redemption in the land of the Buddha was the only admirable reprieve for those who were so oppressed by excessive social order that they could not help but give in to an excessive manner of disorderliness.

This form of taking one's life in order to redeem transgression complemented *seppuku*, or ritual suicide, which occurred out of a samurai's sense of dishonor based on betraying rather than fulfilling his loyalty to his challenged or slain warlord. While both types of suicide represented a concern for shaming those left behind, double suicide also held the promise of attaining buddhahood and eternal spiritual rebirth on an eternal lotus blossom in Buddhist paradise by reciting the *nembutsu* chant (Namu Amida Butsu) at the time of death and receiving the saving grace of Amida Buddha. Yet, even though this act generally included an acknowledgement of the need for expressing respect and a sense of responsibility for the warrior's jilted wife and disrespected family, double suicide was construed by the shogunate as an antiauthoritarian thumbing of the nose at its enforcement of hierarchical order while proclaiming the merits of an alternative lifestyle (or, ironically, way of dying). As a result, the performance of Chikamatsu's plays was restricted or even banned during the Edo period.

With the rise in the popularity of various forms of suicide, ritual death for misbegotten or bereaved lovers or for wayward warriors, as well as the unfortunate demise through execution of those accused of insubordination or disloyalty, occurred when the social, financial, and legal pressures exerted at the proverbial crossroads between the High and the Low City—or the realms of maintaining social connections and giving into a life of disconnections—became unsustainable. However, the situation in Tokyo was not always so bleak since the gap between Yamanote and Shitamachi often resulted in a harmonious interplay of opposites that was celebrated in festivals, performances, and many other examples of productive cultural interaction through communal activities shared by citizens of both districts.

Tokyo Rising or Setting?

Although the original city planning was rooted in Edo-period political and economic objectives, the polarity between High City and Low City has been readily adapted to modernization and continues to govern and greatly affect nearly all aspects of Tokyo's current development and social functions, including the role of sacred spaces and their interplay with an otherwise increasingly secularized world. This is because the urban divisions, as initially created, retain a remarkably fluid and flexible ability to adapt and adjust to ever-changing circumstances, particularly the transition from a warrior society, where commerce was frowned upon, to a vigorous commercial enterprise, referred to at the peak of the postwar economic miracle as "Japan, Inc."

According to famed architect Yoshinobu Ashihara's notion of "the hidden order" underlying the labyrinthine construction of the "amoeba city...with its amorphous sprawl and the constant change it undergoes, [Tokyo is] like the pulsating body of the organism. And as with an amoeba, Tokyo demonstrates a physical integrity and the capacity for regeneration when damaged.

Whether the amoeba city is good or bad, it does persevere."[26] Furthermore, Ashihara argues, the nature of the city is reflected in the structure of its dwellings. Inside traditional Japanese houses, "permanently installed dividing walls were minimal, with most of the space portioned with sliding removable panels. This gave the interior space a singularly fluid quality and profoundly affected Japanese lifestyles and ways of thinking."[27] In addition, outside walls traditionally made of wood or paper slid open to allow easy access to the garden areas outside the main structure. The fluidity between the interior rooms, which helps connect inner and outer realms of the abode, symbolizes an ongoing and free-flowing, albeit contradictory, back-and-forth movement also found in the relation between the once lushly forested and watery realm of the High City and the flat, commercialized division of the Low City, as well as the conceptual, social, and cultural worlds each of the districts represents.

High City

Since the inception of the Meiji era, the Yamanote district has been able to maintain its prestigious status and assert itself as the center of political authority and commercial power, which is the main indicator of success and progress. The shogun's castle has been transformed into the imperial palace, and the elite class of samurai has more or less turned into white-collar professionals or blue-suited executives and salarymen, whose lives, both public and private, are now mainly dictated by the strict rules of corporate culture, with its relentless pursuit of high GNP, instead of a domineering and demanding warlord. The gates and bridges that served as openings and/or barriers for the hilly topography of Edo are still apparent in the transportation system of Tokyo; as noted, for example, the gateway to the Akasaka area is the Akasaka-mitsuke Station, located at what was once one of the lookouts for the shogun's inner dwelling place.

Many of the Yamanote neighborhoods, especially in the central area near the palace and Tokyo Station, exude a feeling of prosperity and sense of well-being even in the tougher postbubble economic times. The High City has been at the heart of international trends in fashion and etiquette, particularly in the areas near Harajuku and Aoyama in the southwest corridor. Harajuku ironically gains some of its luster not only because it is near the magnificent Meiji Jingu but also because it was an American colony during the period of occupation after WWII. The takeover lasted until 1963, when the nearby Yoyogi Park became a centerpiece for the Olympics, which were held a year later. The train station at Harajuku still resembles a New England commuter stop. The promenade leading to the Meiji Jingu along a grand boulevard referred to as Omotesando (literally, "path leading to [a shrine]") is as swanky as any elegant urban shopping district in the world today. In this vicinity, Aoyama nightlife has been at the core of recent influential literary styles, especially prominent novels in the 1980s by younger authors who documented a lifestyle of thrill seeking accompanied by existential despair.

The Yamanote railway system, the high-speed train line inaugurated in the late nineteenth century, conveniently connects all of the major areas of the High City while still demarcating a division with the Low City. The Yamanote Line has six major stations, including the following (see Map 2.3; stations are listed clockwise):[28]

- Tokyo Station, Japan's central train station with a nearby post office situated to the east of the palace and the Nihonbashi bridge, which in the Edo period allowed access to the castle grounds
- Shinagawa Station, gateway to the Shinkansen train line, which parallels the old Tokaido route leading to Tokyo from Kyoto and the western provinces (this was the pathway traveled by the daimyō, who were required to make regular visits to Edo)
- Shibuya Station, one of the primary entertainment districts, especially for the youth pop culture near Harajuku, and gateway to the western suburbs
- Shinjuku Station, with its relatively new city hall and other towering high-rise buildings, in addition to watch stores and entertainment areas
- Ikebukuro Station, a major shopping and commercial district that has been developed in the north-central area of the city
- Ueno Station, which houses a park, a zoo, and museums and also serves as the northeast sector's gateway to Shitamachi

The complex web of social and commercial activities taking place in the vicinity of these stations, each of which has distinctive characteristics and its own kind of personality, indicates that the High City remains the vital core of the city. The stylized, iconic diagram of the Yamanote Line in Map 2.3, which is based on what is often found in various sources, including a pamphlet, a guidebook, and a subway ad that feature oval, rectangular, and circular shapes, transforms what is the much more irregular shape into a perfectly neat symmetrical design. Even though the main sacred sites such as Meiji Jingu and Sensōji stand outside the borders of the High City, temples and shrines abound throughout Yamanote neighborhoods and are keys to understanding the cultural functions of every one of these areas.

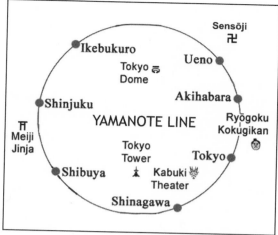

Yamanote Line as a Circle

MAP 2.3

Low City

The Edo period's legacy and sense of social identity also continue to endure in contemporary Shitamachi, which offers sumo tournaments at the Kokugikan stadium, as well as the creations of craftspeople and artists near Sensōji as some of its major tourist attractions. Throughout the modern era, the Low City has been the residence of renowned literary and cultural Figures. Its "who's who" list of writers includes Mori Ōgai (who has a hotel named after him in Yanaka) and Okakura Tenshin (for whom there is a memorial park in Yanaka), in addition to Akutagawa Ryūnosuke, Kawabata Yasunari, Kōda Rohan, Mishima Yukio, Natsume Sōseki, Takamaki Jun, and Tanizaki Jun'ichirō, among many other illustrious names. The literary giants of Shitamachi also include a couple of writers who specialized in tales of the denizens of the Low City, Nagai Kafū, who wrote of the lives of outcasts, and Higuchi Ichiyō.

Higuchi, known as the "modern Murasaki" (author of the *Tale of Genji*), is considered the first prominent female author of the Meiji era. She turned down marriage and moved to Shitamachi in order to write novels and stories about the hardship of geishas in the Yoshiwara quarters. Higuchi became famous for her first novel, published at age twenty in 1892. "In a story called *Growing Up*, she describes the children who live in the shadow of the Five Streets and the festivals of the quarter—the annual summer carnival and the Tori no Ichi— and the gang fights of the children."[29] However, Higuchi became ill and died tragically in her relative youth just a few years later. An Inari shrine and small museum dedicated to her memory stand less than a mile north of Inarichō, and her visage has adorned the Japanese five-thousand-yen banknote.

The neighborhoods of Yanaka, Nezu, and Sendagi, near Nippori Station, north of Ueno, are particularly well known for art galleries and gardens, although these areas are now located inside the confines of the Yamanote train line in Bunkyō ward. Yanaka, which along with Aoyama, near Akasaka, houses one of the four largest cemeteries in Tokyo, is rich in Buddhist temples since many were moved into this area outside of the Yamanote district during the Edo period. This transition was first initiated after the widespread destruction caused by the Meireki fire of 1657, when temple buildings that were made of wood and susceptible to combustion were relocated from the heart of Edo to outlying areas. The dense cluster of Buddhist sites in the northeast sector helped to bolster the spiritual protection of the inner city from the supposedly deleterious effects of the demon's gate. Still known today as a temple town, Yanaka retains much of the old-world, artistic charm.

The Ya-Ne-Sen area, as Yanaka-Nezu-Sendagi is called by its inhabitants, is said to resemble the " 'the real Japan' of *Madame Butterfly*, one of the few areas in Tokyo that escaped the fire raids of 1945, and thus still has the traditional wood-frame buildings, some from the Meiji era, fine old houses with their gracefully weathered, broad semi-clapboard siding, each of which elegantly complements the vast Yanaka Cemetery and the brood of Buddhist temples that make Yanaka an enchanting borough of the past."[30] Here, the Shitamachi of old remains as compelling as it always was in preserving local customs, such as bon-odori dances, cherry-blossom-viewing parties, omikoshi-carrying festivals, and rice-cake-making events. The area features many antiquated shops that sell traditional items, such as tofu, rice crackers, calligraphy brushes and paper, and bamboo ware nestled alongside izakaya restaurants, soba shops, and sentō (public baths), as well as shops that specialize in work shoes (*tabi*) and shirts. In addition, Yanaka houses the Okakura Tenshin Memorial Park, dedicated to the revered Meiji era intellectual who wrote the influential and still-popular *Book of Tea* in English in the early days of the twentieth century and also campaigned for pan-Asian unity (with Japan taking the lead). In addition, there are smaller museums showcasing tradition in their bronze figurines, calligraphy, and Edo utensils.

An interesting example of how the traditional gets linked to the modern is SCAI the Bathhouse, a contemporary art gallery since 1993, housed in an old, unassuming public bath facility—the 200-year-old Kashiwa-yu bathhouse once used by prominent authors who occupied Shitamachi, including Kawabata Yasunari and Ikenami Shotaro, among others. The structure's high ceiling is ideally suited to exhibiting examples of art, while the façade, along with the roof tiles and chimney of the original building, remains for the most part unchanged from the time of their Edo heyday.

The traditional form of entertainment known as *rakugo*, a kind of improvised stand-up comedy with slapstick that draws on cultural humor or is a combination of comic storytelling and pantomime, in which the storyteller sits on a cushion and without any prop except his folding fan tells familiar stories and acts out common situations, can be still be found in Shitamachi and is performed extensively in clubs throughout Yanaka and Asakusa.[31] This atmosphere is shown in Figure 2.3, which evokes a contemporary beatnik flair with a stylized pagoda depicted in the background. Near this street sign, a mechanical portable shrine graces the exterior of an office building and draws nearly as many admirers as a real festival procession, while a rickshaw man (another old-fashioned custom that is not an oddity in Shitamachi) advertises his services with his business card.

In many ways Shitamachi has thrived economically over the years—for example, the first subway line in Tokyo is the Ginza Line, which was originally built in 1927 to connect Ueno and Asakusa. However, much of the traditional atmosphere has gradually deteriorated as the area, which was rebuilt after the devastating effects of the 1923 earthquake and war bombing in the first half of the twentieth century, continues either to decline or to be gobbled up by urban development. The area also preserves the underside of Edo

FIGURE 2.3 "Rhythm & Jive" on "Beat Street"

culture, such as pornography as a legacy of Yoshiwara even after prostitution was outlawed in 1957, as well as the poverty and degradation of migrant workers and the homeless, who live in the wretched day-laborers' warren of San'ya.

The More Things Change...

In the past couple of decades, some commentators have expressed a sense of loss and nostalgia for the fading history and vanishing unique traits of Shitamachi. According to Edward Seidensticker's remarks in the foreword to a book on the history of Tokyo neighborhoods:

> For all the newness of the surface, Tokyo goes on being a conservative city in ways that are important. Hilly Yamanote, to the south and west of the palace, has grown enormously in wealth and importance this last century. It quite overshadows flat Shitamachi, the plebeian eastern parts of the old city, which were the center of the pre-modern mercantile culture. Once the guardian and progenitor of the best in Edo, Shitamachi can scarcely be said to have a culture of its own these days... Yet it goes on being different from Yamanote, and the difference must be seen as a survival from an earlier day. Yamanote is by comparison chilly and scattered. Shitamachi is warmer, cozier, chummier.[32]

Because of the efforts of Seidensticker and many others who have pointed out that Shitamachi is not just a place defined by geography or a physical border but also represents a state of mind, way of life, or cultural attitude, a sustained renewal of interest in salvaging the atmosphere and revitalizing the legacy of the Low City has recently been launched. Recovery efforts have led to the opening of several museums and the rezoning of the area around Sensōji so that it remains vital. In appreciation of the cultural heritage of the area, it is said of the third-generation resident of the area that he "displays a number of premodern qualities and thinks of himself as being open, generous, hot-tempered, quick-witted, inquisitive, generous, and quick to offend and quick to forgive. He is spontaneous and impulsive, both traits one does not associate with the modern Japanese."[33] These are qualities supposedly lacking in the more restrained behavior of the citizens of Yamanote and therefore in dire need of being salvaged.

However, the situation in Shitamachi remains fluid as social conditions are perpetually changing in contradictory ways. On the one hand, the price of real estate is escalating, and signs of gentrification, including high-rises and highways trumpeted as "revitalization projects," intrude on (or enhance) the traditional cityscape. Even Minami Senjū Station, next to the old execution grounds, is experiencing an upscale development trend with the construction of new condominiums. At the same time, urban decay counters efforts to revive the past. A compelling counterpoint to the nostalgia expressed for lost Edo is the "gritty, firsthand account of life for day-laborers in Tokyo's shunned ghetto, San'ya," which is provided in the vivid yet despondent account by Edward Fowler in *San'ya Blues: Laboring Life in Contemporary Tokyo*.[34] Fowler's book demonstrates that there is no escaping the turmoil and challenges faced by the itinerant and homeless residents of San'ya, traditionally an area inhabited by the former outcast community, which is near the infamous Bridge of Tears (Figure 2.4). This designation still appears on street signs and represents an inverted gateway for the troubled and tormented that ironically reveals a kind of holiness or access to sacrality since there are several historically important temples in the area that once specialized in funerals for the downtrodden.

In recent years, with an increasing recognition of and concern for the tormented life of the homeless and decrepit migrant workers who fill the streets of San'ya, the local government has developed new policies and practices in an effort to provide at least temporary social service shelter centers as a halfway house and an avenue to return to mainstream society. One such site is the Taitōryō, which was constructed next to the famous Kan'eiji temple in Ueno Park, where there was some free space just to the other side of the Yamanote Line, although after a few years it was dismantled. However, as Tom Gill notes:

> One of the Tokyo SSCs is Taitōryō, located very close to Ueno Park, facing the famous Kan'ei-ji temple. It has 104 beds and an annual budget of 180 million yen. There was powerful NIMBY opposition to opening the Centre. Consequently it has no nameplate to reveal its function, is surrounded by fences, and outside stairs are concealed behind plastic covers. As one of the staff dryly remarked, people do not want to be reminded of gloomy matters like homelessness when attending funerals at the temple.[35]

This social pattern ensures that San'ya is still imbued with a muen focus, which complements the en focus that is evident in Ya-Ne-Sen. Not far from San'ya, several temples remain clustered between the Minami Senjū and Minowa stations on the Hibaya Line, discussed in greater detail in chapter 4, which once offered respite for prostitutes and criminals who died prematurely, in large part due to living a life of submission or being perceived as insubordinate toward an unjust, authoritarian regime. At Enmeiji temple, built in the 1667 next to Kotsukappara, a statue of the Neckchop Jizō (Kubikiri Jizō), as seen as Figure 2.5, stands amid signs of modernization, as well as urban decay.[36] The 3.6-meter-high statue was erected in 1741, when it was the only consolation available to some of the more than two hundred thousand people who were condemned to execution between 1651 and the late 1800s and were not allowed to receive comfort from the clergy in their final moments before death. A large engraved stone in the foreground of the icon bears the cursive characters "Namu myōhō renge kyō" (Hail to the *Wondrous Lotus Sutra*), the main prayer of the Nichiren sect.

The prominence of death-related religious sites in Shitamachi contributes to a sense of preserving the past while revitalizing the present but without effacing the complexity and authenticity of the melancholy or the tragic as it stands contradictorily alongside the comic, transcendent, or life affirming. In this way, "The city is saved by the inner resilience and the hardened fatalism of its residents, their ability to sustain periods of almost Buddhistic non-attachment and an unshakeable optimism, the belief that a better world follows natural upon destruction."[37]

FIGURE 2.4 Sign at Intersection at the Bridge of Tears

FIGURE 2.5 "Neckchop Jizō" at Enmeiji Temple

NOTES

1. In a very different cultural context, this phrase was coined to characterize the existential painting *The Scream*; see Uwe M. Schneede, *Edvard Munch: The Early Masterpieces* (London: Schirmer Art Books, 1988).

2. Comparable examples abound; to name just a few: Izumo Taisha, the second most important shrine in the country, located in western Japan; Toshogu, the lavishly decorated shrine complex and Tokugawa mausoleum at Nikko, north of Tokyo; the Eiheiji temple, home of the Sōtō Zen sect, founded by Dōgen in the remote mountains of Fukui Province; the Itsukushima shrine in Miyajima, famous for its large torii gate standing in the sea part of each day until the land dries with the tide; and two of the Daibutsu, or Great Buddha statues, one of Vairocana at Tōdaiji temple in Nara, which originated in the eighth century, and the other of Amida at Kōtokuji temple in Kamakura, stemming from 1253.

3. Other, more minor examples in the West might include Salt Lake City, home to the Mormons, or Canterbury, which houses the main cathedral for the Anglican Church.

4. The central city of Kyoto contains the Heian shrine, which commemorates the origins of the imperial capital, the Tōji temple, founded by Kūkai, and the Honganji temples of the Jōdo shin sect. The peripheral areas include notable Zen temples Kinkakuji, Myōshinji, and Ryōanji to the northwest and Daitokuji in the north, as

well as the stilted pavilion of Kiyomizu temple on a lookout peak in the southeast and Sanjūsandendō temple and Fushimi Inari shrine in the south. The outlying districts include Enryakuji temple on Mount Hieizan, which serves as the protector of the demon's gate on the peak northwest of the city, and its rival, Onjōji, on the shores of Lake Biwa in the valley below. Other cultural highlights of Kyoto include the quaint cobblestone streets of the medieval Gion Corner area, which feed into the Yasaka Jinja at the gateway to Maruyama Park. The park houses what may be the world's largest cherry tree, which blossoms in April, auspiciously around the same time as the Buddha's birthday. Another highlight is the Philosopher's Walk, a picturesque path along a cherry tree-lined canal meandering through the base of the Higashiyama (eastern mountains) area from Nanzenji to Ginkakuji, two of the foremost Zen temples (the path was trod every day by renowned early twentieth-century philosopher Nishida Kitarō, who contemplated on the way to his office at Kyoto University).

5. Paul Waley, *Tokyo Now & Then: An Explorer's Guide* (New York: Weatherhill, 1984), p. 207; the caption reads, "Unlike some of the temples of Kyoto, Asakusa Kannon is very much a part of its city." Also, Edward Seidensticker comments that Asakusa is to Tokyo as " 'St. Paul's is to London, or Notre Dame to Paris,' said American Orientalist W. E. Griffis in the late nineteenth century. It was a place that fascinated most foreigners, even Isabella Bird, who did not for the most part waver in her determination to find unbeaten tracks. Griffis was right, though Asakusa was more than a religious center—or rather it was a Japanese sort of religious center, one which welcomed pleasure to the sacred precincts"; in *Low City, High City* (Rutland, Vt.: Tuttle, 1984), p. 207.

6. Kishino Seiryū, *Tokyo no otera/jinja: Nozo toki sampō* (Tokyo: Koseidō, 2008).

7. See Ian Reader and George J. Tanabe Jr., *Practically Religious: Worldly Benefits and the Common: Religion of Japan* (Honolulu: University of Hawaii Press, 1998), pp. 247–249.

8. Hidenobu Jinnai, "The Spatial Structure of Edo," in *Tokugawa Japan: The Social and Economic Antecedents of Modern Japan*, eds. Chie Nakane and Shinzaburō Ōishi (Tokyo: University of Tokyo Press, 1995), p. 124.

9. Ibid., p. 139.

10. For the source of this see Akira Naito, *Edo: The City That Became Tokyo: An Illustrated History* (Tokyo: Kodansha International, 2003), pp. 34–35.

11. Paul Waley, *Tokyo: City of Stories* (New York: Weatherhill, 1991), p. 17.

12. Jinnai, "Spatial Structure of Edo," p. 124.

13. Those samurai who did not serve the shogun did not receive the honorific *o* before their name; see Jean Pearce, *Foot-Loose in Tokyo: The Curious Traveler's Guide to the 29 Stages of the Yamanote Line* (New York: Weatherhill, 1976), p. 37.

14. Roland Barthes, *The Empire of Signs* (New York: Hill and Wang, 1983).

15. Jinnai, "Spatial Structure of Edo," p. 131.

16. Ibid., p. 132.

17. See James L. McClain, John M. Merriman, and Ugawa Kaoru, eds., *Edo and Paris: Urban Life and the State in the Early Modern Era* (Ithaca, N.Y.: Cornell University Press, 1994).

18. Jinnai, "Spatial Structure of Edo," p. 137.

19. There were nine bells in Edo that were rung in *ittoki* intervals, or about every two hours according to modern timekeeping.

20. Masakatsu Gunji, "Kabuki and Its Social Background," in *Tokugawa Japan: The Social and Economic Antecedents of Modern Japan*, eds. Chie Nakane and Shinzaburō Ōishi (Tokyo: University of Tokyo Press, 1995), p. 205.

21. Buddhist clerics received education but renounced family life, yet often duplicated its relational structure in the brotherhood of the temple environment, or instead broke the precepts and married surreptitiously.

22. Jean Pearce, *More Foot-Loose in Tokyo: The Curious Traveler's Guide to Shitamachi and Narita* (New York: Weatherhill, 1984), p. 56.

23. Nam-lin Hur, *Prayer and Play in Late Tokugawa Japan: Asakusa Sensōji and Edo Society* (Cambridge, Mass.: Harvard University Asia Center, Harvard University Press, 2000).

24. Ibid., p. 69.

25. Ibid., p. 14.

26. Yoshinobu Ashihara, *The Hidden Order: Tokyo through the Twentieth Century* (Tokyo: Kodansha, 1989), p. 59.

27. Ibid., pp. 13–14.

28. The Map on the left side of the three includes two more stations on the Yamanote Line, Takadanobaba Station and Akihabara Station.

29. Waley, *Tokyo Now & Then*, p. 206.

30. Lawrence Rogers, ed. and trans., *Tokyo Stories: A Literary Stroll* (Berkeley: University of California Press, 2002).

31. Pearce, *More Foot-Loose in Tokyo*, pp. 61–62.

32. Edward Seidensticker, "Foreword," in Waley, *Tokyo Now & Then*, pp. x–xi.

33. Edward Seidensticker, "Foreword," in Pearce, *More Foot-Loose in Tokyo*, p. 7.

34. Edward Fowler, *San'ya Blues: Laboring Life in Contemporary Tokyo* (Ithaca, N.Y.: Cornell University Press, 1996); taken from the back cover blurb by the *Publisher's Weekly*.

35. Tom Gill, "Whose Problems? Japan's Homeless People as an Issue of Local and Central Governance," in *Contested Governance in Japan: Sites and Issues*, ed. Glenn D. Hook (London: RoutledgeCurzon, 2005), p. 202.

36. There are other such statues in Japan constructed for occasions when Jizō came to the spiritual rescue of victims of war or violence. Also, Tokyo's other main execution ground was in Shinagawa.

37. Stephen Mansfield, *Tokyo: A Cultural History* (New York: Oxford University Press, 2009), p. 254.

LIVING AND DYING

3 AKASAKA IN THE HIGH CITY: BORN SHINTO . . . LIVE INARI . . . DIE BUDDHIST

The Conundrum of Religious Institutional Structure

This chapter weaves together a descriptive analysis of the historical and cultural background, as well as contemporary functions and the atmosphere of some of the main sacred sites in the neighborhood of Akasaka, and accompanies it with a critical discussion of Japanese religious institutional structure. By examining a variety of shrines and temples that are prominent and not so prominent (but in their own way equally important for understanding the role of sacred space), I explore the conundrum involving the particular type of religious pluralism whereby almost everyone in Japan acknowledges an affiliation with both the Buddhist and the Shinto traditions, but very few admit feeling much loyalty or commitment to a particular institution.

My analysis revisits perennial questions about the interaction of the two major religions: How do they operate in relation to one another in modern Japan as seen in light of a fifteen-hundred-year history of syncretism? Are linkages a matter of combining somewhat disparate forces, or does a more fundamental, underlying bond support the traditions that must be identified? At first glance, the focus here on several major Shinto shrines in Akasaka, which support an emphasis on life by helping patrons pursue the blessings of health and wealth, and on local Buddhist temples with cemeteries, which foster an emphasis on death through rites of mourning and memorials, would seem to reinforce the insightful and to a large extent indisputable dictum "Born Shinto . . . die Buddhist." As indicated in the introduction, I insert the phrase "live Inari" so as to highlight the underlying connections and disconnectionsthat cut across sectarian divisions rather than focus on the ritual specializations of the respective traditions.

From *Shinbutsu Shugō* to *Shinbutsu Bunri* and Back

An examination of the particular Akasaka sites will support the emphasis on living Inari. Thus, I first offer an overview of the long-standing historical commonalities and combinations that have linked the major religious institutions through the notions of assimilation (*honji-suijaku*, literally, "original ground-trace manifestation") and the unity of foreign buddhas and local gods (*shinbutsu shugō*). Over the course of a millennium and a half since its introduction to Japan from the mainland, Buddhism, as an imported faith that claims universal truth based on the wisdom of dharma and the compassion of buddhas, has coexisted and been inseparably linked with Shinto, which has functioned as the indigenous belief derived from autochthonic practices. The traditions enjoyed centuries of joint participation in temple-shrine complexes that shared many of the same ritual functions in pursuit of sacramental purification and the maintenance of social relations in this world and the next, or the realm of the spirits.

When Buddhism first began to make its presence felt, beginning in the sixth century CE, the doctrine of honji-suijaku was created to justify the incorporation of its deities through a fairly systematic approach toward redefining and reencoding native gods. According to this standpoint, indigenous divinities that had gained a significant following before Buddhism was introduced were no longer seen as discrete spiritual entities separable from the imported theology but as heretofore unrecognized projections or manifestations of the fundamental essence or reality represented by corresponding yet superior Buddhist gods. An important corollary was that Buddhist deities were classified into various gradations indicating their degree of spiritual power and extent of sway over the native domain. Of particular importance was the notion of the avatar (*gongen*), which refers to the appearance of a buddha or bodhisattva who chooses to manifest in the earthly realm by taking on a localized material form, often as an animal or some other aspect of nature. As part of the process of assimilating imported ideas and icons into their pantheon, the Japanese tended not to distinguish between what was Buddhist and what was of South Asian origin more generally, so that numerous non-Buddhist deities stemming from the continent (that is, of other South Asian or Hindu derivation), including monkey, snake, and elephant gods, were assimilated as avatars.

In this way, the term Shintō, or "way of the gods," as opposed to Butsudō, or "Way of the buddhas," was used to contrast bodhisattvas, avatars, or heavenly beings, esoteric or exoteric, which are explicitly Buddhist, with all other deities, whether indigenous or otherwise lumped together with native gods and spirits. The general pattern is that the animal or natural form is considered to represent the messenger of a more abstract level of deification that has the capacity to serve as custodian or protector for an individual or a larger

FIGURE 3.1 Inari Icons with Buddhas

community of devotees, as well as their sacred spaces. Therefore, nearly all Buddhist temples incorporated a local avatar as a guardian spirit, and nearly all Shinto shrines also had foreign tutelary deities installed into the site.

Japanese gods are invariably ethically ambivalent in encompassing positive and negative energies. They can have a mischievous or even demonic power that agitates and annoys or deludes and deceives the victims of their pranks. However, if appropriated and incorporated into the larger pantheon through the doctrine of assimilation, their disruptive power and destructive status are radically reclaimed and reoriented to reflect the purity of genuine spirituality and compassion. Figure 3.1 shows the fox, a notorious shape-shifter that can tempt and betray unwary souls. The fox appears in various divine forms as manifestations of Inari, which are considered avatars or guardian messengers of the buddhas. Beneath the foxes on the stone pillar are the sculpted buddhas, which represent a higher plane of theological being. The seductive energy of deceit is thereby transformed into the divine power of protection.

In the classical period, additional doctrines were formulated to buttress the approach of assimilation, including Ryōbu Shinto or Dual Shinto, which refers to an inherently shared quality of native traditions with Buddhism. During the thirteenth century, as an example of the mixture of faiths, Zen master Dōgen—who, despite a strict emphasis on the practice of zazen meditation, highlighted the role of miracles and supernatural intercession in his view of religiosity and whose Eiheiji temple today contains an Inari shrine—wrote the following verse, which is emblematic of shinbutsu shugō in addressing the matter of fertility festivals held at local shrines:

Sanae toru	Transplanting rice seedlings
Haru no hajime no	At the beginning of spring—
Inori ni wa	For that prayer
Hirosetatta no	We celebrate the festival
Matsuri o zosuru	At Hirose and Tatta shrines.[1]

Obverse tendencies also emerged over time, such as doctrines that attempted to reverse honji-suijaku by asserting the preeminence of indigenous deities. During the Edo period, the National Learning (*Kokugaku*) movement proclaimed the supremacy of Shinto ideals, which reflected the essence of Japan as a national polity, as opposed to corrupt imported ideologies like Buddhism and Confucianism. Despite these trends, the basic pattern of assimilationism and the oneness of universal buddhas and native gods, which were seen as complementary icons of the respective religious traditions, persisted and prevailed until the Meiji period. Temples and shrines generally occupied the same compound, and the priests for both institutions were often one and the same person even though Shinto stressed the primacy of this-worldly family life and Buddhism represented a path of renunciation of worldly concerns.

Modern Separatist Trends

Beginning in the late nineteenth century and lasting for about eighty years, the traditions were for the most part decoupled, largely due to political agendas that advocated the nationalism and militarism that led up to WWII. Significant changes in official policy toward religion greatly affected the assimilative pattern by reflecting the dramatic shift in the domestic affairs and foreign policy of modern society, especially with the

rise of State (Kokka) Shinto as an ideology that embodied native traditions and sustained the empire of Japan.[2] The official authorization of
Shinto was attached to an orchestrated government and media attack on
Buddhism as an unworthy foreign cult. A campaign that attempted to
ensure the separation of gods and buddhas (*shinbutsu bunri*) was undertaken, which compelled priests and shrines to declare themselves affiliated
with one tradition or the other, for they could no longer represent both at
the same time.

This trend was reinforced by several other key developments, including
a distinction that was ordained between State Shinto and other forms of
the native tradition, such as Imperial (Kyūchū), Shrine (Jinja), Folk
(Minzoku), and Sect (Shūha) Shinto; a government-promoted crusade
against Buddhist imagery (*haibutsu kishaku*), which resulted in the
destruction of numerous icons and other ritual artifacts; and a new rule
that required Buddhist priests to marry and eat meat (*nikujiki saitai*) in
order to reduce their other-worldly status.[3] These transitions were accompanied by a rise in both lay Buddhist and eclectic New Religious movements, many of which refashioned ritual elements in a way that continued
to detract from and further erode the long-standing fabric of Buddhist-
Shinto amalgamations.

Since the end of the war, the relatively short-term separation of Shinto and
Buddhism has largely been overcome through widespread efforts to reunite
indigenous and imported gods, as well as the temples and shrines that house
them. The interaction of traditions was reinvigorated, or at least the obstacles
that interfered have been removed, so that the bridges that link them have for
the most part been repaired on a case-by-case basis. Therefore, with the
exception of nativist/nationalist trends at the end of the nineteenth and in
the first half of the twentieth century, throughout most of Japanese history
Shinto has been defined not so much for what it is but in terms what it is not.
That is, Shinto has been understood as a grab bag of deities, icons, and rituals
that are not Buddhist but that have been so interwoven with Buddhism over
the centuries before the Meiji era and again after WWII that it is hard to decipher where the line for one tradition leaves off and the other seems to begin.
The continuing impact of honji-suijaku is invariably felt in modern temples,
which incorporate some nativist elements such as torii gates and water-purifi-
cation rites, along with examples of naturalized or localized gods, who are
seen as messengers. The impact is also felt in contemporary shrines, which
evoke Buddhist symbols such as incense and bells in support of deities of
Buddhist origins, which are seen as avatars.

Contours of the Akasaka Neighborhood

Akasaka sites provide important case studies that demonstrate the ongoing effects of assimilation. This fascinating neighborhood, located in the heart of Tokyo, contains several important commercial and residential, as well as public and private, subdivisions. As a notable representative of the society of the Yamanote district, Akasaka is particularly, albeit somewhat surprisingly, well suited for this study of religious institutions for various reasons. Located just below the Detached Palace, which in the Edo period was the home of Tokugawa lineal clans, including the Kii clan, which produced the eighth shogun, Yoshimune, in the eighteenth century, Akasaka is primarily known for its proximity to the imperial quarters and the capitol buildings.

The neighborhood also houses a profusion of diverse sacred spaces, both at the edges and in the midst of this ultramodern central-city locale, which are affiliated with yet reflect a commonality that transcends the major traditions. These sites consist of several important Shinto shrines situated on the main thoroughfares and commercial avenues on the perimeter of the neighborhood, which highlight the area's concerns for attaining prosperity and protecting the state. In addition, numerous smaller Buddhist temples that provide graveyards that serve as vehicles for rites of mourning are tucked away down alleys in the largely residential interior sector of Akasaka and are regularly patronized by members of families from the area and beyond it in cases where relatives have moved away over the years.

A tour of Akasaka (Map 3.1) begins at Akasaka-mitsuke Station, where the Ginza and Marunouchi subway lines converge and underpasses link to the nearby Nagatachō Station, close to the capitol buildings. This was originally one of the thirty-two lookout towers (*mitsuke*) that helped to defend the shogun's castle from intruders or invaders. Built in 1636, this tower was one of the most fortified defenses in the city and led to what was at the time the village of Shibuya down the road and other points west. The tower also helped to separate the plebian population from the elite classes of the daimyō and the samurai, whose status was deserving of privilege but who, it was feared, might use their power to threaten to subvert or rebel against the establishment. As discussed previously, Akasaka is one of the primary areas where the Tokugawa shogunate situated powerful warriors for the dual purposes of social elevation and political oversight in an intriguing example of how to "keep your friends close but your enemies closer."

Much of the area has a military history stemming from the Edo through the Meiji periods, when an army base was located on what is now the Tokyo

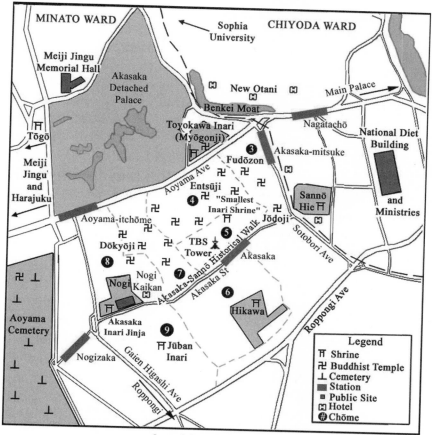

MINATO WARD

Sophia University

CHIYODA WARD

Meiji Jingu Memorial Hall

Akasaka Detached Palace

New Otani

Main Palace

Benkei Moat

Tōgō

Toyokawa Inari (Myōgonji)

Nagatachō

National Diet Building

Fudōzon

Akasaka-mitsuke

Meiji Jingu and Harajuku

Aoyama Ave

Entsūji

"Smallest Inari Shrine"

Sannō Hie

and Ministries

Aoyama-itchōme

TBS Tower

Jōdoji

Sotobori Ave

Dōkyōji

Akasaka

Akasaka-Sannō Historical Walk

Aoyama Cemetery

Nogi

Nogi Kaikan

Akasaka St

Hikawa

Roppongi Ave

Akasaka Inari Jinja

Jūban Inari

Nogizaka

Gaien Higashi Ave

Roppongi

Legend

⛩ Shrine
卍 Buddhist Temple
⊥ Cemetery
▮ Station
▪ Public Site
Ⓗ Hotel
● Chōme

Sacred Sites in Akasaka

MAP 3.1

Broadcasting System (TBS) Tower, and this legacy still has a resonance in the area. Throughout WWII, barracks were spread all around Akasaka, as well as in nearby Aoyama and Roppongi, where soldiers congregated off hours for recreation and today prominent war leaders are honored in shrines. Also, with theaters in the vicinity, along with other signs of a vibrant entertainment district in Akasaka, the bluff where the TBS Tower is situated affords the passerby an occasional glimpse of a celebrity or performer.

Akasaka remains impressive and influential as a bastion of social and political power because it is an upscale, blue-suit business district populated by high-rise building and hi-tech corporations near places vital to the structure and governance of the capital city. A resident or visitor emerging from the stairs that lead from the arcade below Akasaka-mitsuke Station finds that this is a dynamic urban crossroads and an exciting area to stroll around. The station stands across from one of the former palace moats, once a much longer waterway linking Akasaka-mitsuke to other main castle gates; today the district features boating and cafés, with major hotels nearby, including the New Otani, Akasaka Prince, and Excel Tokyo. The area also houses prestigious shops, restaurants, and businesses near the national ministry buildings. Akasaka is located near Sophia University to the north, and to the south stands Roppongi, a renowned arts and recreation center for a younger crowd but which has become rather seedy of late. To the northwest lies Meiji Memorial Hall, and a little farther away are the majestic Meiji Jingu, as well as the Harajuku neighborhood, famous for its exotic youth culture.

Known as a "playground for adults for over a century," Akasaka encompasses an entertainment area that includes first-class restaurants with an international atmosphere that in many ways seems like a holdover from earlier times. This area has long been a center of political dealings. Here, high-level leaders visit a *ryōtei*, or a luxurious traditional Japanese restaurant, where VIPs gather to meet for a fabulously expensive meal hosted by geisha in order to network and complete backroom deals. Akasaka first developed this style at the end of the nineteenth century, when Shimbashi to the east of the palace became increasingly exclusive and expensive. As an observer noted a couple of decades ago, "Akasaka, given its proximity to Nagata-chō, the bailiwick of the prime minister and the other political heavy lifters, has always attracted government bureaucrats and pols and been the natural site for *ryōtei* politics..."[4]

The area's customs are changing, but until recently it was not uncommon for a fashionable geisha to be spotted being swept away in a horse-drawn carriage on her way to one of these exclusive rendezvous sites, which have been reduced significantly in number and cost by recent budget restrictions and greater scrutiny of possibly scandalous practices. As part of the reforms associated with the 1993 prime ministerial elections, which were convened after several major scandals that exposed the way in which corrupt *ryōtei* politics were infecting the highest levels of leadership in the land, it was reported that the newly elected "Mr. Hosokawa, whose stated aim is to make Japanese politics more accountable, has instructed his colleagues to avoid the clandestine world of Akasaka's *ryōtei*, just around the corner from the Diet, the Japanese parliament. Instead, he has instructed politicians to use hotel lounges or parliament offices for their meetings."[5] Over the years, Akasaka clubs and night spots have also catered to foreigners, although this is often tainted by a reputation for luring and fleecing the unsuspecting naïve tourist with promises of erotic escapades. At the same time, this neighborhood also includes a sizable, quiet (*shizuka*) residential area with single homes and condos, as well as a variety of trendy but less prestigious public and commercial enterprises.

Overview of Sacred Sites

My study specifically deals with the locale that includes Akasaka 3–4–5–7–8–*chōme* (city districts) in Minato Ward, a rectangular expanse that is bordered by the Aoyama Cemetery to the southwest and Nagatachō Station, along with government structures, to the northeast. Taking a closer look, the neighborhood includes three main subdivisions:

a. 3–chōme, the *ryōtei* entertainment and shopping district located between Akasaka-Mitsuke Station to the northeast and Akakasa Station to the southwest, which includes two major shrines and several temples
b. 4–, 5–, and 7–chōme, the inner (*oku*) district of Akasaka, which stands in the shadow of the TBS Tower and is mostly residential, with some cafés and shops and a couple of dozen minor temples that are mainly graveyards
c. 8–chōme, a commercial area with a post office and a park located near Aoyama-itchōme Station to the northeast and Nogizaka Station to the southwest, which encompasses a large shrine and several small temples.

This chapter also refers to Akasaka 6– and 9–chōme, where other important sites stand just beyond the borders of the neighborhood. These include a couple of important Inari shrines and a large cemetery.

Ironically, the considerable cultural charms and religious significance of this vital historical neighborhood appear to be lost on some promoters of tourism, one of whom has announced:

Probably the only actual sight in Akasaka is the Hie Shrine, located atop a little hill at the edge of the area. Reached by a steep flight of stairs under a veritable tunnel of orange torii, the shrine grounds are an oasis of tranquility in the middle of Tokyo and, in good weather, a popular place for a lunchtime picnic. Once a year, the shrine holds the rather modest Sanno Matsuri festival, featuring the usual panoply of music, dancing, yatai stalls and sake.[6]

To be sure, Sannō Hie Jinja, which stands on the main street, which leads south from Akasaka-mitsuke Station, is a sprawling complex that traditionally was a protector of rulers, and today its huge forested area spreads nearby and is considered to be the spiritual protector of the Diet. Shrine rituals celebrate Sannō Gongen, a deity represented by a monkey, and also include devotion to Inari; both gods are seen as promoters of fertility and defenders of government ministries located near the compound.

Sannō Hie Jinja is no doubt the most famous and visible of sacred spaces in the neighborhood, with its two grand entrances, each with a large torii gate (one traditional, with steps climbing a hill, and the other modern, with an escalator).[7] However, this shrine is by no means the only notable site in Akasaka, nor does it stand alone in providing rites to acquire benefits or make political connections or in serving as a location of comfort and sanctuary in an otherwise secular setting. As another commentator recent notes, in addition to noteworthy Inari shrines, the neighborhood contains many other religiocultural gems, including modest yet active Buddhist temples scattered throughout the interior sectors, as well as parks and other public places:

> I have since discovered that a stroll through the area has rewards that extend beyond the transient pleasures of overpriced restaurants and grog houses. A few minutes from the Akasaka Mitsuke subway station there is a Buddhist cemetery all but hidden on a steep slope that rises up from a busy street, and next to it a holy place dedicated to the steadfast Acalanatha [Fudō Myōō]. From higher up the hill [comes] the sound of someone practicing the samisen. A few minutes away from narrow walkway climbs, Telegraph Hill-like, to the top hill on which sits one of the serendipitous pocket parks that are sprinkled about the city. A sign informs the visitor that the park used to be the Tokyo residence of the lord of Hiroshima domain during the Edo era...One does not expect to find a small tree-shaded park sitting atop a hill in fast-track Akasaka, yet here it is, right next to the studios of the Tokyo Broadcasting System and placidly overlooking the busy streets below.[8]

Leading southwest from the station toward the Detached Palace grounds lies Toyokawa Inari, which features a display of red lanterns lit up at night, which lends the place an Edo-like festive atmosphere readily apparent to the pedestrian. Additional sites in Akasaka are hidden from view behind another kind of structure or down an alley, such as the largest Buddhist site in the area, the Shingon sect's Akasaka Fudōzon temple mentioned earlier, and Nogi Jinja, dedicated to General Nogi, which includes a garden and an Inari wedding shrine in the same compound. To the east of Akasaka Avenue lies Hikawa Jinja, another large but rather dank compound, and the route toward Akasaka Station is part of a lengthy urban cultural walkway that was designed a few years ago as part of the four-hundredth anniversary of the founding of Tokyo in 1603.

Sannō Hie Jinja: Guardian of the State

The oldest and most enduring shrine in Akasaka and perhaps all of Tokyo, Sannō Hie Jinja is variously known as Hiyoshi Sannō-sha, Hiyoshi Sannō Daigongen-sha, Edo Sannō Daigongen, and Kōjimachi Sannō (for its former location), and worshippers often refer to it affectionately as Sannō-sha or Sannō-sama. This shrine has a very interesting political history, and its ritual functions shed light on the issue of how religious institutional connections are affected by modifications while sustaining the intentions of a site's original symbolism in light of modernization. Technically located at 2–10–5 Nagatachō in Chiyoda Ward, the shrine has two grand entranceways on Sotobori Avenue at the southeastern edge of Akasaka in Minato Ward. The third main gate leads from the subway stations at Tameikesannō, once the site of a beautiful lake with sacred waters and lotus blossoms, and at Kokkaigijidōmae, the stop in front of the National Diet Building. This is also near Toranomon, or the Tiger's Gate, which was the southernmost lookout of Edo castle and was originally connected by waterways to Akasaka-mitsuke.

Officially designated a first-class government shrine (*kanpei-taisha*) from 1871 through 1946, Sannō Hie Jinja has long held strong political connections with rulers extending from pre-Edo leaders to the Tokugawa shogunate, the imperial household, and the current prime ministry. Although Buddhist temples were the protectors of the state in earlier eras, that role is now reserved for Shinto, even in the postwar period. This emphasis on governmental connections touches base, for better or worse, with the role of *ryōtei* politics, held just a block away in Akasaka. The shrine is also highly valued because its museum holds a sword that is a National Treasure, in addition to fourteen Important Cultural Assets, including thirteen swords (the collection has a total of thirty-one swords) plus one *naginata* (samurai pole weapon).

Hie Jinja provides one of the three great festivals of Edo, which proceeds through downtown Tokyo toward the palace grounds on June 15 in every even year as the only parade in Japan that receives the privilege of entering the imperial gates. The Sannō Matsuri has been held since 1681, when it was regularly attended by the Tokugawa shoguns because the shrine housed the guardian deity of the city of Edo. The Kanda Myōjin Matsuri—also known as an example of a Tenka Matsuri, or a Grand National ceremony held every other year—is a celebration by townsfolk in the Low City style (although it takes place inside the Yamanote Line). The Sannō Matsuri, which originated in the High City, on the other hand, is an elegant affair noted for its sobriety and pageantry rather than boisterous atmosphere.[9] The procession originally consisted of forty-five festival floats, with three sacred palanquins carrying three gods. Followed by singers and dancers, the formation entered the castle grounds. Since 1885, the tall floats have not been able to travel the streets of Tokyo due to the presence of electrical street overpasses. Today, the festival procession, which moves for thirty kilometers through the business districts of Ginza and Kyōbashi to reach the palace, consists of a parade of about five hundred people clad in the costumes of the imperial court and carrying three omikoshi.

Historical Background

Although the early history and origins of religious practice at the shrine remain obscure and somewhat contested, Sannō Hie Jinja seems to stem from beliefs first held on Mount Hiei in Shiga Prefecture. The site derives its name from the deity enshrined within, Oyamakui-no-kami, the god of Mount Hiei, more commonly known as Hie-no-kami. In the early part of the ninth century, when Kyoto was growing as the new capital, Mount Hiei became the headquarters of the Tendai sect, established by monk Saichō in the northeast corridor in order to protect the city's demon's gate. Saichō, who had recently returned from a pilgrimage to China, helped open hundreds of Buddhist temples that either replaced or assimilated indigenous shrines. In founding one of these temples on Mount Hiei, Saichō dispossessed the local (Shinto) deity and considered it necessary to build another shrine in or near the new temple to placate the offended god. Hence, Hie Taisha was constructed on the eastern slopes of Mount Hiei, where the native deity, Sannō Gongen (King-of-the-Mountain Avatar), could be worshipped. Subsequently, "Tendai temples were built all over the land, and in many cases Hie shrines, dedicated to Sannō Gongen, were built on the temple grounds for protection."[10] Thus, branch sites of a belief located in Shiga Prefecture proliferated throughout the country, and one of these eventually found its way to Edo, which was at first a backwater but was destined to become the major city of Japan.

According to a medieval record, at the beginning of the Kamakura period a man named Edo built a Sannō Hie Jinja to serve as the guardian deity of his residence on the grounds of the present palace because his estate belonged to the mother shrine on Mount Hiei. The shrine has played a spiritually protective role for all of the varied occupants ever since. In 1478, Ota Dōkan, a samurai poet-monk, constructed Edo Castle at the same spot and also re-created a Hie shrine in the compound as a guardian of the fortress. The first shogun, Ieyasu Tokugawa, began ruling Japan from Edo Castle and was a patron who worshipped the site's deity as the guardian of Edo. In 1607, Sannō Hie Jinja was moved outside of Edo Castle to Hayabusa-chō, near the present National Theater (Kokuritsu Gekijo) in Kojimachi. This location was to the southwest of the castle, also considered a potentially dangerous geomantic direction, for if the evil spirits failed to gain entrance from the northeast, then they would try from its obverse side, which is known as the reverse demon's gate (*ura kimon*). To the northeast corridor of Tokyo, Kanda Myōjin was a protector shrine, and the Tendai priest Tenkai, abbot of Kita'in in Kawagoe, constructed Kan'eiji in Ueno in imitation of Enryakuji temple on Mount Hiei, making it imperative that the opposite part of the city should also be guarded.

After Sannō Hie Jinja, along with much of the city of Edo, was destroyed by the Meireki fire in 1657, two years later shogun Ietsuna Tokugawa rebuilt the shrine at its present location in Akasaka, farther to the southwest than

FIGURE 3.2 Hie Jinja's Torii Amid Modern Buildings

Kojimachi. The new shrine buildings were one of the city's finest examples of the *gongen-zukuri* style of architecture; the early Tokugawa shoguns favored its vermilion-lacquered finishings. This style consists of a complex roof system in which the *haiden*, or hall of worship, and *honden*, or inner sanctuary, are connected. Today, Hie Jinja also features one of Tokyo's most attractive monuments (Figure 3.2), a torii gate erected in 1821, which still stands even though much else was destroyed by fires. On its two copper-plated posts are the four Chinese geomantic animals: the blue dragon (east) and black tortoise (north) are on one post, and the red phoenix (south) and the white tiger (west) are on the other.[11] The large gate, which leads uphill through a tunnel of smaller gates to the main buildings, has a pediment-like apex, which is a feature peculiar to the Sannō torii, one of ten main styles of gates.

Ritual Functions

Sannō Hie Jinja does not rely only on a long and noteworthy national background for its appeal because it is also a site that features numerous kinds of healing rites and fortune-telling practices as performed by priests and shamans; in addition, it serves as a well-rounded cultural center and social gathering place for Yamanote residents and visitors. The shrine is one of the most popular for Japanese families to visit during the Shichigosan rite of passage, a festival in which young boys wear a *hakama* and girls a *kimono* for the first time; here, wedding ceremonies are frequently conducted in solemn fashion according to traditional Shinto rites.

The main shrine gate leading from the Toranomon entrance encloses the statues of two monkeys, which are avatars or messengers of Sannō Gongen, perched on a hill looking north toward Akasaka-mitsuke and south over Tameike. On one side, the mother monkey is holding her child since the deity has a reputation for granting fertility and ensuring childbirth, and pregnant women often come here to pay wishful homage to the stone statues.[12] In addition, on these premises the Kyōgoku daimyō clan built an important Inari shrine, which has long been the rival for attracting fox worshippers of the nearby Toyokowa Inari and Hikawa Jinja shrines.

Across from Toranomon near the top of a steep hill stands Kompira-sama, a shrine that is annexed to Sannō Hie Jinja and celebrates the god of mariners and safe navigation in the middle of Tokyo. This site is affiliated with the original Kotohigarū site in Shikoku, also built by the Kyōgoku clan, where it was once used as a beacon for ships making their way through the busy waters of the inland sea. Of Indian origin (Sanskrit: Kumbhira) and often associated

Table 3.1 Nogi Jinja Ceremonies

Cherry Blossoms	In early April, a tea ceremony is held under a cherry tree, and *sencha* green tea is prepared.
Kencha Ceremony	On June 16, *kencha*, or "tea offerings to the gods," is made, and high-quality cold green tea is prepared in the prayer hall.
Tanabata	In August (or the seventh lunar month), a tea ceremony is held at the main corridor for Tanabata (Star Festival); high-quality cold green tea is prepared with bamboo shoots, and slips of poetry are included.
Chrysanthemum Festival	On September 9, a tea ceremony is held in the main hall, and high-quality cold green tea and a special chrysanthemum drink are prepared.
7-5-3 Ceremony	In November, a tea ceremony is held where *ema* are hung, and *kōcha*, or black tea, is prepared.

today with an elephant, Kompira was originally an aquatic god, crocodilian in form, who helped sailors in difficulty, but nowadays the benefit has transferred to businesspeople and politicians who pray for good fortune in their public ventures and personal affairs. The shrine is also popular with people who vow to stop drinking, smoking, gambling, and other debilitating vices. All three spiritual animals at the Sannō shrines—the monkey, fox, and elephant (like the dove as a messenger of Hachiman or the dog for Suitengu, among many other examples)—are instances of honji-suijaku that support of the forces of life and prosperity.

In addition to promoting rites for well-being, the shrine regularly holds dozens of cultural activities. Table 3.1 lists some of the many annual Sannō Hie Jinja cultural events, including tea ceremony celebrations, which are usually associated with Buddhist temples:[13]

These activities show the multifaceted aspects of the shrine's ritual functions, which go beyond distinctions of sacred and secular, as well as of Buddhism and Shinto. However, since so many other sites in this neighborhood provide similar ceremonial and cultural services, the distinctive appeal of Sannō Hie Jinja cannot be separated from its role as a spiritual guardian and protector of the city and state rulers even though this function has changed dramatically over the centuries from pre-Edo clan leadership to the era of the shogun and modern imperial postwar government institutions.

Nogi Jinja: A War Hero's Suicide

Like Sannō Hie Jinja, which was founded for political functions, Nogi Jinja, located at 8–11–27 Akasaka in Minato Ward, combines associations with the state with popular religious rituals that interweave the symbolism of life and death. The shrine was created to honor Gen. Nogi Maresuke, a famous early twentieth-century hero of two wars who was trained in the West and lived in a hybrid-style compound in Akasaka's once military district. Nogi committed *seppuku* along with his wife when the Meiji emperor passed away in one of the most famous cases in Japanese history of *junshi* (or following one's lord into death). The general enjoyed a special friendship with and had great respect for the emperor, whom he visited dozens of times during the final days of his life. Expected to be among the most esteemed of the thousands of mourners at the funeral, Nogi and his wife informed the dignitaries that he was sick that day but did not disclose the real reason for their absence.

As the ruler's body left the Imperial Palace for interment in Kyoto on September 13, 1912, Nogi's wife slit her throat (according to a theory, Nogi did this) while he performed a traditional seppuku or disembowelment ceremony that eerily took place just around the time the procession was heading past his home for a stop at the Aoyama Cemetery, where a Buddhist bell would be rung 108 times to signal the end of an era. Both Nogi and his wife wrote traditional thirty-one-syllable *waka* poems in honor of the occasion. A number of other shrines honor Nogi in Chōfu, the town in western Honshu where he was raised, and elsewhere in Japan, including near the site of the Meiji emperor's burial in Kyoto.[14] The Akasaka site is particularly notable for its very popular wedding shrine, which draws upon the attraction of the war hero's tragic story.

In what had long been a military part of town, Nogi Jinja is one of two shrines that are dedicated the memory of a Meiji leader who played a crucial role in both the Sino-Japanese War of the mid-1890s and the Russo-Japanese War a decade later. These revered figures take on the status of a local god (*kami*), and their shrines are decorated with attractive gardens and today host wedding ceremonies, in part to raise funds for maintaining the grounds. The other site is Tōgō Jinja, built in Harajuku in 1940, around the beginning of the Pacific War. The shrine memorializes Admiral Tōgō Heihachirō, who vanquished the Russian navy in 1905 in the Straits of Tsushima in an extraordinary victory for the Japanese, who were never expected to be able to defeat a European rival in warfare. In an upbeat contemporary way, some signs near the shrine read as if it were the English words "to go." As with Nogi, other shrines honor Tōgō in various parts of Japan, including Fukuoka and near Tsushima.

During his lifetime, General Nogi was widely known as the "emperor's samurai" and was thought to epitomize the ideal of combining Japanese spirit with Western technology (*wakon yōsai*) in a country that was obedient to the Meiji emperor yet open to foreign influence.[15] As commander of the Third Army, Nogi finally succeeded in capturing Port Arthur from the Russians but only after losing sixty thousand of his troops, including his two sons, who were his only heirs, in a Pyrrhic victory. He refused to participate in the traditional Japanese custom of adopting nonblood relations to carry on the family name, thus making him, in effect, a nonrelational person (*muenbotoke*) despite his otherwise prestigious social status.

In a classic example of Japanese tragic heroism, whereby sincerity in the face of defeat earns higher marks from one's peers than apparent or short-lived success, after feeling disgraced by his war effort Nogi requested permission from the emperor to commit seppuku but was turned down. Instead, Nogi was appointed president of the Gakushu-in school (which later became a university), where for a few years he was responsible for training the emperor's grandson, a child who would eventually reign as Emperor Hirohito. As indicated in a statue on the compound in which he is portrayed in Western clothes and bending over to praise a poor young boy he once taught, Nogi was thought to have had a special affection and knack for teaching children, but he knew then he was only biding his time until the moment was right for seppuku.

Even though it was atypically performed in private quarters, Nogi's suicide was a remarkable spectacle of self-willed death and a highly provocative event that shocked the masses, who were surprised to see this Edo-style behavior while it seemed that the country was adjusting to modernity. The general's secret life of despair over his failures while everyone else considered him triumphant was commented upon evocatively in literary works by two of the most renowned Meiji-era authors. This includes several stories by Mori Ōgai, a close friend of the general whose writing style seemed to shift significantly as a result of his death, and Natsume Sōseki's most famous novel, *Kokoro*, written in the early years of the Taishō era as a chronicle of the final days of Meiji culture.[16] For Sōseki, Nogi's suicide became a role model followed, for better or worse, by several characters he eloquently depicts, including the antihero Sensei, who confesses his own suicide in a lengthy epistle written to the novel's first-person narrator, who is devastated by the loss.

Ritual Functions

The compound of Nogi Jinja (Map 3.2) exists on several levels covering a slope that leads down from Nogizaka Station on the Chiyoda Line. At the top of the hill and standing on Gaien Higashi Avenue, which runs from Aoyama-itchōme Station to Roppongi Station, is Nogi's former home, which was once situated across the street from army barracks and is now the centerpiece of the shrine. Built in 1889 as a modest black clapboard structure reflecting the tastes of an austere man, the house was designed by the general based on a French barracks he had once inspected and admired in Europe when he had lived there as a student. Although the shrine was built at the homesite, based on concern for the probable effects of negative spiritual energies caused by his untimely death, defense ministry officials were obliged to relocate it across the street from the original location.[17] Destroyed in a 1945 air raid, the house has been rebuilt to highlight the spiritual purity of Shinto simplicity. The architect for the project, Hiroshi Oe, also designed the Nogi Kaikan wedding hall (Figure 3.3) in 1969 as a red brick building with stained-glass windows to reflect the type of architecture that was popular in the early years of Meiji rule.[18]

Like the red lanterns at Toyokawa Inari, this part of Nogi Jinja transports the visitor and enlivens the whole neighborhood with nostalgia for an earlier era. The blood-stained suicide clothes of Nogi and his wife are on display

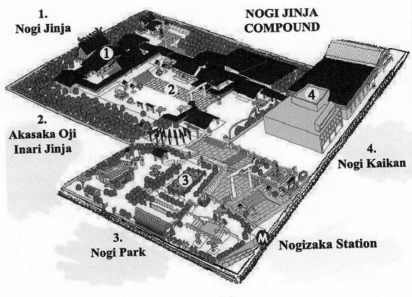

MAP 3.2

FIGURE 3.3 Nogi Kaikan Wedding Hotel

every September 12 and 13 to mark the anniversary of their deaths, when visitors may enter the house and also see the tatami living room and bedrooms furnished with Western-style furniture of the day. Adjacent are the brick stables, also built in 1889 and where Nogi kept the white horse that Russian Gen. Anatole Stoessel gave him after the Japanese victory at Port Arthur. Across the street in what was once the Japanese War College, which was occupied by U.S. military forces for a period after the war, there long stood the headquarters of the Japanese Self-Defense Forces.

The Akasaka Ōji Inari Daimyōjin Jinja, to give its full name, is a hall for marriage ceremonies that was added to the compound because all religious sites these days must be able to support themselves and raise money through commercial enterprise or from the receipt of charitable gifts.[19] A large stone torii leads from the Aoyama Avenue entrance, and at the top of the steps, on the left, a row of small but impressive vermilion torii gates with votive banners lead to a shrine with a prayer hall, as well as the spirit hall, which contains the general's disembodied spirit, although he and his wife are interred in Aoyama Cemetery down the road. Western visitors have wondered why anyone would want to hold a wedding in a site associated with the morbidity of Nogi's suicide, but the Japanese clearly see this as an enhancement rather than a detriment. When the wedding shrine is not being used for its main purpose, it often houses cultural events, such as the performance of *rakugo*, an Edo-period form of comic entertainment much more associated with the Asakusa area in Shitamachi than Yamanote.

Toyokawa Inari Jinja: Potpourri of Worldly Benefits

Life-oriented and death-oriented rites are interconnected in a different way at Toyokawa Inari, or Myōgonji, temple located on Aoyama Avenue adjacent to the Detached Palace at 1–4–7 Moto Akasaka in Minato Ward. This is a registered Sōtō Zen Buddhist institution that generates a substantial amount of revenue for the sect from donations and gifts received from practitioners who pursue practical benefits, yet to most people, including many of its patrons, as well as casual visitors or tourists, it is better known as a Shinto shrine that offers a wide variety of crossover ritual practices and icons. In addition to Inari, which is said to be accompanied by Dakini-shinten, an esoteric female deity imported from India that rides on a flying white fox, a number of other Shinto and Buddhist deities are enshrined in the compound, including Shichifukujin, Kannon, and Jizō. On ceremonial occasions, Zen monks trained at the sect's main monastery at Eiheiji temple chant sutras for the benefit of devotees; they can also be seen sweeping and performing chores as part of their discipline, although zazen meditation is not practiced on the premises.

Historical Background

Like Sannō Hie Jinja, the history of Toyokawa Inari, which remains vibrant in the modern period, is based on the premodern transfer of the power and authority of a treasured sacred space from central Japan to Edo. In this case, the Tokyo site is a branch temple (*betsuin*) of the main temple/shrine compound located in Toyokawa City in Aichi Prefecture, which is about a half-hour train ride from the Toyohashi Station on the Shinkansen train line and a couple of hours south of Nagoya, an area traditionally known for its complex web of magical fox tales.[20] According to the foundation legend (*engi*) and other lore, a thirteenth-century Zen monk named Kangan Giin, who was the third son of Emperor Juntoku and a prelate in Dōgen's Sōtō sect, had a profound spiritual experience (*reiken*) while visiting China to show the deceased master's writings to his former colleagues at the prestigious Mount Tiantong (Jp. Mt. Tendō) temple, located in Mingzhou (present-day Ningbo) near the Southern Song dynasty capital in Hangzhou.[21]

Like several other prominent Dōgen disciples, Giin had been a follower of the proscribed Daruma sect of early Japanese Zen, which allowed for the widespread assimilation of local gods. In the midst of a storm during the boat ride home, he envisioned the deity Dakini-shinten carrying a bale of rice on its back and riding a white fox as a benevolent kami (*zenshin*) and a protector deity (*chinju*) of the Buddhist dharma.[22] Based on his vision, Giin had a statue of Dakini-shinten constructed. In addition to other branch temples in Osaka, Yokosuka, and Sapporo, numerous locations of the cult are referred to as "divided spirit sites" (*bunreisho*), in which the spiritual power has been transmitted from a parent to a daughter shrine through an icon, which is ritually animated and empowered.[23]

According to fairly reliable accounts, a statue of Dakini-shinten was brought to Tokyo in the Edo period by Ōoka Tadasuke, also known as Ōoka Echizen, the son of a minor retainer of the shogun who rose to the rank of daimyō through his administrative skills rather than political connections. Once a disciple of a priest from Aichi's Myōgonji temple, Ōoka was summoned by Tokugawa Yoshimune to become the magistrate for this part of Tokyo (Map 3.3), where he served for nearly twenty years (1717–1736), considerably longer than the average tenure. Across the street from his residence he established the branch temple as his tutelary shrine, which was moved in the 1880s and rebuilt yet again after WWII. It is said that Dakini-shinten has been kept continuously in the shrine as a hidden image of buddha (*hibutsu*) that is restricted from being seen by anyone other than the high priest, and this provides a powerful attraction for ritual participants.

Part of the continuing appeal of the site in Akasaka is that Ōoka, who led a very interesting career as a judge and political reformer, is the subject of countless Kabuki plays and detective stories, many of which were no doubt borrowed or translated from Chinese tales about Judge Dee but have now become part of contemporary Japanese culture, with English versions also available. Depicted as "Solomon in a kimono":

> Ōoka-sama is the prototype of the wise Asian magistrate dispensing justice with omniscient magnanimity and a touch of humor, as when he made two brothers whose perpetual quarreling had ended in fisti-cuffs wait together some time in a freezing cold room with only a small brazier for heating. Shared adversity eventually had the brothers reconciled, and much more effectively than any number of blows from judicial rods. There is an Aesop-like quality to this and some of Ōoka-sama's other cases.[24]

Furthermore, Ōoka Tadasuke is known for showing great skill as an administrator who, working with Yoshimune, instituted several significant social reforms that made for considerable improvement in people's lives in the Edo period. These changes included organizing the first public fire brigades in a city that was always vulnerable to devastating conflagrations; using a cheaper, light type of roof tile that was neither combustible like shingle and straw nor likely to brush people who were fleeing from one of the seemingly inevitable fires; and founding a clinic in the shogunal herb garden in Koishikawa for poor people not eligible to receive medical treatment. A small shrine to the magistrate stands to the left of Toyokawa Inari's main hall and is a point of departure for many visitors who seek practical benefits at the shrine.

Ritual Functions

Both the Aichi and the Tokyo locations reflect a deliberate strategy by the Sōtō sect to promote the sites as prayer temples (*kitō jiin*) that offer a potpourri of rites for protection and gains in the material realm. The temple-shrine in Aichi, which enshrines a thousand-armed Kannon and the Sixteen Rakan and also has numerous statues and ritual portraits (*chinsō*) of founder Giin, is known primarily for its very crowded and exuberant omikoshi-

MAP 3.3

carrying festivals, in which adults and children wear costumes or traditional garb, while some believers don oversized fox masks. The more austere Tokyo site, which shows the mixture of Buddhism and Shinto by enshrining a statue of Kodakara Kanzeon Bosatsu, a Kannon with a baby in her arms to whom people pray for the birth of healthy children and prosperity for the future family line, and Migawari Jizo, a self-sacrificing manifestation of the bodhisattva,[25] bestows several kinds of worldly benefits amid the hustle and bustle of Akasaka's modern lifestyle. These include financial stability, commercial prosperity, safety during overseas travel, protection from evil, and success on exams. The shrine also features biannual festivals to pray for travel safety (*kōtsū anzen*), with the main celebration taking place every twenty-second day of June. In addition, the compound houses a cultural center, the Akasaka Tokyo Toyakawa Bunka Kaikan, which offers calligraphy and tea ceremony, and a hall for wedding receptions, conventions, and other public affairs, both religious and secular.

The primary ritual activity at Toyokawa Inari in Tokyo begins to the right of the main temple hall at a large modern building where members of the public apply for permission to have prayers said on their behalf by temple priests for success in business and travel, as well as recovery from illness. As in many Buddhist temples, since the whole of the *Great Wisdom Sutra* (*Dai hannya kyō*) cannot be read in full, an abbreviated version is substituted, and the rest of the scripture is skipped over but evoked through divine intervention. In front of the hall, which is guarded by two red-bibbed statues of the fox, stands a fortune-telling booth that features sales of omikuji and ema, as well as yin-yang and astrological readings.

Recently, Toyokawa Inari invented the Yūzū Inari shrine, which refers to worshipping the deity in support of "financing, adaptability, flexibility; *yūzū shihon* is circulating capital."[26] This new form of Inari, which resonates with the character the fox deity has had for centuries as a fertility symbol, is considered the deification of the wish-fulfilling jewel held in the left hand of Dakinishinten. According to temple literature, Yūzū Inari responds to the " 'worsening economic state of affairs in the world and the beginning of Japan's post-bubble economic dark clouds,' which could be improved 'through the boundless compassion of the buddhas in the granting of the continued circulation of money.' "[27]

In sum, Toyokawa Inari is brimming with life-based rituals that cover marriage, fertility, prosperity, and celebration, so that in this setting Buddhism seems to be taken away altogether from the image of dealing with death and is associated instead with health and wealth. However, in addition to emphasizing an affirmation of life, both the Aichi and the Tokyo sites feature a fox-spirit grove (*reikozaka*) with at least several dozen small statues that are offered as memorials in honor of the deceased by replacing the traditional Buddhist stupa in commemorating death. This is but one of numerous examples that demonstrate an inseparability of rituals for living and dying in the heart of Yamanote religiosity.

Additional Akasaka Sites with Life and Death Rituals

In addition to the three major shrines located on the main thoroughfares, the area also has a number of other important sites, including the modest, modern-looking Jūban Inari and Hikawa Jinja, the Aoyama Cemetery, and the Akasaka-Sannō Historical Walkway, as well as more than a dozen small Buddhist temples. These sites help to illumine the significance of traditional sacred space in terms of the importance of death-related rituals taking place in the midst of the life-oriented High City and in relation to contemporary cultural treasures that are part of the national and urban legacy.

Hikawa Jinja located at 6–10–12 Akasaka in Minato Ward is a shrine of particular historical value that was established in the mid-eighteenth century as the tutelary shrine of Yoshimune that also served all of Akasaka. Yoshimune is the leader whose name is most closely connected with the development of the neighborhood in the early modern period. Built under the shogun's direction in the 1730s, the buildings of Hikawa Jinja display a starkness and sobriety of simplicity that reflect Yoshimune's stern character, and this aesthetic stands in great contrast to the splash of color and decoration preferred by earlier Tokugawa shoguns.[28] However, shrine buildings created according to the *gongen* style favored by most of the Tokugawas can also be seen in the configuration of the prayer hall, a connecting hall, and the main hall.

The primary entrance to Hikawa Jinja lies on the northern, Akasaka end of the compound. Several subsidiary shrines and a damp rocky garden stand on either side of a flight of stone steps. Some structures like the *komainu* statues predate the shrine and were brought from another site, but the gate that leads into the shrine courtyard is a *yakuimon*, or gable-roofed construction, with two additional posts supporting the main structure, which dates from the last decades of the nineteenth century. On the left of the shrine courtyard as one faces the prayer hall stands a small building containing votary paintings by Meiji-era artists, including the famous decadent floating world print (*ukiyo-e*) by painters Tsukioka Yoshitoshi, Kawanabe Shōsai, and Shibata

Zeshin, in addition to the seventeenth-century Tokugawa court painter Kanō Tan'yū. These works are exhibited only during the shrine's festival, which takes place on September 15, with a full-scale *matsuri* held every other year during odd-numbered years.

Another set of sites that helps to transform the secular aspects of cultural heritage into a sense of the sacred—or, conversely, reflects the lack of any gap between realms—is the Akasaka-Sannō Historical Walkway, which stretches along Aoyama Avenue and is linked to similar street paths in other neighborhoods. The walkway features signposts set periodically along the street and at other noticeable spots—although they may end up being overshadowed by more prominent signs or features of the cityscape—that remind and instruct passersby about important points of interest. These include a variety of religious and nonreligious spaces, some of which are well known and sought out while others are more obscure and likely would be overlooked without this way of calling attention to them. Created as part of a citywide campaign to celebrate the four-hundredth anniversary of Edo in 2003, the walkways are promoted by tour guides, subway advertisements, and other inducements such as classroom lessons, all of which foster an appreciation of the paths. Visitors to an area often meander along the course while looking out for new places to eat or shop or various other cultural heritage sites in addition to sacred spaces offering worldly benefits. Strolling along these walkways can create the effect of a minipilgrimage, especially if multiple religious places are visited en route.[29]

While all the sites discussed so far reflect life affirmation, it is important to recognize the death and memorial component, which is also found abundantly in Akasaka. Sometimes the seemingly polarized religious elements are very much intertwined, as at the Aoyama Cemetery (Aoyama Reien), which can be reached from the Gaienmae, Aoyama-ichome, or Nogizaka subway stations. The cemetery, which is twenty-six thousand square meters in size and has a central lane bordered by two hundred cherry trees, covers an expansive stretch of territory between Gaien Higashi and Gaien Nishi avenues, which extend to the east and west, respectively, of the Meiji Jingu area. Established in 1872, this is the largest public space in Tokyo; it is organized in a grid pattern with crisscrossing roads and also serves as the evacuation point for Minato Ward residents. The one hundred thousand graves come in a variety of styles and ornaments, mostly in the traditional Japanese style of raised stone gardens with fences. Aside from the usual graveyard architecture, there are mausoleums and triumphal arches, statues, obelisks, and rocks. Famous Japanese politicians and artists are buried here, including assassinated

Prime Minister Inukai Tsuyoshi and politician Ōkubo Toshimichi, along with authors Kunikida Doppo, Ozaki Kōyō, Saitō Mokichi, and Shiga Naoya. There is also a section for foreign dignitaries (*gaijin bochi*), which contains numerous European and American graves, primarily of engineers, diplomats, academics, and Christian missionaries from the Meiji era.[30]

The cemetery, which represents a verdant oasis set against the background of Shinjuku skyscrapers and other high-rise buildings on the periphery, consists of smaller valleys and hills, as well as shady groves and open spaces, providing a mix of natural views and access to the tombs. This huge park in the heart of Tokyo offers a respite from noise and congestion, and there are always people walking their dogs, jogging, sitting on benches, or taking pictures, as found in any major metropolitan park, but others are there to tend graves, arrange flowers, and offer incense. This stands in contrast to the Western custom, whereby visits to the cemetery are somber, mournful, and almost never recreational.[31] Given the high level of public activity in Aoyama Cemetery, it seems that most visitors agree on the intriguing resonance between the graveyard and the modern cityscape, which appears off in the distance. Although plans to alter the use of this space are generally resisted, underground passes have been built as part of modernization even though it is said that this would disturb and disrupt vengeful spirits of the deceased. The newer Oedo Subway Line, completed in 2000, passes under the cemetery, and it is said that reports of crimes are higher in the area, while quite a few businesses have relocated, and some former patrons now tend to avoid walking here because of fear of retributive spirits.

Conclusions: The Significance of "... Live Inari..."

The presence of the Aoyama Cemetery, which borders on Akasaka and is often compared to the equally prominent Yanaka Cemetery in Shitamachi—the former has served the imperial family, while the latter caters to the Tokugawa clan—shows that death is not ignored in Yamanote. Whereas in Inarichō death rituals are highlighted first and foremost even though the neighborhood also houses several shrines of a contrasting atmosphere, in Akasaka it is the four main Inari shrines that are most visible, as the graveyards of small temples are harbored in the interior sections (*oku*) amid the houses and apartments. In the context of sacred urban space, this can be considered the inner sanctum of the neighborhood, akin to the role the *butsudan* plays in the household. Although the temples in this part of the neighborhood are known primarily to those who choose to seek them out for ancestor veneration, they play a crucial role in the religious and social fabric of Akasaka since they are frequented by families for ongoing rounds of *haka mairi* (family graves) on holidays and anniversaries, as well as for irregularly scheduled or spontaneous visits.

Folk Religiosity

A study of Akasaka sites demonstrates the need to go beyond the "never the twain shall meet" outlook that characterizes the conventional dichotomous view of "born Shinto, die Buddhist" in order to reach a more holistic and integrated standpoint regarding institutional structure. Ian Reader's book *Religion in Contemporary Japan* (1991) provides a useful description of Shinto rites of passage such as naming a child on the seventh day after birth (*miyamairi)*, the Shichigosan 7-5-3 festival for children who are seven, five, and three years of age, held in November, and wedding ceremonies, which are often elaborate affairs sometimes combined with a pseudo-Christian rite. The book also describes annual rituals such as New Year's (*Oshogatsu*) and ceremonies for special occasions like groundbreaking for new business and civic ventures (*jichinsai*). In addition, Reader depicts Buddhist rituals for funerals and memorials, such as visiting family graves by returning to the ancestral village (*furusato*), often during the spring or autumn equinox (*Ohigan*) or the ghost festival (*Obon*), or by venerating at the home altar (*butsudan*) ancestors who are also commemorated through their posthumous ordination names (*kaimyō*) inscribed on spirit tablets (*ihai*).

At the same time, Reader seeks to transcend the maxim by pointing out that, despite the fact that rites such as weddings and funerals are mainly associated with one or the other tradition, the functions of naming babies and awarding posthumous names reveal important parallels in that both commemorate an initiation to a new stage of existence (or nonexistence). He also shows against the stereotype that New Year's celebrations are held at Buddhist temples and that *kamidana* is more or less a Shinto version of the Buddhist altar. Furthermore, Reader demonstrates that making pilgrimage (*mairi*) to various sorts of sacred sites is a common element in both religions, whether undertaken as an individual spiritual journey or as a trek in collaboration with family members or other kinds of groups or associations.

In the following vivid account, in part metaphysical and in part personalized, Reader points to the need to go beyond the basic institutional formula by stressing the significance of the intertwining of Shinto and Buddhism:

The core of shared actions and underlying cosmological attitudes is expressed through the medium of different religious traditions at different times, providing the Japanese with a sense of fluidity in which they can interact with different parts of the whole, depending on need. Each part of the whole also provides the ground for action according to different parts of the lifestyle of the community and individual...the Japanese may pray at the *kamidana* and *butsudan*, go to the shrine at New Year, the temple at *obon*, the church at Christmas, and then during a life crisis may go to a new religious group. As a Japanese student told me, her parents sent her to a Christian school because of its good academic reputation, bought her Buddhist amulets and prayed at Shinto shrines before her examinations, and celebrated New Year, *obon* and Christmas.[32]

This is in accord with Michael Pye, who argues, "The key point is to differentiate between a general level of religiosity [or] the 'primal religion' of contemporary Japan, and the specific religious communities and their teachings."[33]

In *Practically Religious: Worldly Benefits and the Common Religion of Japan*, Reader and coauthor George Tanabe emphasize that it is crucial to refer to a basic or primal level of religiosity, although they tend to reject such tried and true designations as "traditional religion" and "folk religion." The authors believe that these terms can be taken to suggest a division between the elite and the ordinary dimensions of religious practice and to implicitly deny the importance of doctrine, text, and scriptural tradition. Furthermore, the terms may indicate a static or unchanging nuance irretrievably lost to modernity, while evoking the polemics of Japanese identity generally associated with the controversial nativist ideology of Nihonjinron.[34] According to Reader and Tanabe, the word *tradition* "is redolent with a sense of nostalgia and speaks of the past rather than of the present, of the untouched and the pristine, of stasis rather than dynamism."[35]

In considering how to define the underlying linkage between traditions based on locating a basic layer of religiosity, Reader and Tanabe also criticize depictions such as "syncretistic," "assimilative," and "combinatory," which may imply that two autonomous traditions have somehow been joined or united. Instead, they favor the use of "commonality" or "common religion,"[36] which encompasses the various customs and practices that are broadly accepted within a culture, including scriptural influences and liturgical traditions, as well as artistic and iconographic legacies that have shaped sites and rites:

[T]his common religion involves common acceptance of various spiritual entities, such as gods (*kami*) and buddhas, as well as ancestral spirits and spirits of powerful humans who have become deities after death. It also includes the idea that such spirits can confer protection and success on the living and that petitioning for such benefits is a fundamental and highly ethical religious value.[37]

One of the main concerns I have with the Reader/Tanabe approach, which I discuss more fully in chapter 4, is the way they identify the notion of common customs almost exclusively with the pursuit of practical benefits. The authors argue, "At the heart of this common religion is the practice of seeking this-worldly benefits. This common religion provides an open-access, total-care system for its members."[38] I will show that numerous additional historical, cultural, emotional, and financial factors affect religious motivation for the Japanese, so that *genze riyaku* is to be considered one key but by no means the only element when seeking to provide an exhaustive explanation of the topic.

Moreover, the Reader/Tanabe approach to commonality, I feel, fails to capture fully the most basic level of religiosity underlying yet embedded in nearly all forms of ritual practices in spite of apparent sectarian divisions. *Practically Religious* leaves much unsaid about the complexity of institutional structure and the degree to which Japanese ritual participants move back and forth among various institutions not just during major life cycle events or annual holidays, which is the way the process is usually described, but on a continuing basis and even within the course of a single day of religious activities. That diverse practices occur regularly in between the main rites of passage of childbirth, marriage, and death points to a seamless, fluid, and flexible realm of folk religion (*minkan shinkō*) that supports productive, integrated interactions between native and imported traditions taking place to a greater extent than a strictly functional definition of institutional structure is able to suggest.

While the term *shinkō* is often understood to refer to a cult or a less well-organized and perhaps fledgling religious movement (in contrast to a more established sect [*shūkyō*]), I am using it here in a much broader sense to indicate a pervasive yet diffuse degree of religious practice that underlies and sustains both of the major traditions. In that sense, I concur with the assessment of renowned folklorist Hori Ichirō:

It is true, of course, that weddings and festivals are usually Shinto affairs while funerals and requiem services are Buddhist. In these and other ways the organized religions participate in the customs and usages of folk religion. More to the point, it is within the frame of reference provided by folk religion that the organized religions have made their way into Japanese society. Only as they accommodated themselves to folk religion and its implicit norms did the institutional religions find acceptance and begin to exercise influence on people in their daily life. Any attempt to understand the role of Shinto, Buddhism, and other religions in the lives of Japanese people will of necessity be obligated to come to terms with folk religions.[39]

According to Brian Bocking's summary of the meaning of the term, *minkan shinkō* "may be defined as a developing substrate of folk-religious beliefs in Japan which incorporates elements from, yet transcends official distinctions between, 'Buddhism,' 'Shinto,' 'Taoism,' 'Confucianism,' 'Christianity,' etc., and…represents the true, indigenous and persistent character of 'Japanese religion.'"[40] This approach concurs with that of Ama Toshimaro, who argues that the key to understanding religion in Japan is to clarify the distinction between founder-based and folk religions, which were not created by a specific leader "but came into existence naturally, and were handed down as an inheritance from ancestors as an unconscious process."[41] For Ama, the fact that many Japanese maintain that they are not interested in adhering to a religious belief despite their sectarian affiliation(s) is less relevant than the existence of a set of folk beliefs, which constitute "the real character of Japanese religious sentiment." He concludes by suggesting that "although Japanese people profess to having no religion, they do not dismiss religion out of hand in the way that atheists do. It is rather the case that people who profess to a lack of religion are often very enthusiastic believers in their own particular form of folk religion. For those Japanese who gain peace of mind through folk religion, there is no need to select specific doctrines from other founded religions."[42]

This view is also supported by Miyake Hitoshi, who expresses concern that "Japanese intellectuals generally, and scholars within Buddhism and Shinto more often than not, have either ignored or looked down on folk religions." Like Hori, Miyake seeks to resuscitate the term by demonstrating its fundamental significance for understanding what underlies and interconnects the two main traditions.[43] Observations of religious practices at Akasaka's sacred sites, however, lead me to disagree with Miyake's emphasis on cosmological ritualism based on the rotation of seasonal and annual cyclical ceremonies as the key to understanding the round of folk religious practices, including life-cycle rites of passage. Instead, I stress the role of ritual practices happening on a daily basis such that a sense of spontaneous participation often occurs in response to personal affairs, ranging from a family crisis or financial concerns to mood swings and stress at the workplace. In a modern urban setting this involvement occurs at various sites that retain some of the archaic cultural resonance but also operate according to contemporary rhythms suitable to a largely secular environment.

The layer of folk religion as the basis for the interrelation of Buddhism and Shinto is as evident in ceremonies for dying as in rituals for living. Although Shinto is more devoted to rites for life, according to some interpretations, including those offered by purveyors of Buddhist altars, the practice of using a butsudan in the home is not limited to or primarily Buddhist; rather, the "altar *transcended* not only established Buddhist denominations but all organized religion." As John Nelson notes of a butsudan dealer (discussed in chapter 4) that has been very successful in its recent marketing campaigns, "The [Yagiken Company] believed that the veneration of family ancestors (*senzo sūhai*) was fundamental to Japanese culture and society, existing long before the foreign religion of Buddhism made its appearance in 538 C.E. They referenced data from a survey of people visiting cemeteries to clean and maintain family graves (*haka mairi*) which indicated between seventy to eighty percent did not have strong ties to any Buddhist sect."[44] It can further be said that, while featuring death rituals, Buddhism also deals with life rituals in the sense that the afterlife is a form of life for departed loved ones. By cultivating values of self-discipline and moderation in one's own behavior as a way of connecting with and enhancing the plane of existence of venerated ancestors, the realms of living and dying are interwoven on many levels.

Why Inari Shinkō?

Inari shinkō refers to one of the main examples of folk religious practice (but certainly not the only one), which takes place on various occasions occurring between, as well as during, the major rites of passage. All of the main shrines in Akasaka are affiliated with Inari worship but in very different ways and with no specific linkage to one another, although they each have connections with prominent Inari shrines in other parts of the city or throughout the country. For example, Toyokawa Inari is a branch of the main Sōtō Zen temple-shrine in Aichi Prefecture, and Sannō Hie Jinja has an affiliation with Fushimi Inari in Kyoto, while both Nogi Jinja's Akasaka Inari Jinja and the Hikawa Jinja are both linked to other shrines in Tokyo, including Ōji Inari

Jinja, site of the mythical "fox wedding" depicted in a Hiroshige print. These complex networks of affiliations demonstrate the attraction and diversity of a powerful form of folk religious practice that cuts across sectarian divisions. As Stephen Mansfield notes of Tokyo's sense of the sacred, "Inari shrines are the most visible expressions of a world where strange spells and transmutations are common."[45]

On the other hand, although many of the main sites in Akasaka involve Inari worship, which seems to be by far the largest example of a shinkō, with more than forty thousand shrines small and large throughout Japan, ranging from the expanse of Fushimi Inari mountain in the southwest corner of Kyoto to a single torii gate or fox statue elsewhere, there is no intention here of asserting the superiority of Inari over other local or assimilated gods. Reflecting the fact that the doctrine of *honji-suijaku* is alive and well in modern Japan, many other native or assimilated deities, such as Hachiman, Hakusan, Kishibōjin, Shichifukujin, and Tenjin (Suguwara no Michizane), are quite common, along with distinctively Buddhist icons that have become folk gods, like Daruma, Hotei, Jizō, and Rakan.

Inari, which is almost always represented in the image of a magical fox, standing by vermillion torii gates with votive banners, whose magical powers have been tamed and transformed into something beneficial, resembles a number of other gods symbolized by an animal. These include Sannō Gongen, represented by a monkey (which similarly represents fertility), Kompira-sama by an elephant, Benzaiten by a snake, and Hachiman by a dog. Many other nonhumans, including birds, fish, and amphibians, in addition to anthropo-morphic mythical creatures like *kappa* or *tengu* are similarly used in religious rituals. Unlike the monkey, elephant, and snake, which are animal avatars derived from India, the fox god Inari (and other examples such as dog, badger, cat, and *tengu*) is indigenous although somewhat influenced by continental icons and attitudes.

Therefore, the use of the phrase "live Inari" refers to customs or practices habitually carried out within a worldview of myth and magic found in both Buddhist and Shinto contexts. It is not meant to refer to just this one icon as opposed to an array of other devotional objects in the vast pantheon of Japanese religion but is being used here as an emblem of a larger ritual frame-work. Inari serves as a placeholder for an overarching sense of unified religi-osity that involves practices of fortune-telling and divination or offering prayers to obtain benefits, as well as the exorcism of invasive or vengeful spirits, which crosses over apparent sectarian categories based on function, history, or location.

Furthermore, "live Inari" is not strictly associated with Shinto as it is by no means excluded from but is very much evident in every one of the branches of Buddhism.[46] Indeed, many of the supposed examples of Shinto practice can also be found at various Buddhist sites. In addition to syncretistic theology and iconography, some of the ritual elements that intersect the religious traditions both at public spaces and in household worship include torii gates and altars or platforms, the presence of water, bells, and incense as purification devices, and *omikuji* and *ema* tablets used as examples of divination or for amulets. The effect of these commonalities is that a participant's religious experience at diverse sacred sites is often more or less the same, regardless of the institutional label.

Three main types of assimilative ritual patterns seem to be in evidence at sacred sites today. One example includes cases where a shrine and a temple that were once interfused but were separated during the Meiji period continue to exist symbiotically side by side as divided yet interdependent entities. For example, at Ōtori Jinja shrine near Inarichō, a famous autumn festival is held. This celebration is also supported by Chōkokuji, a Nichiren temple once part of an integrated compound that now stands advantageously next door. A second example is the case of Nezu Jinja, an Inari shrine located near Yanaka, which includes the prominent display of distinctive Buddhist symbols such as the swastika, traditionally an auspicious indicator of spiritual presence imported from mainland Asia. Third is the case of Toyokowa Inari in Akasaka, which represents a prime but by no means unique instance of full-fledged syncretism, whereby the distinctions between traditions seem to dissolve and disappear altogether, thus revealing an underlying layer of folk religiosity.

Nationalism versus Culturalism

An important aspect of Japanese folk religiosity that is evident in various Akasaka shrines and temples is their foundation in nation-building elements that encompass the role of state politics and class structure in addition to the impact of these elements on a communal intellectual legacy. Historical and political forces, which have greatly contributed to the establishment and further development of the religious sites, are crucial for understanding their overall significance as sacred spaces. The main shrines, as well as smaller temples, generally have deep roots in premodern or Meiji society and reflect the influence of heroic individuals like Yoshimune, Ōoka, or Nogi, and this affects the way they are viewed by casual visitors and devotees alike.

The sacred sites in Akasaka exhibit some important historical differences. Sannō Hie Jinja probably stems from the early medieval-period centuries prior to the growth of Tokyo. It has been relocated and rebuilt many times, and the current structures were constructed between 1958 and 1967, when sufficient funds were raised from donors following destruction from an air raid during WWII. Nogi Jinja derives from the early twentieth century, yet it too has been reconstructed since the war. Toyokawa Inari and Hikawa Jinja both maintain that they have Edo origins, although only the latter can validate that it has more or less continuously occupied the current location since the eighteenth century.

Regardless of the historicity of the claims, much of the sites' appeal in attracting visitors is that they try to replicate the atmosphere, or at least what it is imagined to be, of an Edo-period religious environment, thus bringing the sacred past into the secular present. The attraction of Akasaka's religious sites, which are visited on a daily basis by ritual participants who may come purposefully but often walk in from the street informally on their way to and from the workplace for individual prayer or to take part in festival cycles, is not just a matter of adherents' selecting a particular ceremonial function or favored icon, although this certainly plays an important role in terms of which locations they choose to patronize. Akasaka's shrines and temples may seem like a throwback to a different era and suddenly thrust the visitor into a realm of folklore and supernaturalism and thereby offer a sense of relief and release, or at least distance and distraction, from the contemporary world, in which the wrestling with vengeful spirits continues to determine the course of one's life and explain the trajectory and meaning of day-to-day activities.

Yet the sacred sites in the neighborhood can also be appreciated in conjunction with modernity as suggested by a guidebook's map (Map 3.4) outlining a recommended walking tour, which is to take just thirty-four minutes from the time one arrives at Akasaka-mitsuke Station, near Toyokawa Inari, until reaching the destination of Nogizaka Station, adjacent to Nogi Jinja. In taking this path, the pedestrian visitor walks through the heart of Akasaka and visits the small graveyard of Hōdoji temple, in addition to parks, museums, and places of historical interest, rather than covering the periphery along the major thoroughfares. This trip culminates not with the shrine in honor of General Nogi but with the new commercial development of Tokyo Midtown a few blocks away, demonstrating once again the powerful interweaving of sacrality and secularity.[47]

Folk religious spaces and symbols are multivalent based on complex historical factors, and each particular symbolic element takes responsibility for

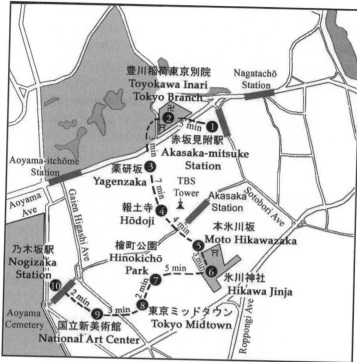

Akasaka Walking Tour (34 min)

MAP 3.4

representing or enhancing a ritual function or degree of spiritual resonance. The process of participation seems to reflect a longing for collective social identity and a sense of solidarity with a communal cultural character. Clarifying the intricacy of the background and its vicissitudes, along with the diversity of holy functions, illuminates how and why so many sacred sites coexist and compete for attention in what would appear to be a predominantly secular part of the city that lacks interest in recovering traditional religiosity.

A key question that arises is whether the emphasis on national identity, past or present, constitutes a form of nationalism such that folk religion may be seen to represent an attempt to essentialize diverse and divergent cultural elements in a way that betrays nativist leanings and longings by promoting an agenda of Japanese exceptionalism derived from an entitled sense of authenticity or ethnic/racial superiority. As Reader and Tanabe indicate, it must be acknowledged that an approach based on identifying a primary layer of folk religion can be criticized for several reasons. First, this view has often been advocated by nonacademic folklorists in describing the customs of their specific areas in a way that reflects local biases. The more systematic approach to folklore studies taken by the prominent school of ethnography initiated by Yanagita Kunio and Origuchi Shinobu, which has been influential on Ama, Hori, and Miyake, has also been attacked for conflating a romanticized and idealized view of traditional customs with discussions of national (or racial) identity, as well as for using this view in support of counterarguments to modernization.[48] This standpoint may tend to view folk religiosity either as a form of practice that preceded Buddhism and Shinto chronologically and thus enjoys an enduring and unchanging state of constancy or, at the opposite extreme, as a random collection of local data that tries to capture and label any and all curious customs and superstitions that cannot easily be categorized as either Buddhist or Shinto.

While appreciating these criticisms and seeking to distance myself from possible political implications of some of the views regarding folk religion, my observations suggest that there is a basic difference between interpreting Japanese rites in terms of the state politics of nationalism and the everyday social behavior of what I refer to as "culturalism." As a matter of fostering various levels of cultural identity, Japanese folk religiosity involves establishing and maintaining connections (*en*), or webs of deep, karmically driven relationships between individuals and their counterparts, who participate jointly in navigating the realms of sacred and secular, this-worldliness and other-worldliness, life and death, and human and natural.

This is a primary element of Japanese society, in which nearly everyone strives to avoid the lowly status of the unattached or unaffiliated (*muen*). According to Winston Davis, the success of any Japanese religious movement largely lies in upholding these connections, "be it a relationship with the gods, nature, society (this life) and the afterlife. To live a good afterlife we need to keep these relationships, or we would become *muenbotoke* [unrelated soul]. Family or friends are needed to do the afterlife rituals for you. And the family and friends feel responsible to do it or because if not keeping their duty and souring the relationship with the dead, they risk having an angry ghost."[49] This emphasis on the human-centered context of relationships also diverges from the way Miyake tends to focus on the animistic and divinity- or kami-centered nature of folk beliefs.

In the Japanese context, nature plays a crucial role as a realm facilitating crossovers between contradictory realms. Naturalism is thus a key part of culturalism as a major factor in Japanese folk religiosity since gods are often rulers of a natural domain and animals are seen as the mascots or messengers of many deities. Many temples exist in scenic natural surroundings and are usually meant to be built on a mountain; in a city where there is little elevation a temple is still referred to as a "mountain" (san). Nevertheless, all shrines and temples are surrounded by some element of greenery, which creates a sense of serenity even in the midst of the concrete jungle of Tokyo. Although natural space has been reduced significantly in modern times, the essence of the sacred encompassing the qualities of minimalism and rusticity (*wabi-sabi*) is felt within the walls of the temple or shrine through nostalgic festivals and ceremonies that offer reprieve from and escape to an alternative worldview. That is why adherents' strong commitment to elements of practice supports the maintenance and continuity despite severe challenges experienced in modern times by traditional sacred sites, which continue to serve as both ritual milieus for devotees and a kind of refuge or oasis offering sanctuary for the more casual visitor.

NOTES

1. Steven Heine, *The Zen Poetry of Dōgen: Verses from the Mountain of Eternal Peace* (Mount Tremper, N.Y.: Dharma Communications, 2005), p. 121.

2. H. D. Harootunian, *Things Seen and Unseen* (Chicago: University of Chicago Press, 1988).

3. See Richard Mark Jaffe, *Neither Monk nor Layman: Clerical Marriage in Modern Japanese Buddhism* (Princeton, NJ: Princeton University Press, 2001); and James Edward Ketelaar, *Of Heretics and Martyrs in Meiji Japan: Buddhism and Its Persecution* (Princeton, NJ: Princeton University Press, 1990).

4. Lawrence Rogers, ed. and trans., *Tokyo Stories: A Literary Stroll* (Berkeley: University of California Press, 2002), p. xxvii.

5. Terry McCarthy, "Japan Bids Sayonara to Geisha Politics," *Independent* (Nov. 28, 1993).

6. "Japanese Lifestyle," http://www.japaneselifestyle.com.au/tokyo/akasaka.htm (accessed Jan. 7, 2010).

7. All three entryways to the shrine feature steep stairways, which is characteristic of East Asian sacred spaces that seek to challenge and test the dedication of devotees, even in a contemporary urban environment. Atago Jinja in southwestern Tokyo is also known for its imposing flight of stairs.

8. Rogers, *Tokyo Stories*, p. xxviii.

9. John H. Martin and Phyllis G. Martin, *Tokyo: A Cultural Guide to Japan's Capital City* (Tokyo: Tuttle, 1996), pp. 69, 75–78.

10. Paul Waley, *Tokyo Now & Then: An Explorer's Guide* (New York: Weatherhill, 1984), p. 48.

11. Ibid., pp. 48–50.

12. Paul Waley, *Tokyo: City of Stories* (New York: Weatherhill, 1991), p. 222.

13. See www.hiejinja.net/jinja/kouza/bunka/hiyosi/index.html (accessed May 8, 2010).

14. Doris G. Bargen, *Suicidal Honor: General Nogi and the Writings of Mori Ōgai and Natsume Sōseki* (Honolulu: University of Hawaii Press, 2006), p. 35.

15. See Robert Jay Lifton, Shūichi Katō, and Michael R. Reich, *Six Lives, Six Deaths: Portraits from Modern Japan* (New Haven, Conn.: Yale University Press, 1979).

16. See Bargen, *Suicidal Honor*, for a discussion of this and also for the role these writers played in chronicling Nogi's life and death; she points out, for example, that the wife of Sensei, the main, suicidal character in *Kokoro*, is named Shizu (literally, "quiet") after Nogi's wife, Shizuko (which includes the diminutive "ko," almost universally used in girls' names until the past couple of decades).

17. The inscription reads as follows: "*General Nogi's Residence and Stable*—Erected in 1902, the Nogi residence was home to General Nogi Maresuke and his wife until September 13, 1912, when on the day of the Emperor Meiji's funeral, the couple committed ritual suicide in order to follow their emperor to the grave. Built in the style of the French army buildings that impressed Nogi so much during his student days in Germany, the Nogi residence is noticeably different from many lavish Meiji Period homes built either entirely in Western-style or with Western-style drawing rooms. General Nogi's home is a simple, unadorned structure befitting a soldier. Making use of the slope on which the building stands, part of the wooden house, which covers 168 square meters and is roofed with Japanese tiles, is actually underground. The general's stable, also a single-story structure roofed with Japanese tiles, was constructed in 1889 before the house itself was built. The stable, 12.5 meters long and 4.5 meters wide, is a narrow building divided into four sections, which were used to house the general's horses and to store feed. A sturdy brick structure, the stable bears witness to the great care the general took of his horses." See also Francis Dorai, ed., *Insight City Guide Tokyo* (Singapore: Apa, 2007), p. 111.

18. Waley, *Tokyo Now & Then*, pp. 386–387.

19. Martin and Martin, *Tokyo*, pp. 249–252.

20. This institution enshrines at least three forms of the fox/rice deity, which are considered mutually supportive as protector gods for the temple-shrine complex and its followers: the Buddhist deity Dakini-shinten, depicted as a female bodhisattva sitting astride a flying white fox and enshrined in the Dharma Hall; the indigenous Inari fertility deity known as Toyokawa Inari, held in the Shrine Hall; and a variety of small fox icons that are guardians of these primary images.

21. Steven Heine, *Zen Skin, Zen Marrow: Will the Real Zen Buddhism Please Stand Up?* (New York: Oxford University Press, 2008), pp. 96–104.

22. There are countless similar legends, including one that has Dōgen saved by the appearance of Kannon during a typhoon while crossing the Japan Sea on his return from China.

23. As with other examples of the Inari cult, including Fushimi Inari, the head temple charges the off-site locations for the privilege of being awarded a spirit; see Ian Reader and George J. Tanabe Jr., *Practically Religious: Worldly Benefits and the Common Religion of Japan* (Honolulu: University of Hawaii Press, 1998), especially pp. 145–146.

24. Waley, *Tokyo Now & Then*, pp. 372–374.

25. Martin and Martin, *Tokyo*, pp. 80–82.

26. Karen A. Smyers, *The Fox and the Jewel: Shared and Private Meanings in Contemporary Japanese Inari Worship* (Honolulu: University of Hawaii Press, 1999), p. 48.

27. Ibid., p. 125.

28. Waley, *Tokyo: City of Stories*, p. 221.

29. See *Edo Tokyo sanpo* (Tokyo: Ninbunsha, 2003).

30. Richard Jeffery, "Aoyama Cemetery: Gaienmae," http://tokyoq.com/weekly_updates/tqoole/cemetery.html (accessed Apr. 10, 2010).

31. There is evidence that things are changing in some Western countries. For example, a report shows that in Norway recently, despite signs at cemeteries indicating there are laws against this, "More and more of the capital's residents use the city's cemeteries as parks. It is not unusual to see people who sunbathe or barbecues near the headstones." Unfortunately, a corollary serious social problem that has emerged is that, along with the joggers, dog walkers, and picnickers enjoying themselves on sunny days, junkies have been leaving syringes behind near graves. See http://www.vg.no/nyheter/innenriks/artikkel.php?artid=10003532 (accessed July 13, 2010).

32. Ian Reader, *Contemporary Religion in Japan* (Honolulu: University of Hawaii Press, 1991), pp. 51–52.

33. Michael Pye, "Rationality, Ritual, and Life-Shaping Decisions in Modern Japan," in *Japan and Asian Modernities,* ed. Rein Raud (London: Kegan Paul, 2007), p. 24.

34. Michael Pye notes that:

    confusion has been provided in the older literature by a miscellany of statements about "popular religion," "syncretism," "superstition," etc., terms which can make a specialist in the study of religions quite upset when poorly or inappropriately used. Space does not allow a systematic treatment of this terminology here....In terms of a general theory of Japanese religion, it is not so very difficult to provide the necessary correlations. The key point is to differentiate between a general level of religiosity, which I have called the "primal religion" of contemporary Japan, and the specific religious communities and their teachings. (Ibid., p. 24)

35. Reader and Tanabe, *Practically Religious*, p. 28.

36. Ibid., pp. 25–32.

37. Ibid., p. 29.

38. Ibid., p. 31.

39. Ichirō Hori, "Folk Religion," in *Japanese Religion: A Survey by the Agency for Cultural Affairs*, ed. Ichirō Hori, Ikado Fujio, Wakimoto Tsuneya, and Yanagawa Keiichi (Tokyo: Kodansha, 1972), pp. 121–122; see also Ichirō Hori, *Folk Religion in Japan: Continuity and Change*, ed. Joseph M. Kitigawa and Alan L. Miller (Chicago: University of Chicago Press, 1994).

40. Brian Bocking, *A Popular Dictionary of Shinto* (Surrey, UK: Curzon, 1996), p. 123.

41. Toshimaro Ama, "Interview with Hisashi Kondo," *Japan Plus: Asia-Pacific Perspectives* 4(3) (2006), p. 36.

42. Ibid.

43. H. Byron Earhart, "Introduction," in *Shugendō: Essays on the Structure of Japanese Folk Religion*, ed. Hitoshi Miyake (Ann Arbor: Center for Japanese Studies, University of Michigan Press, 2001), p. 5.

44. John Nelson, "Household Altars in Contemporary Japan: Rectifying Buddhist 'Ancestor Worship' with Home Décor and Consumer Choice," *Japanese Journal of Religious Studies* 35(2) (2008): 305–330.

45. Stephen Mansfield, *Tokyo: A Cultural History* (New York: Oxford University Press, 2009), p. 240.

46. See Barbara Ambros, *Emplacing a Pilgrimage: The Ōyama Cult and Regional Religion in Early Modern Japan* (Cambridge, Mass.: Harvard University Asia Center, Harvard University Press, 2008).

47. *Tokyo: Shitamachi, Yamanote Wokkingu* (Tokyo: JTB, 2008), pp. 156–159.

48. Hashimoto Mitsuru, "*Chihō*: Yanagita Kunio's 'Japan,'" in *Mirror of Modernity: Invented Traditions of Modern Japan*, ed. Stephen Vlastos (Berkeley: University of California Press, 1998), pp. 133–143.

49. Winston Davis, *Japanese Religion and Society: Paradigms of Structure and Change* (Albany: State University of New York Press, 1992), p. 24. The term *botoke* (or *hotoke*) in *muenbotoke* literally means Buddha but is generally used to refer to an ancestor spirit.

4 INARICHŌ IN THE LOW CITY: IM-PRACTICAL WORLDLY BENEFITS

The Conundrum of Religious Motivation

This chapter examines the role of fifty shops selling butsudan supplies, along with a rich variety of temples, shrines, and other sites of historical or cultural significance, in a distinctive Shitamachi locale (Map 4.1) in order to treat the conundrum of religious motivation, or why and how Japanese people who express a surprisingly low level of belief are driven to exhibit a high level of practice. This discussion represents a follow-up and complement to the previous chapter's examination of institutional structure through viewing religious places in Yamanote. When taken together, the aim of these two chapters is to use the microlevel of analyzing sacred sites in particular Tokyo neighborhoods as representative case studies that constitute a vehicle for probing and reevaluating the macrolevel regarding the overall meaning and significance of religiosity in contemporary Japan. Considering the two conundrums of religious structure and motivation in tandem helps answer the overriding question about sacred space: What makes religiosity tick in an increasingly secular environment that would seem to detract from and cause it to deteriorate?

In a city recognized for numerous areas around town with a host of specialty shops ranging from technical supplies like electronics, watches, and cameras to cultural refinements such as stationery, dolls, and antiquarian books or other needs like kitchenware and shoes (both offered nearby in Shitamachi), Inarichō features a long row of Buddhist and Shinto implement establishments, which are now mostly retail although some remain wholesale (ton'ya-gai). These shops primarily sell altars, a miniature household shrine in which Buddhist images and memorial tablets are placed so as to be installed in homes as the centerpiece of commemorations for deceased ancestors, in addition to other kinds of mortuary ritual accessories or Buddhist furnishings (butsugu).

Some of the Inarichō shops cater to the butsudan requirements for particular sects, including Nichiren, Zen, and Pure Land, while others are pansectarian; some specialize in a boutique fashion in a specific style or ornamentation, such as beads, bells (Figure 4.1), or drums, while others, like the seven-story Nakagawa Company building, function like department stores (*depaato*) by distributing a wide variety of products for funerals and related ceremonies. Many of the enterprises have only a single shop in this neighborhood, while the Isshindō Company has multiple storefronts here with branches in other parts of town serving parishioners from nearly fifteen thousand temples from around the country. Also, in the midst of butsudan row (Map 4.2) are stores that sell other items like barbershop supplies, including hairbrushes, as well as art galleries and the ubiquitous McDonald's and other native and foreign restaurants.

Almost all of the Inarichō storefronts were destroyed during WWII bombing, but in the rebuilding of the neighborhood following this loss, the shopkeepers decided to band together to create an Association of Ueno-Asakusa Buddhist-Shinto Altar Shops. This organization began forming in 1955 and subsequently was legally established and has been very active since 1970. In recent years, the organization has maintained its own website (www.

FIGURE 4.1 Buddhist Bells at Inarichō Butsudan Shop

Association of Over 50 Buddhist and Shinto Altar Shops

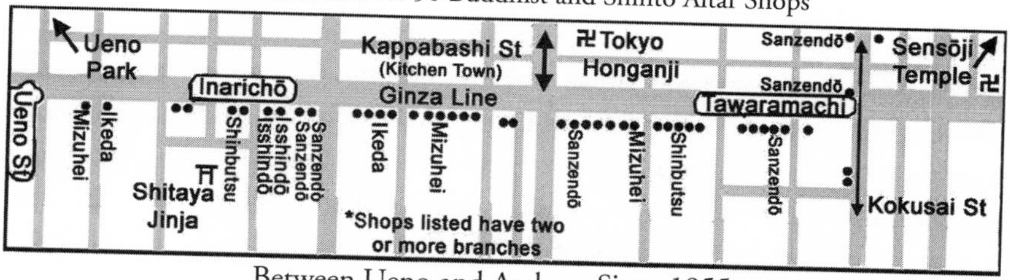

Between Ueno and Asakusa Since 1955

MAP 4.1

shinbutsugu.jp) with links to all of the different commercial entities it represents, plus historical information about the rituals they service and other features such as blog chats that offer personal anecdotes about funerary customs and habits.[1] A banner from the association's internet home page makes an upbeat promotional pitch for the row of butsudan shops located between Ueno and Asakusa.

In light of increasingly strong competition from butsudan stores in other parts of the city, which often sell products with an innovative design that appeals to today's modern, fashion-oriented consumer, as well as more general social changes that challenge and may threaten the continuation of traditional funerary practices, the shopkeepers' common website is designed to present a unified front for the thriving but challenged industry by promoting each of Inaricho's companies. Map 4.1 translates and adapts from the website by showing the locations of the shops between the Inarichō and Tawaramachi stations on the Ginza Line, almost all of which are on the south side of the street, so that, by facing north, the precious wood used for the altars, often timber dried and seasoned for long periods, is not directly exposed to the sunlight in order to prevent damage from warping. Maintaining the website is an intriguing part of the evolving quality of butsudan practices, which 90 percent of the population follows in one way or another. These kinds of modifications show considerable flexibility and leeway in preserving yet updating older ritual functions.

Practicality or Im-practicality

The lead query regarding the matter of religious motivation is, what supports and sustains the unflagging interest and active involvement of ritual adherents in practicing traditional rites? Why are apparently antiquated customs performed at numerous sacred sites throughout Tokyo, still vigorously maintained, given the advances of modernization, which inevitably disrupts and distracts from participation? Relating this to the question of institutional structure, which factors stimulate the commitment to observances for the deceased in death-oriented, other-worldly ceremonies such as making a purchase at a butsudan shop in Inaricho near Asakusa, as well as the enthusiasm for religious activities for life-oriented, this-worldly aspirations encompassing festivals and various forms of worship such as praying at an Inari shrine in Akasaka? Assuming that many of the same motivational factors drive both life-affirmation and death-affirmation rites, to what extent can a combination of the incentives be considered a product of an integrated realm of folk religions that underlies the Buddhist and Shinto traditions?

The main topic for discussion and debate regarding religious motivation in recent scholarship has been to consider whether ritual behavior is carried out by the Japanese primarily for the sake of gaining practical worldly benefits (*genze riyaku*), as Ian Reader and George Tanabe claim in *Practically Religious*, or whether different or additional spiritual and emotional factors (referred to as *anshin*) are at work on the individual or personal, as well as the group or community, levels.[2] Although Reader and Tanabe do not deal specifically with funerary rites, they argue for a "total-care system" that covers "every individual need and requirement...throughout one's life, from birth to death and even the afterlife," so that dying also has a pragmatic, this-worldly dimension in promoting gains for the living here and now by appeasing ancestor spirits.

By focusing on the aim of reaping a benefit from religious observances, *Practically Religious* suggests the priority of practicality and material reward as opposed to attaining peace of mind (*anshin*, or having "one's mind put at ease," *anshin dekita*). The concept of anshin, which Reader and Tanabe tend to dismiss as a construct rather than a realistic goal that ritual participants pursue, refers to broad-based psychological and sentimental rewards. These can be obtained through the inner comfort and consolation provided by funeral ceremonies. These rites allow for appropriate grieving and for maintaining connections with familial lineage and cultural heritage, or a sense of communing with and subduing vengeful ghosts and spirits in a fashion that recalls premodern exorcism practices.

Which aspect, the practical benefit or the impractical reward, inspires Japanese people to line up for hours in a traffic jam waiting to get to a temple for an *Obon* or *Oshogatsu* celebration or to spend tens of thousands of dollars on elaborate memorial rites? Or is the dichotomy of practical versus impractical motivation yet another, externally imposed chimera that clouds our understanding of religious practices, which, according to Reader in another publication that may sound contradictory, are based on developing a "strongly reciprocal element in the relationship between humans and [divine forces]." This connection is attained by constructing through ingrained patterns of giving and receiving a "matrix of reciprocity, of creating obligations, receiving benevolence and responding with gratitude [in a way that] mirrors standard social relationships within Japanese society in general."[3]

Inaricho and Its Environs: Ring of Necropolis

Although the two neighborhoods discussed in this book are both emblematic of larger religio-cultural trends in their respective divisions of the city, studying Inaricho as representative of the religiosity of Shitamachi is somewhat different from looking at its counterpart as exemplary of Yamanote society. Akasaka in Minato Ward is a self-contained yet multifaceted area where several major shrines dominate a cultural landscape otherwise identified mainly with commercial, political, and entertainment interests. In contrast to the role played by that area in the High City, Inaricho in Taitō Ward is known not so much for any special or outstanding religious sites as for its multitude of butsudan stores. These shops, in addition to a variety of other death-related temples, as well as life-related shrines elsewhere in the vicinity, resonate with a network of diverse aspects of sacred and secular space in various parts of the Low City. The sites create a sense of social connections that reflect the notion of *en*, but they must also be understood in terms of their proximity to a cluster of *muen*-related temples near the old execution grounds in Minami Senjū.[4]

Watashitachi no Shitamachi ("Our Low City")

The importance of Inaricho framed in a broader sociohistorical context is the way it highlights how Shitamachi harbors a remarkably complex cultural legacy that encompasses contradictory elements of holiness infused with commercialism, the fine arts inseparable from plebian forms of recreation, a deep sense of continuity with the past linked to itinerancy and constant change among some residents and social functions, and the joys of celebration and aspiration mixed with the sorrows of defeat and desolation. All of these societal factors help to shape the approach to death and memorials that connect to other-worldliness in the shops and temples of Inaricho, as seen in light of shrines dedicated to life and the performance of rites associated with this-worldliness in neighboring locations.

The historical background that might help to explain why a concentration of butsudan shops exists in Inarichō is obscure, but the origins of Inarichō no doubt date from the Meiji era, if not earlier, due largely to the confluence of temples situated in Shitamachi beginning in the seventeenth century. Traditionally, the Low City was the area in the northeast corridor, or demon's gate of Tokyo, where the shogun placed undesirable elements such as marginalized people, including "day laborers, litter-bearers, tinkers, hawkers, mendicant entertainers and sometimes mendicant priests, the occasional masterless samurai, and all the riffraff of the city,"[5] as well as taboo endeavors like working at the execution and cremation grounds in addition to prostitution and theatrical shows, often considered risqué and subversive by authorities.

Despite the seemingly secular qualities developed in Shitamachi during the Edo period, Edward Seidensticker comments on the pervasiveness of religious sites, including temples with graveyards, many of which were moved to this district after the Meireki Fire of 1657 and no doubt helped give rise to the prevalence of altar shops in Inarichō, as well as the area's general death-oriented cultural context:

> Asakusa and Shitaya, from what is Ueno Park to the Sumida, were part of the zone of temples and cemeteries extending in a great sweep around the Tokugawa City. One could have walked from where the northernmost platforms of Ueno Station now stand nearly to the river, passing scarcely anything but temples...Edo was a zoned city, and among the zones was one for the dead. Not wanting them too near at hand, the shogunate established a ring of necropoles at the city limits. Many temples remained at the end of Meiji and a scattering remains today, making Asakusa and Shitaya the most rewarding part of the city for the fancier of tombstones and epitaphs. A late-Meiji guide to the city lists 132 temples in Asakusa Ward and 86 in Shitaya.[6]

Today, according to Paul Waley, dozens of temples still stand in this vicinity, "at least 150 in all. Any short detour into the backstreets will reveal small unassuming temples, most of them little different from normal houses."[7]

The term *Shitamachi* has been used to refer to a very large region of east-northeasterly Tokyo. The distinction between Yamanote and Shitamachi probably stems from the late seventeenth century, first appearing in print in the *Edo sangoyu* of 1690, with the Low City originally referring to areas below and toward the flatlands east of the castle, including Ginza to the south and Kanda to the north in what is now the Chiyoda Ward.[8] The Kanda area, with its major shrine, Kanda Myōjin, guarding the northeast sector of the city, complementing Sannō Hie Jinja in the southwest, epitomized the twin lifestyles of Shitamachi: the emerging, highly disciplined yet entrepreneurial merchant or townsman (*chōnin*) class who cultivated *en*, and the free-spirited yet down-to-earth outlook of the more independent, non-householder or itinerant denizens of the district, who occupied the realm of *muen*. Over the next century the "downtown" of Tokyo was extended eastward to include Ningyōchō in Chūō Ward, the original theater town and licensed quarter with the famous Suitengu Jinja, and then northeast to the Ueno-Asakusa area.

As the city continued to spread to the other side of the Sumida River, Shitamachi eventually came to encompass not only the Taitō and the Arakawa wards, which represent the area most closely associated with Low City society, but also the Kōto Ward to the south, including Fukugawa, which was an early Shitamachi neighborhood where Bashō resided, and the Sumida and Adachi wards, near the shores of the Sumida River. Also, farther to the east, the Edogawa Ward, as well as the Katsushika Ward near the Edogawa River, became part of Shitamachi. The latter part of the city has been famous for the past few decades as the milieu of the eccentric antihero Tora-san, featured in the longest-running (1969–1995) movie series in world history, *Otoko wa tsurai yo* ("It's Tough Being a Man"). Tora-san was to have grown up in the neighborhood of Shibamata in Katsushika Ward, and as a baby he was bathed in the divine waters of the local temple, Taishakuten (a.k.a. Daikeiji), known today as a major ritual center and tourist site.[9]

Affirming Death and Life in the Inarichō Geocultural Triangle

The geographical area selected for this study of sacred space is much more limited than the full expanse of Shitamachi and focuses primarily on the legacy and social symbolism of the death-oriented customs found in and near the row of butsudan shops at Inarichō. Butsudan row extends from about a block east of Ueno Station along Asakusa Avenue, past Inarichō Station and the intersection with Kappabashi Street's Kitchen Town, and toward Tawaramachi Station at Kokusai Avenue as the eastern boundary several blocks away from Sensōji. This area runs from Higashi Ueno 5–6 to the west through Moto Asakusa 1 to the east.

My methodological gaze, however, extends beyond Inarichō proper to include a geocultural triangle filled with religious sites that have diverse

cultural resonances, as well as apparent contradictions, in relation to butsudan row. This territory starts with the nearly half-mile stretch of Inarichō
storefronts in Taitō Ward, which stand in the center of a locative hypote-
nuse, and reaches to three main areas. The first is Ya-Ne-Sen, which encompasses Ueno Park and Yanaka on the west side, with its artist-quarter
ambience, that spills over into western Bunkyō Ward near Tokyo University
and its plethora of death-oriented temples. The next is Minami Senjū Station
to the north of Inarichō in Arakawa Ward, with its group of temples recall-
ing the age of persecution and punishment in the Edo period. The third is
Asakusa to the east in Taitō Ward, with its paradoxical elements of prayer
and play, in addition to various life-oriented shrines. All of these areas contribute important, albeit somewhat conflicting and continually shifting, religious connotations regarding the function of this-worldly and other-worldly
sacred sites and rites.

The basic polarity involving the role of life affirmation taking place in the
shrines of Yamanote and death affirmation taking place in the shops and temples of Shitamachi also plays out within each of the neighborhoods in these

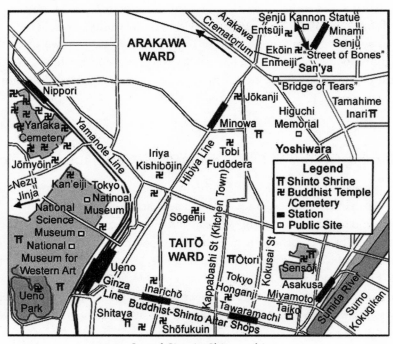

Sacred Sites in Shitamachi

MAP 4.2

districts. As discussed in chapter 3, Akasaka contains many cemeteries adjacent to places that perform rites to obtain prosperity and longevity, and the subareas of the Inarichō geocultural triangle include a variety of sacred sites that promote the forces of life near butsudan row and temple graveyards. Seeing the interaction between the apparent opposites of living and dying in the Low City is crucial for understanding the broader issue of motivation for participating in religious observances in both Yamanote and Shitamachi.

The complexity of the multiple polarities encompassed by Japanese religiosity is highlighted in the Inarichō area, where the role of commemorating death embraces two divergent functions. One is for those who have *en*, or are surrounded by a web of productive human relationships based on family ties that connect the living to the souls of the departed, who will be memorialized at the time of death and in perpetuity; Ya-Ne-Sen epitomizes this approach. The other is for those who are *muen*, or are without relationships to family or other supporters and, therefore, die without having anybody who is meaningful remaining behind to remember them or grieve for the absence of their lives; Minami Senjū represents this outlook.[10]

Given the importance associated with the performance of funerary rites, as well as the considerable expenses these practices demand, it is not hard to imagine that many people's worst fear is falling out of grace with their family or with society at large. The grim fate of muen status befalls those who are forced to lead lives of desperation, in addition to members of the outcast community, whose own relatives will likely suffer discrimination regardless of what rituals are conducted on their behalf. On the other hand, it should be noted that the term *muen* itself covers a polarity since it can have the most positive of connotations if it refers to a lifestyle based on dedication and commitment to achieving a high-minded spiritual or artistic ideal. This is the case of a highly disciplined wandering monk, mountain ascetic, poetic recluse, or some other lone pilgrim or traveler who cuts himself off from the distraction and corruption of conventional society in order to concentrate on attaining a sense of release from the ordinary world.

En Approach in Ya-Ne-Sen

The *en* approach to death memorials is epitomized by Inarichō shops, which cater to the needs of concerned families, and also by the nearby Yanaka Cemetery (Yanaka Reien, literally "spirits garden," which was originally called Yanaka Bochi or Yanaka Graveyard, a less appealing name that was changed in 1935). This site was established in 1872, along with Aoyama Cemetery near Akasaka, in order to supplement the small cemeteries of various Buddhist temples with the opening of public burial grounds. The Yanaka Cemetery was built by Meiji authorities on land confiscated from the largest temple in the area, Tennōji, which still retains its own graveyard and has a Great Buddha statue that was installed in 1690 to resemble the famous Daibutsu icon located in Kamakura. With an expanse of more than a hundred thousand square meters hosting about seven thousand graves, a small section of Yanaka Cemetery that stays closed to the public is dedicated to the family of the fifteen Tokugawa shoguns of Japan, including the last shogun, Tokugawa Yoshinobu, also known as Keiki.

There are, however, important indicators of life affirmation in Ya-Ne-Sen. Like the burial grounds in Aoyama, Yanaka Cemetery is particularly famous for its beautiful cherry trees, which in April completely cover its paths so that its central street is often called Sakura Dori, or Cherry Blossom Avenue. The cemetery is adjacent to Yanaka's temple town, which in turn leads to this locale's famed artists' district. Other notable temples include Jōmyōin's collection of eighty-four thousand donated statues of Jizō (only a percentage is available), who holds a sponge gourd in his left hand and is considered to be a healing Buddha with a specialty in coughs and asthma, as well as the concerns of pregnant women and the protection of children, the dead, and travelers. The temple also dispenses scrub brushes for washing away one's pains.

Many of the sites combine Buddhist and Shinto elements, although not to the extent of the institutional indivisibility found in Toyokowa Inari. These include Nezu Jinja, a major Inari shrine with its two-story vermilion gate resembling Sensōji's Kaminarimon and a Buddhist swastika, and Daienji temple, dedicated to Kishibōjin, a deity that is supposed to aid childbearing. Daienji, which also honors the memory of beautiful Osen, an Edo-period tea waitress who was a leading model for a *ukiyo-e* print artist, distributes scrub brushes for women in order to free them from ailments, and also features a Shinto-like chrysanthemum festival every November.[11] At Eikyūji temple, there is enshrined Meki, a yellow-eyed Fudō, who cures some diseases and is one of many such esoteric Buddhist deities in Tokyo that are commonly named for the color of their eyes.

Bordering on Yanaka stands Ueno Park, once the sanctuary of the shoguns and now the largest public park in the country. Today the park houses many temples and shrines from the Edo period, including Kan'eiji, along with smaller religious sites. However, Ueno is better known for important modern museums and schools of the arts, in addition to a zoo and an amusement park near a honky-tonk shopping district and a railway hub. The area was designed by the founding abbot, Tenkai, who wanted to emulate Kyoto's northeast corner environs, so he constructed Shinobazu Pond and Bentendō, an island built in the water in dedication to the goddess Benten, in order to replicate Lake Biwa and Chikubushima Island, which along with Mount Hiei helped to protect Kyoto spiritually from the intrusion of malevolent forces through the demon's gate. He also created Kiyomizu Kannon-dō, located above Shinobazu Pond and modeled after Kyoto's famed Kiyomizu temple. Long the departure zone for travelers headed for points north, such as the way station at Senjū or the festivities farther afield at what was once the Tokugawa shrine in Nikko, Ueno historically "was crowded and bustling with entertainers and customers of the shops," many of which "were known as *hotoke-dana*, 'Buddha stores,' because, perhaps, of their proximity to Kan'eiji." As part of the inseparability of sacred and secular in this area, it is said that some of the Buddha stores also "sold those services in which the *kekoro* [prostitutes] specialized."[12]

Muen Approach in Minami Senjū

On the northeasterly side of the Inarichō geocultural triangle extending into Arakawa Ward stands Minami Senjū, once the shogun's Kotsukappara execution grounds, where criminals, many of whom were political prisoners or victims accused of insubordination, were punished with decapitation, burning, or even crucifixion. As Paul Waley notes, the Senjū area (Map 4.3), with its famous bridge (Senjū Ohashi), was long considered a kind of last outpost for travelers heading out of Tokyo, including Bashō, who "described his departure on a journey to the north of Japan recorded in his masterpiece *Narrow Road to a Far Province*. Bashō had made the relatively short but exhausting trip from his house in Fukagawa by boat up the Sumida River in the company of his friends. From here the poet set out along the road to the north, stopping on his first night at a place called Sōka in Senjū, and said, 'When we disembarked at Senju, my heart grew heavy at the thought of the thousands of miles that lay ahead, and tears welled from my eyes on leaving my friends in this world of illusion.'"[13]

At the southern end (*minami*) of this area in a space that was the size of a football field, from the 1600s to 1873 a couple hundred thousand people were executed or died while in jail and were interred in shallow, unmarked graves. Most of the bodies were just covered in sand instead of being properly buried, so that birds and animals would be able to pick at their remains, and newspapers today occasionally report the discovery of bones whenever road construction is undertaken in the area. Most of the original execution grounds now lie beneath the train tracks, and what remains is tightly fit into a small corner between the JR Jōban Line, a railway freight yard, and the road in front of Minami Senjū Station. To the north of the station stands what was known as the Street of Bones, or Kotsu Avenue,[14] where the skeletons of the executed were laid out or their severed heads were displayed on poles to intimidate possible subversives.

Another infamous site just to the south of the station, the Bridge of Tears, where families would bid farewell to criminals being led off to their capital punishment, lies today at the unfortunate heart of another kind of suffering. Across the bridge area, to the northeast of Inarichō, stands San'ya, with its flophouses and largely itinerant residents' reliance on public subsidies and welfare, as well as the area of the Yoshiwara, or former licensed quarter situated by the shogun in the northeast corridor of the city as an emotional outlet for citizens. This part of the cityscape, also populated by members of the *burakumin* community, formerly outcast until antidiscrimination laws were passed in the early part of the Meiji era, reveals dire signs of urban blight, which is perhaps the worst in all of Tokyo, yet is still moderate in comparison with ghettoized sectors of many U.S. cities.[15]

In the Edo period, outcasts whom the shogunate moved from the more centrally located Nihonbashi to what is now Imado chōme just north of Asakusa, took occupations considered taboo and shunned by the mainstream society, such as working the execution grounds, removing ashes from crematoria, or trading in leather products, especially footwear. Today, *burakumin* operate many shoe and rag shops in this area, and the nearby Tamahime Inari Jinja at 2–13–2 Kiyokawa in Taitō Ward offers the Konkon Kutsuichi, or shoe fair, every spring (April 25–26). Another shrine in the area, Imado Jinja, is said to be the birthplace of the Beckoning Cat, or Maneki Neko.

Side by side with this activity, a couple hundred "soaplands," massage parlors, and "love hotels" are serviced by several thousand women as part of what was once Yoshiwara, which at one point in history was a plush area where behind closed doors the austere values of the elite samurai class were set aside for nights of pleasure seeking and escapism, which required refined surroundings. However, "By 1890 the law permitted women who did not wish to remain with Yoshiwara to leave the enclave. That same year the Salvation Army arrived in Tokyo and published a tract called *Triumphant Voice* encouraging the denizens of Yoshiwara to flee and offering them help."[16] Furthermore, once modernization began and money, once scorned, was valued, luxurious entertainment could be found in other parts of the city like Akasaka, where business and political leaders conducted their affairs at expensive *ryōtei*. With this shift, Yoshiwara gradually became a kind of palace of sleaze.

Minami Senjū is now primarily a modern transportation hub, but a cluster of Edo-period temples remain in the vicinity. These reveal the muen approach to death and dying, such as the so-called Neckchop Jizō and the Dump Temple, which once catered to the dispossessed and downtrodden, including sick and impoverished prostitutes, criminals, and outcasts. Near the station's south exit, close to the Street of Bones, are two important muen sites. One is the Jōdo sect's Enmeiji at 2-34-5 Minami Senjū in Arakawa Ward, which features the Neckchop Jizō, which provided sanctuary for the executed and now stands amid a dilapidated graveyard just below the train tracks. Down the street are the revamped Ekōin grounds at 5−33−13 Minami Senjū in Arakawa Ward, which is dedicated to those who lost their lives in fire and other tragedies. Ekōin is a branch of the original temple in Ryōgoku, near the sumo stadium across the Sumida River, which is also dedicated to the memory of the dispossessed. The branch temple's cemetery contains memorials to Nezumi Kōzō, a famous burglar executed in 1832; nationalist teacher Yoshida Shōin, executed in 1859; and Takahashi Oden, a murderess who had the distinction of being the last criminal to be executed by decapitation in 1879.

According to a commentator, "Reading the memorial markers is to share the sorrows of the past. 'People who died at sea.' 'To aborted infants.' 'Ninety unclaimed citizens from the 1923 earthquake.' 'Those who died in prison.' One, from 1895, notes that 'fifty yen has been provided for eternal maintenance.'"[17] Ekōin was destroyed twice, once in the 1923 earthquake and again as a result of WWII bombing, but was rebuilt shortly after the war. Across from this temple is the Himawari (Sunflower) Jizō, dedicated in 1982 to the "Yama men" (day laborers), which is available for those who have died with no relatives or friends to claim them. Twice a year memorial services are conducted for these men.

Jōkanji, a Jōdo temple located at 2−1−12 Minami Senjū in Arakawa Ward is another important muen burial site near Minowa Station on the Hibiya Line, one stop south of Minami Senjū. Jōkanji, which literally means "the temple of serene silence," is also known as the Dump (or Throwaway) Temple (Nagekomidera) since many dead prostitutes from Yoshiwara, where the mortality rate was exceptionally high, were tossed into a communal grave after dying of illness or starvation. Probably more than eleven thousand girls at an average age of twenty-two years were disposed of in this way:

Behind the temple hall, incense still burns at the memorial stone for the unfortunate women. So moved was the author Nagai Kafu by this reminder of the sorrow of life in the quarter that he wrote the following lines in his diary: "If anyone considers erecting a monument to me when I die, let him choose a spot here among the leaning crumbling stones of the courtesans." [Quoted from Seidensticker, *Kafu the Scribbler*, p. 143] A commemoretive plaque, not quite of the sort Kafu had stipulated, does indeed now stand in front of that of the wretched courtesans.[18]

A statement from one of the victims reads, "I was born to live in hell and to be buried in Jōkanji temple." A Jizō stands with the stark engraved caption "Muen Graves" (*muenbaka*). However, like Ekōin but in contrast to Enmeiji, the temple was recently restored, and to the unknowing passerby it presents itself as more or less like any other contemporary religious site.

Like Jōkanji, Entsūji is a small temple at 1–59–11 Minami Senjū in Arakawa Ward, which has also historically cared for the spirits of otherwise unprotected deceased parties, such as criminals or young geisha suffering from venereal disease. Affiliated with the Sōtō Zen sect, Entsūji features a large golden Hyaku Kannon statue that was originally constructed in the Edo period. Rebuilt recently, Kannon now adorns the main streets near the station. This impressive icon reveals the importance of Buddhism in the cultural context of muen funerary rites and seems to highlight the degree of concern and compassion that has emanated from the depths and despair of Japanese society in the early modern and modern eras in a way that contrasts with cynicism about elements of greed often associated with funerary customs.

The muen sites are all featured on the Arawaka Ward's official website (www.arakawa-unet.jp/sightseeing/index.html) and have become a source of pride for this section of Shitamachi. Sometimes referred to as "the darker side of Tokyo,"[19] Arakawa has a rich though unfortunate history and is in the process of modernizing but seeks to honor its legacy. Rounding out the sacred space of the Minami Senjū area are several sites whose origins predate the Edo period, including Nikkeiji temple and two large shrines that continue to feature grand festivals, Kumano Jinja and Susano Jinja, which stand on the pathway leading toward the Senjū Ohashi Bridge. The Arakawa Ward's tourist division promotes a walking tour of all of the sites, one of several itineraries it recommends, which indicates a sense of pride in the beneficent role the religious sites have historically played in the otherwise rather sordid social history of the area encompassing the interactions of life and death orientations.

Arakawa Walking Map

MAP 4.3

Life-Oriented Sites in the Neighborhood Interior

The atmosphere of Shitamachi once again changes dramatically heading to the southeast point of the Inarichō geocultural triangle and toward the Asakusa Sensōji temple district, which, with its complex associations regarding the integration of prayer and play, is a bastion of held-over yet ever-vanishing early modern resources and artifacts.[20] Asakusa for centuries "was the kaleidoscopic center of the city's insatiable quest for diversion,"[21] serving as the gateway to Yoshiwara and the home of the kabuki theater in a bygone era, as well as a dynamic movie theater district in the twentieth century. Still today, according to Jean Pearce, even more so than the Ya-Ne-Sen area, "Asakusa is the Japan that all tourists dream of seeking, the woodblock print come to life, the painted teacup a reality,"[22] because it is here that one experiences the floating world and its various pleasures of picnics and outings, poetry writing and arts. Sensōji temple, which enshrines an unseen icon of Kannon,[23] features a giant *koro* (incense burner), where people stand and draw the smoke to their body with their hands, which is believed to cure all illness and turmoil, "from thinning hair to cancer, from business problems to broken heart… Although medical science in Japan is rated among the foremost in the world, such ancient, deep-seated beliefs still exist, comfortably, side by side with science."[24]

Shitamachi is for the most part a working-class neighborhood whose historical and recreational attractions remain very atmospheric in reflecting a bygone era. In addition to religious sites, which populate the quarter with an emphasis on memorials, many other sites emphasize the achieving of life goals, which complements the way Akasaka's shrines stress life but also include temples with graveyards large and small. Returning toward Inarichō Station, one passes the nearby Miyamoto Taiko Drum Museum and shops, which are a yearlong center of cultural activities. Also standing in the midst of the Inarichō triangle are several relatively small but very popular shrines, which can easily fill the streets on a ceremonial occasion. One of these is Shitaya Jinja, an Inari shrine located in the heart of butsudan row at 3–29–8 Higashi Ueno in Taitō Ward, where it promotes the benefits of prosperity and happiness. Even the butsudan shops help to support life affirmation by distributing yearly almanacs (Figure 4.2) that predict one's outlook and prospects for attaining good fortune through constructive interactions with family members both in this world and in the spirit realm.

A number of sites in the Yanaka, Shitaya, and Asakusa areas, including Asakusa Sensōji, serve as representatives of one of the Shichifukujin, or Seven Gods of Happiness or Good Fortune. These deities are usually associated with Shinto because they are typically not thought to be part of the Buddhist pantheon, except for Hotei, the Laughing Buddha; however, all but one are of Indian origin, and five of these six are originally Hindu. There is a long-standing tradition since the Edo period of visits undertaken as a kind of minipilgrimage to each of the seven temples or shrines during the period from January 1 to January 7 as part of New Year's festivities, but rites and festivals regularly take place at these sites all year long.[25] The Shichifukujin route is one of many examples in Japanese religiosity in which pilgrimage for religious purposes and recreational touring appears to go hand in hand, so that the secular neither overpowers nor succumbs to, nor is it disguised as, the sacred, but the realms blend together naturally.

The various sites providing rituals for the attainment of *genze riyaku* include several smaller shrines that offer opportunities for worship and participation in festivals that attract remarkably large crowds at certain times of

FIGURE 4.2 2008 Almanac for Year of the Rat

the year, in addition to a couple of temples dedicated to life affirmation at the rather drab-looking Iriya no Kishibōjin (aka Shingenji temple) at 1–12–16 Shitaya in Taitō Ward, which was built in 1659 during the Edo period by monk Nichiyu. Dedicated to Kishibōjin, the Indian Buddhist goddess of children and mothers, who figures prominently in many temples throughout Japan and is worshipped in rites for childbearing, people come here to ask the god to watch over their children's health and to protect them from misfortune. During the Meiji period, the temple became famous for its Iriya Asagao (Morning Glory) Festival, held for three days every July, which draws hundreds of thousands of visitors to this small facility. In earlier times, the morning glory was raised for its seeds, which were used as medicine, and it was also valued for sentimental reasons. A famous poem translates, "Asagao taking hold of the well bucket, I ask a neighbor for water," so as not to disturb the flowers.[26] At nearby Tobi Fudōdera temple, the esoteric Buddhist deity is said to cure stomachaches and also aids those planning to travel by air ("Tobi" refers to flying).

One of the main examples of a shrine on the Shichifukujin pilgrimage route in the Inarichō vicinity is Asakusa Ōtori Jinja at 3–18–7 Senzoku in Taitō Ward, next to Chōkokuji temple, which used to share its compound. This site is well known for holding the Tori no Ichi (Day of the Rooster) festival at least twice every November as an autumnal celebration that resembles American Thanksgiving. During the festival the shrine offers rites for the genze riyaku of commercial prosperity and business success. People flock to the food stands and trinket booths, which extend for blocks, all the way to Asakusa, nearly a mile away.[27] The shrine at most other times of the year seems at once unassuming in being sparsely populated with underused grounds and a bit garish in its design, which features bright red enshrinements. However, like Iriya Kishibōjin, it is mobbed during festivals, which celebrate the gods Ebisu and Daikoku, in addition to Ōtafuku, whose bloated face and satiated expression give testimony to the benefits of prosperity.

The festival probably stems from the Edo period and is based in part on an association made between the shrine's name and the sign of the Chinese zodiac. In earlier times, it was a chance for the women occupying Yoshiwara to enjoy some free time in the general community. Today, nearly everyone attending is looking to buy different sizes and styles of *kumade* (or bear's claw), a bamboo rake, which can cost anywhere from $10 to $1,000 (the bigger the investment, the bigger the payoff) and is said to help the purchaser rake in the money if placed on an office wall. Also sought after are other *engimono*, or charms, such as cranes, turtles, and gourds, all of which are symbols of wealth and abundance.[28]

In another fascinating geocultural juxtaposition that dramatizes the profound interaction of death- and life-oriented forces in the Low City, the Kappabashi Street Kitchen Town (also referred to as the Food Wares Street) lies perpendicular to Asakusa Avenue on Kokusai Avenue, standing perpendicular to the heart of Inarichō's butsudan row.[29] Kitchen Town is home to more than 170 shops that produce and sell plastic display-food models (*sampuru*) and utensils, along with many different kinds of kitchen and restaurant supplies from all over the world, including bakery equipment and ingredients; Japanese, Western, and Chinese tableware and furniture; china and laquerware; packaging and decorative goods; chefs' coats and cutlery; *noren* (shop curtains); bamboo wares; sweets; refrigerators and refrigerated showcases; and much more.

Established in 1912 as a feature of modern, internationalized Tokyo, Kappabashi is a more recent urban development than Inarichō, but it is a larger and probably much better known area, one more likely to appear in a tourist guide and a prime place to visit for those interested in food after the Tsukiji Fish Market.[30] A temple located near this area, Sōgenji (or Kappadera) at 3–7–2 Matsugaya in Taitō Ward, provides rites for genze riyaku, where mythical kappas appear as friendly creatures compared to the better-known mischievous kind, and supplicants with business problems usually buy a small kappa figurine at the temple office and leave it at the altar.[31]

At the intersection with butsudan row, an oversized rooftop head of an Italian chef, who, complete with hat and moustache, epitomizes the culture of

FIGURE 4.3 Kappabashi's Chief Chef

Kappabashi, oversees the corner, where a majority of Buddhist altar shops are situated (Figure 4.3). Because of their proximity, the general Kappabashi and Inarichō area is a place where people can get their needs taken care of all at once for the material world by buying household goods, as well as items for the spiritual realm. Some people go to Inarichō to buy a Shinto altar (*kami-dana*), or a shelf used in the home to enshrine a tutelary divinity of the clan or village in order to consecrate their new abode. At the same time they may buy supplies to outfit the kitchen, arguably the main room of the household, at a Kappabashi store.

Others visit butsudan row around the time of a death in the family but may also go to a shop in Kappabashi to buy long-lasting plastic flowers for their altar since, in this fast-paced era, there may not be enough time to maintain the requisite vase on a daily basis. It appears, however, that the parties involved may not always fully recognize this fascinating cultural juxtaposition. For example, the Tokyo Kappabashi Dōgu Street Promotion Union has its own website (www.kappabashi.or.jp), which highlights Kitchen Town's proximity to the colorful pagoda at Sensōji rather than to Inarichō, which stands right before its eyes. I have also spoken to visitors to one of the two shopping rows in the area, who said they were not aware of the existence of the other set of stores, although there is at least one shop in the vicinity that sells both religious implements and food supplies.

Viewing the row of butsudan shops as part of a network of temples and graveyards not only near former execution grounds and current crematoria but also close to shrines, entertainment, museums, and the arts highlights the role of commemorating death and memorializing deceased ancestors not as a practice that is detached or separate from but one that is fully integrated with the continuing challenges, struggles, and aspirations of human existence. Shitamachi's emphasis on death, which takes place in a vibrant urban environment that also celebrates various life goals ranging from the finest in the literary and fine arts to street festivals featuring traditional comedy and theaters of eroticism bordering on the pornographic, functions as a vehicle to communicate and maintain connections on both the en and muen levels with the afterlife in a way that is key for the living.

Part of the cultural symbolism for this interaction of contradictory elements revolves around Inari, the magical shape-shifting fox, which is crucial to the sacred spaces of both Akasaka in the High City, where one seeks worldly benefits, and Inarichō (literally "Inari town") in the Low City as a road that transports participants to the otherworld, or the realms of the divine and the underworld. No doubt packs of foxes, which usually live just on the outskirts or borderline of human habitation, long lurked around their dens in forested areas in nearby Ueno Park. More significantly, as Karen Smyers points out, "Foxes not only live on the boundaries, they cross them. And by crossing, they challenge them. The cultural elaborations of the fox in Japan position it to mediate between the human and the animal and the human and the divine."[32] Thus, the fox came to be associated with both the life force of seeking prosperity and healing through the blessings of a mischievous but benevolent deity and the death force of either appeasing or exorcising ghosts and spirits intermediated by the same boundary-crossing god. When combined, both sets of associations make for rites that are useful and essential for enabling one to become fully human.

Inarichō Shops in Ritual Context

The practice of installing a butsudan in the home and observing prayers on a daily basis is one important part of the whole package of Buddhist funerary rites, which stands at the very heart of the controversy about Japanese religious motivation. I have referred to this matter as a kind of inverted Mark Twainesque disconnect in that nearly everybody performs rituals, and yet, although people generally acknowledge that they do this, practically nobody talks about why or wants to admit that they believe in their efficacy. Andrew Bernstein points out that a recent survey of Japanese adults shows that more than half of the respondents claimed not to believe in any religion at all, but nearly 90 percent said they performed regular grave visits, while more than three-quarters "offered incense and flowers to their ancestors at the family Buddhist altar (*butsudan*)."[33]

As John Nelson shows in evoking the film *The Funeral*, in many cases once a death occurs, which is often sudden and unexpected, "family members are compelled to undergo a crash course in the culture and costs of funerals, mortuary rituals, burial practices, and periodic commemorations that focus on the salvation of the deceased person's spirit."[34] There are many basic guidebooks on the market with titles like "What Is the Wake?" or "Funeral Practices of Our Ancestors." Much of the ignorance of or indifference to a family's religious affiliation no doubt is a postwar phenomenon, and the dying out of a remembrance of or adherence to tradition is in large part a result of the current forces of secularization.

Japanese Way of Death

Not only are Buddhist funerals nearly universal, whether or not their symbolism is well understood,[35] but they are also costly and time-consuming affairs. Over the course of history since the Meiji period—following an era of relatively unpretentious funeral ceremonies—the government has tried to regulate and prevent these rites from becoming excessively expensive and sumptuous by encouraging modesty rather than showiness, especially for the procession sometimes referred to by the traditional term, *nobe-okuri*, which means "sending off to the fields." Using this term may recall a simpler, agrarian era and imply something effortless and heartfelt, but the actual practice was generally carried out in an elaborate and ostentatious manner as a kind of spectacle during the Meiji period, although this trend more or less died out during the Taishō period, when nobe-okuri was replaced by the streamlined *kokubetsu-shiki* (farewell ceremony).[36]

Despite significant alterations in the way funerary practices are conducted, overall interest and involvement in, as well as expenses for, these rites remain quite high. Even now, amid severe post-economic bubble financial concerns and constraints, there is a "keeping up with—or outspending—the Tanakas" phenomenon that continues unabated, causing already elevated levels of spending to remain quite substantial.[37] Recent changes reflect a basic sense of the fluidity of Japanese religiosity, which allows for adjustments to traditional customs without necessarily sacrificing the popularity or costs related to carrying them out. The panel from the brochure of Sōjiji temple, one of the two main temples of the Sōtō sect located in the town of Tsurimi, near Yokohama, advertises burial plots in its prestigious and limited sacred grounds, which range (depending on size) from around $12,000 to four or five times that amount, by also touting the beauty of the "various colors of the four seasons" (Figure 4.4).

As with weddings in Japan, which are expensive ceremonies for which customs have changed considerably but still draw on ancient traditions, each item of the funeral ranges widely in price but altogether can cost more than $80,000. The main mortuary ritual elements, which also require significant donations given to the service-providing temple and its priest, include the following:

- ritual bathing of the corpse (*yukan*) for purification as a preliminary preparation for the burial, which is a crucial first step since the dead body is considered an impure and taboo entity
- the wake or nightlong vigil, which is attended by friends and relatives, presided over by a priest, and centered on a funeral arrangement with a portrait of the deceased and an inscribed wooden memorial tablet (*ihai*) featuring the family's ordination name

FIGURE 4.4 Sōjiji Temple Burial Ad

- the funeral itself (usually held the day after the wake), during which a priest chants esoteric Buddhist verses and bestows a posthumous ordination name (*kaimyō*, also known as *hōmyō* or *hōgo*) on the deceased, who is now considered a buddha (*hotoke*), for which a fee is charged to the bereaved in a ritual that has become increasingly controversial because of the taint of corruption and the discrimination of outcasts[38]

- the funeral procession, during which a hearse takes the body, followed by the attendants, to the crematorium (*kasōba*), which has traditionally been one of the most elaborate and expensive stages of the mortuary rites
- the cremation, which has long been the preferred burial option in Japan since Sakyamuni is said to have attained buddhahood (*jōbutsu*) this way and is still carried out by 98 percent of the population; this is accompanied by the family's bone-picking ceremony, in which chopsticks are used[39]
- the burial at the cemetery, which includes the land-use fee and price of a stone marker, which may resemble a traditional Buddhist stupa. The bereaved have several new options for disposing of the remains in response to limited space and the escalating cost of realty by, for example, scattering the ashes in the sea or the hills (*shizen sō*, or natural burial, which is increasingly popular in part because the Japanese appreciate communing with nature), placing them in a high-rise cubicle or on the roof of a skyscraper, or using a miniature coffin and grave.

The prices for each item of the funerary process can fluctuate considerably based on a variety of factors, but rough median estimates of current costs calculated in approximate dollar values are shown in Table 4.1:

In addition, there are costs for the hearse, coffin, and other items that can be costly, such as apparel, which must be uniformly black for men and women and worn just once. The total price of the funeral, which includes elements such as posthumous names and home altars with their accoutrements not common in most societies, is considerably higher than the cost of burial in the United States, maybe even by three or four times the amount. However, one factor that offsets the overall cost of the funeral is condolence gifts: "It is customary for people to make a monetary offering to those holding ceremonies, including funerals, to ease the financial burden of such events. The amount

Table 4.1 Funeral Costs

Funeral (bath, wake)	25,000¥
Temple donations	10,000¥
Kaimyō	10,000
Cremation	5,000
Burial plot	10,000
Ihai	10,000
Butsudan	10,000

paid often depends on how close the contributor was to the deceased and how old the person is. When a colleague dies, the amount can range from [$300] to [$2,000]. When parents and siblings die, family members may pay more."[40]

Following the burial, memorial services are to be conducted on the seventh and forty-ninth days subsequent to the time of death. After this, remembrances are held on a monthly, yearly, or longer cyclical basis, including regular family visits to the grave (*haka mairi*) during the annual holidays of *Obon*, *Ohigan*, and *Oshogatsu*, which venerate ancestors in spring, summer, fall and winter, in addition to other occasions referred to as *nenko hōji*. This term covers yearly memorials on the day of dying (*shōtsuki saga*) or on other auspicious days according to the almanac, as well as on a grand cycle spanning 3, 7, 13, 17, 23, 27, 33, 50, and 100 years after death; following this milestone, memorials are mainly observed every fifty years. Traditionally in Japan, the memorial for a death anniversary took priority over birth anniversary celebrations. Each of these occasions incurs additional expenses through providing gifts or travel funds for family members or donations to the clergy, as well as for the upkeep of the burial grounds and the butsudan with its implements.

Butsudan Shinkō

While much of the attention is on the immediate aftermath of the death, as well as remembrances held many years later, an essential part of funerary rites has the family of the departed purchasing the butsudan, which is a wooden cabinet with doors that enclose and protect a religious icon, typically a statue or a scroll, and that are opened to display the image during daily or cyclical memorial observances. In many ways, the butsudan (Figure 4.5) has a special place in the whole mortuary process because over time it becomes the primary focus of ancestral veneration rites, such that it is considered a cult, referred to as *butsudan shinkō*, practiced on a daily basis (*mainichi no shinkō*).[41]

According to Nelson, the altar is traditionally important in Japanese families with regard to the afterlife because it creates a sense of continuity with parents and grandparents, who are intimately involved in helping to guide one's behavior in the near future:

> Like the central server of a computer network connecting and channeling information from diverse sources, the authority of the family altar used to embody and encode the teachings of the Buddhist sect

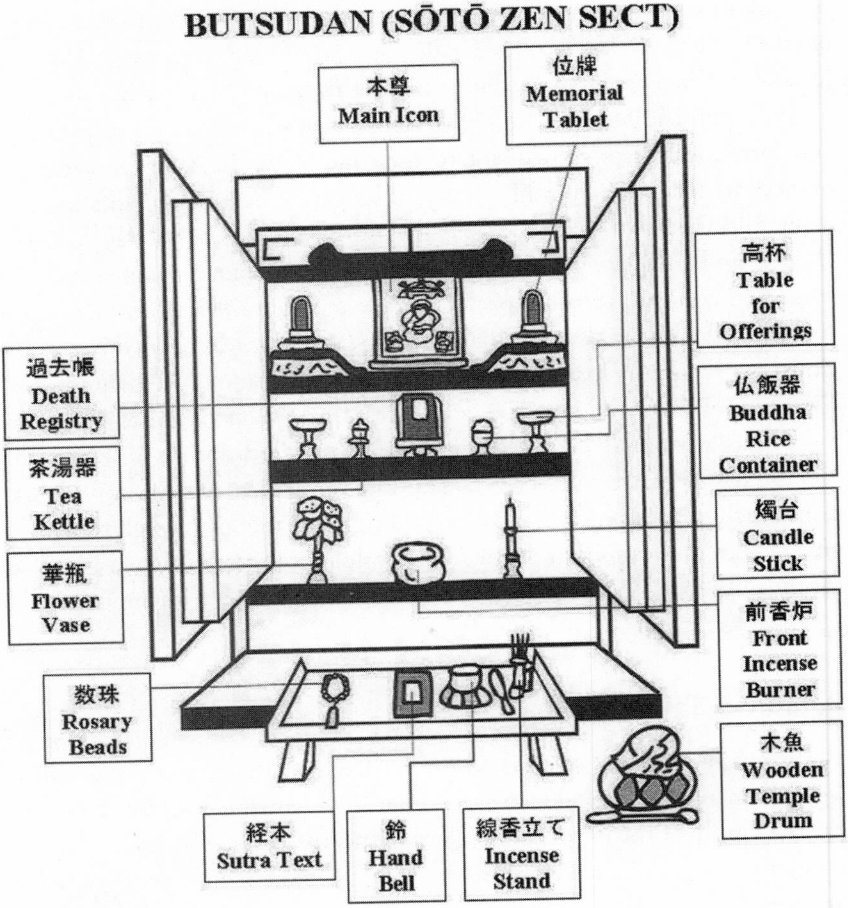

BUTSUDAN (SŌTŌ ZEN SECT)

本尊
Main Icon

位牌
Memorial Tablet

高杯
Table for Offerings

過去帳
Death Registry

仏飯器
Buddha Rice Container

茶湯器
Tea Kettle

燭台
Candle Stick

華瓶
Flower Vase

前香炉
Front Incense Burner

数珠
Rosary Beads

木魚
Wooden Temple Drum

経本
Sutra Text

鈴
Hand Bell

線香立て
Incense Stand

FIGURE 4.5

with which a family was affiliated. Altars were accessible to each family member, though usually only the head of the household would conduct prayers on Buddhist holidays (such as *Obon* and the equinoxes) and on death-day anniversaries (*meinichi*). His wife (or mother if living) attended to the altar on a day-to-day basis, making sure that offerings, incense, and candles conveyed the family's esteem into the spirit realm. Visitors would often first pay their respects before the altar prior to any casual conversation or business.[42]

Although Japan is considered secular, it is a culture where one has access to the inner sanctum and to the holy of holies every day right in one's own home.

On special occasions throughout the year, it is said that ancestral spirits return to their earthly home. Families light welcoming fires at the gates of their houses to guide the souls on their journey to their earthly abode, place lanterns indoors, clean their household altars, make various food offerings, and pray for the repose of the spirits.

Historical Background

A very brief historical overview of the evolution of butsudan shinkō indicates that over the centuries Japanese religiosity absorbed and merged elements of Buddhist memorializing stemming from Indian religious practices with East Asian ancestor rituals derived from ancient Chinese customs. This was probably initiated as long ago as the seventh century, around the time of the introduction of Buddhism from the mainland. As recorded in an oft-cited passage from the *Nihon Shoki* of 720, during a time of sociopolitical turmoil and natural disasters Emperor Tenmu was said to have proclaimed that "in every house a Buddhist shrine should be provided, and an image of Buddha with Buddhist scriptures placed there. Worship and offerings of food [were to be] made at these shrines."[43] It is likely that in the early centuries the altar was almost exclusively a ritual item for use by the elite classes of society.

During the medieval and early modern periods, the altars became more commonly used by individual families at various levels on the social ladder, who probably also held a *kamidana* in the home. As the centuries went by, it became common for evangelical Buddhist monks known as *hijiri*, who were often not affiliated with a particular sect, to help align the butsudan according to a family's or a clan's religious preferences and sensibilities, as well as the laws of geomancy. As Nelson describes the history, by the early twentieth century there was a gradual movement from housing the altar in an externally located structure (*jibutsudō*) to a room within the home (*butsuma*) devoted to Buddhist-style ritual and ancestral spirit veneration.

The construction of Buddhist altars is not uniform and varies depending on the sect, although the size generally is around 60 cm for the width of the bottom of the frame and 130–185 cm for the height. The butsudan are refilled on a daily basis along with other decorations, often with the guidance of an almanac's explanation of auspicious and inauspicious days. The main elements of the butsudan generally required by Buddhist denominations include a candleholder, flower vase, incense burner, and water or tea bowl. The centerpiece of the altar is a primary object of worship—either the main Buddha icon (*honzon*) of the sect or, for some denominations, a scroll (of the Nembutsu for Jōdoshin, the Daimoku for Nichiren, or the Mandala for Shingon)—that is usually placed in the center next to an image of the sect's founder, the ihai, and/or the register of the family's deaths. Most butsudan also have a wooden drum (mokugyo), rosary beads, bells made of bronze or wood, a copy of a sutra, gilt lotus flowers, and perhaps an image of one of the main bodhisattvas, Kannon or Amida.

Nelson explains that the primary aim of the arrangement of accessories is to create an ethereal, heavenly atmosphere: "Every single item on the altar—from its main and subordinate images, to its use of color and form to evoke the paradises of the Pure Land or Nirvana, to its array of candles, flowers, incense burners, and icons—is produced in countless workshops throughout the country."[44] In an ideal scenario, Buddhist icons and symbols are thought to mediate between heaven and earth. However, this understanding of the role of the butsudan may be jaded or diminished by secularization so that today many people value the design rather than the other-worldly spirituality of the altar, while looking upon religion not for a role in communicating with spirits but only as fulfilling a specific liturgical function that is valued primarily for social reasons. As an interesting mixing of secular with the sacred, the most recent trend is to treat and evaluate one's purchase of the butsudan as part of the home's décor rather than as a specifically ritual device.

About a third of the altars sold today are for first-time buyers, and the rest are replacements or upgrades. As with all funerary items, the price of a butsudan can vary widely from less than $1,000 for a simple product to $10,000 or much higher, even five or seven times that amount for custom models, to which is added the expense of some of the accessories that must be replenished over time. The cost of the altar is largely determined by the quality of its materials (whether traditional wood and fine finishings or engravings are used) and production values (whether it is handcrafted or of a customized design). The construction of more expensive altars uses precious and usually darker shades of wood, such as sandalwood, ebony, rosewood, and Chinese quince, with lacquered gold or silver and metal fittings, whereas ordinary products are made of mulberry and keyaki (a type of zelkova).[45] Beginning in the early twentieth century, less expensive tropical woods imported from countries in Asia such as Thailand and Indonesia became popular, and now these cheaper items outsell the traditional products by three or four to one. Superior memorial tablets are made of Japanese cypress (hinoki), and the finer drums are made by hollowing out a block of camphor wood (kusunoki), but in both cases, other less costly materials, such as nettle tree and Judas tree (katsura), can also be used. Today ceramic altar implements are sometimes used, and plastic has recently been introduced and adopted for making some of the parts.

In the 1970s, butsudan companies in Japan began commissioning parts or whole products first from Taiwan and eventually from China, South Korea, Thailand, and Vietnam. More recent trends include having work done in Brazil for sale to the Nikkeijin (Japanese-Brazilian) population or in Europe, including Italy and especially Denmark, in order to take advantage of the cosmopolitan feel of sleek Scandinavian design. As in the case of other trades that are unique to Japan, such as making tatami mats, bamboo blinds, and household fixtures, ancestral altars and ritual implements suffer from a shortage of qualified native craftspeople in part because it is no longer a lucrative or desirable profession. Japan must now rely on mass-produced imports, which account for one-third of the finished butsudan products available for sale, and this trend in turn discourages the children of altar makers from pursuing such a livelihood.

Traditional and Contemporary Butsudan Styles

Butsudan available in the shops of Inarichō, formerly a wholesale district, are not necessarily at the high end of the market, but this type of product can easily be purchased there, if desired, through the special ordering of a custom design. Many of the shops highlight this option in their advertising. At the same time, the shops of butsudan row are very much in the traditionalist camp in the sense of favoring more archaic styles that feature old-fashioned kinds of wood with gold lacquering. Yet, even here in the midst of the Edo mentality, which infuses much of the Low City, the winds of change have been blowing, caused largely by the nuclearization of the family and the graying of society, and stores in the area are struggling to keep up with the challenges demanded by shifting societal trends that tend to promote more au courant styles. These new types of butsudan (Figures 4.6 and 4.7) are for the most part made outside of Tokyo, yet are commonly being sold in locations in and around the city, although those stores are usually situated in more fashionable neighborhoods outside the boundaries of Shitamachi.

Altars can be bought in stores all over the country. There are nearly a thousand shops in all of Japan, and it is said that many of the best altar products are made in Takaoka in Toyama Prefecture on the Japan Sea coast or in Nagoya in Aichi Prefecture in central Japan, but Inarichō is still the only place where so many establishments are concentrated in one locale. However, this in no way

FIGURE 4.6 AND 4.7
Examples of Traditional and
Contemporary Altars; the
Contemporary Butsudan
Photo is Courtesy of John
K. Nelson

guarantees that butsudan row has a monopoly on the market in Tokyo, which is still growing, at least for now, or can rest on its laurels because the forces of secularization and the pressures of greater competition ensure that the customs of purchasing and outfitting altars are transitioning from the old-fashioned, traditional way (*dentō butsudan*) to a contemporary fashion (*gendai butsudan*).

These societal changes, which greatly affect the ways that both local and nationwide funerary practices are conducted, including the size, style, price, placement, and function of the butsudan, are occurring both inside and outside the individual home where the altar is installed and maintained. The main causes of transition involve shifts in demographics, space, finances, and lifestyle. First, the effects of population decline in Japan, which have become quite dramatic in recent decades and may be leading inevitably to a severe crisis in the workforce, create important challenges regarding funerary rites involving the numbers as well as the roles played by the deceased, the bereaved, and the priest. A diminishing birthrate accompanied by an aging populace means that the number of people dying is going up for the time being, but the family members who care for the departed by tending to altars and graves is going down in number and becoming less interested in or likely have less time to uphold the customs of the past, while the clergy continues to be depleted or to remain remote and detached from the lives of their congregants.

Second, changes in the perception and actual use of physical space affect both burials and the role of butsudan. As Shifra Horn notes in *Shalom Japan*, her account of an Israeli diplomat's family life in Japan, "the spiraling price of land in Japan has turned the issue of burial into a luxury. A decent burial, close to a religious temple, might cost as much as twenty to forty thousand dollars... These issues have fired the imagination of Japanese, who are always trying to come up with new and original ideas for giving their dead a decent burial. A temple in the port city of Kobe turned its roof into a burial site, with each well-aired and sunny tomb going for a price of $4000."[46] Inside the home, where the amount of available space is also shrinking in overcrowded cities, the size of the altar tends to be smaller or, since there is not an additional separate room to keep it where the geomantic proportions and directions can be carefully laid out, the altar is often picked primarily for the way it fits in with the surrounding furniture in the main living area of the house or apartment. Many of the butsudan row websites make a point of alerting consumers that "because housing has changed in recent years," adjustments have been made in the way the manufacture and sale of altars is being handled.

The newer senses of interior space are invariably linked to economic recessionary concerns, which are also related to postmodern lifestyle considerations, which means that people want to spend less money and be sure that they are making a pragmatic decision in the purchase of a butsudan rather than reacting on the basis of inherited ideas. At the same time they think about keeping the cost down, as opposed to the ostentatious quality shown by past generations, predilections for decorating the home are being significantly affected these days by questions of taste, as well as the matters of time and convenience for maintenance in addition to regard for any impact on the environment.

To sum up the rapid changes that have manifested since WWII but especially in the postbubble decades, traditional funerals referred to in *The Price of Death* by Hikaru Suzuki as *sōshiki* have focused on ritual purification of a contaminated corpse in order to enable the soul to attain buddhahood in the afterlife rather than to become a malevolent spirit, and these ceremonies have been performed by priests for families assigned to their danka.[47] New types of funerals, or *sōgi*, freed from superstitious (*meishinteki*) beliefs about ritual purity, are largely commercially driven enterprises that provide professional goods and services by a host of businesspeople, which can include clergy who have had to retool their approach by focusing on the needs of the living according to the demands of the marketplace.

However, in contrast to Suzuki and some other scholars who highlight the distinction between traditional funerals based on ritual and contemporary ones based on convenience, I emphasize that the differences may exist more on the surface than beneath it. Traditional services were not just mechanical functions wholly lacking in emotional depth, and newer styles by no means guarantee the integrity of individualism that is implied by the suggestion that they are nonsuperstitious. Furthermore, premodern elements persist and in many ways are fulfilled in the sōgi approach, which is usually not selected due to some kind of rejection of the spirit of the sōshiki approach. In any case, it is clear that the major new trend resulting from the factors of societal change that is found around the country has been the increased sales and popularity of contemporary butsudan. Some altar retailers go even further than modifying the traditional design by making the butsudan part of an innovative modular or integrated décor or by devising new products such as quality urns for disposing of the ashes without a conventional burial.

As John Nelson shows, the Yagiken Company, based in Osaka but with numerous branch stores throughout Japan, including greater metropolitan Tokyo, is one of the main corporations marketing the newer designs that have caused some of the Inarichō shops to initiate their own gendai butsudan campaign since 2008 as a kind of retaliation. However, during repeated visits to butsudan row over a period of several years, I did not find examples of products that tried to resemble the kind of innovation seen in Figures 4.6 and 4.7.

One of the most interesting developments is that the Yagiken Company not only creates a variety of newer designs with different kinds of wood but also aggressively promotes a distinctive rationale that has made important inroads in altering the whole concept of what a butsudan is and does. The altar is no longer a ghost of the past (pun intended) but a "living" (*ribingu*) device that relates to the individual's needs instead of the requirements of a Buddhist sect. The approach has two main components, one of which is to break with tradition by claiming a universal standpoint that is not necessarily even linked to Buddhism. "In fact," Nelson notes, "as I was told by a 'sales consultant' at the Yagiken showroom in Kobe, the word *butsudan* is rarely used. The altar is a special place where, regardless of religious affiliation, a conversation could be held with a departed loved one (*ohanashi dekiru basho*) or where you could put your hands together (*te o awaseru basho*) in a gesture that may be interpreted as either prayer or respect."[48] The other component is to reconceptualize the significance of repentance (*kuyō*) or contrition regarding one's feelings about the deceased in an upbeat, more sublime, and less moralistic way instead of fearing the reprisal of spirits, so that the altar takes on "the role of a place where you can meet loved ones who have passed away (*shinda hitotachi ni aeru basho*)."[49]

The Yagiken Company was so successful in its native land, often by using non-Japanese looking models in their ads and demos, that it has tried to gain a foothold with an international marketing campaign by opening a branch in the heart of Manhattan, which was unsuccessful and closed after a short period.[50]

Apparently, the idea of communing with the souls of the deceased runs counter to Judeo-Christian religiosity (a *New York Magazine* piece referred to this as "ancestor-worship chic"),[51] and the company had insufficient numbers of Asian and Asian American buyers at that location. Unlike other examples of Japanese pop culture successfully imported to the United States, much of which depends for its marketability on a non-Western worldview, this example of a global strategy was not viable. On the other hand, as shown in Map 4.4, the company's sales plan for opening new branches in Tokyo has taken off. The majority of stores are located in the newer western suburbs, where the Tamagawa Cemetery is located, by far the largest burial ground in the Tokyo metropolitan area. Whether intended or not, the Yagiken branch shops stand apart from any direct intrusion into the vicinity of Inarichō.

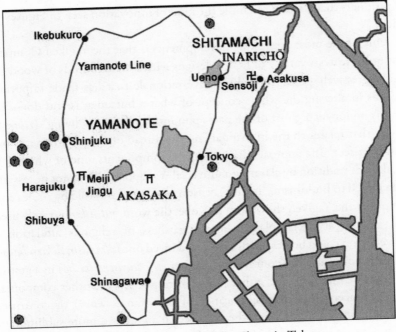

Yagiken Company Butsudan Shops in Tokyo

MAP 4.4

All-Purpose Discounted Funerary Plan

Another trend in response to recent societal changes, to which the Yagiken Company belongs, is for the various components of the industry, including temples, funeral parlors, crematoria, and purveyors of butsudan, to join forces and combine with secular interests in a networking web rather than to rely on a fragmented and sometimes overlapping or conflicting marketing approach or to continue to dig in their heels to preserve an ever-fading tradition. In one example, new technology is used for funerals. For instance, the Mitsui Company is teaming up with the largest Buddhist undertaking firm to develop live broadcasts of funerals for family members too busy to attend in person.[52] An additional tactic is to provide deep discounts for consumers: One company offers a significantly marked down, all-in-one service whose cost is cut from an already cheap price of less than $2,000 to half of that. The ad for this (Figure 4.8) does not include the butsudan, but a buyer of such a plan may also be likely to invest in an inexpensive altar selected primarily for pragmatic, as well as aesthetic, reasons such as furniture, rather than for emotional or spiritual goals.[53]

In reaction to the newer trends, Inarichō shops generally emphasize their long-standing tradition of skilled artisanship, often going back many

納棺

Placing in the casket

納 Placing in the casket:
Cost for placing the body in the casket using protective materials. **15,750**

Dry Ice: 15kg/1Day **8,355**

Consumables:
Waterproof sheets, disinfectants, etc. **5,250**

Transfer: **18,260**
From the place of death to the crematorium by hearse

Casket: 180cm **51,500**

Personnel expenses:

One person on day 1
transportation of the deceased, handling of the deceased, arrangements, crematorium reservation.

One person on day 2
guidance at the crematorium, payment processing.

火葬 Cremation

24,300
Cremation fee

Hearse

Free
Waiting room:
Place for waiting during the cremation

Cremation certificate: **400**

Urn **6,000**
approx. 21cm paulownia wood box including cover

1,440
Storage charge:
Charge for storing the casket for 1 day.

52,000

Regular total price ~~¥183,255~~ Mizue funeral center (Crematorium)

Minimum Plan standard price ¥ 95,000-

FIGURE 4.8

generations to the Meiji era or even before that to the Edo period, as well as the personal touch their sales personnel and workers can offer through discussions about the family's particular concerns and their ability to create "original"—yet still basically traditional—designs that address those interests and anxieties during a time of turmoil. The shops may specialize in the use of exotic wood (*karaka*), the requisites of a sect, or accessories such as drums, bells, or beads. Alternatively, the larger stores can offer a one-stop shopping experience along with delivery and maintenance services.

At the same time, nearly all of the Inarichō stores appear to be hedging their bets with a nod to the growing popularity of contemporary butsudan by stressing that they, too, can produce altars that are made of different kinds of imported materials and in a variety of styles. Some of the shopkeepers are also now willing to negotiate from a price list in order to avoid the appearance of stacking the sales deck. They may also collaborate with others in the funeral industry, from priests to gravediggers. It is also telling that even the traditionalist shops refer to options for "selection" of "original" types of "design" by citing these words in *katakana*, a Japanese syllabary, apparently as a tip of the hat to the effects of modernity and globalization.

Table 4.2 sums up some of the major differences involving functionality, production, and sales between traditional altars, valued for a sense of pride in artisanship that opens up a spiritual connection to the ancestor realm, and

Table 4.2

	Traditional	Contemporary
Ceremony	Sōshiki	Sōgi
Origins	seventh century	New era (*atarashii jidai*)
Spirituality	Haunting of spirits	Kuyō (contrition of bereaved)
Target	Deceased	Ribingu (living)
Function	Memorial	Kaguchō (furniture)
Purpose	Duty, responsibility	Aesthetic décor
Institution	Sectarian	Universal
Work Ethic	Handicraft	Interior design
Source	Japanese forests	Foreign (SE Asian, Danish, etc.)
Materials	Dark, heavy	Light, sleek
Shopping	Specialty shop or depaato	Gallery or boutique
Marketing	Independent agents	Industry-wide network
Purchase	No bargaining	Price lists offered

contemporary altars, which highlight the newer way that death is being seen as closure to life, primarily relevant to those still alive.

Conclusions: What Price Benefits?

The final section of the chapter returns to the second main conundrum being considered in this book: What drives the Japanese to continue to find ways of accommodating and frequently enthusiastically sustaining, while continually adjusting and modifying, traditional funerary practices and other kinds of rituals that remain a deeply rooted (and costly) part of modern society? Also, is the motivation for death-oriented religious practices at sacred sites in Tokyo neighborhoods based on some of the same principles that inspire participation in life-oriented rites? If so, how does this contribute to an understanding of the first conundrum (discussed in chapter 3) on the relation between Buddhism and Shinto?

This-Worldly versus Other-Worldly Benefits

As previously mentioned, in *Practically Religious* Ian Reader and George Tanabe stand out as the strongest and most eloquent advocates of a commonly held view that religions in Japan service both life and death rituals based consistently on the pursuit of practical this-worldly benefits. According to these authors, "the pursuit of benefits unites all,"[54] whether rich or poor, and this covers every sector of urban and rural society regardless of any other class divisions. Furthermore, they argue, "genze riyaku is not just a vital element that survives...transitions but a core organizing principle around which temples function and develop. It is also a principle that can provide doctrinal focus and definitions of faith."[55] While there is much of merit in these assertions, in evaluating the Reader/Tanabe approach, two aspects need to be provisionally separated: first, whether benefits are predominantly this-worldly or other-worldly; and second, whether they are pursued for practical purposes or for other reasons.

My response to the first question is "yes," in that benefits gained from funerary rites have a this-worldly impact since one's relation with departed souls—although this would appear to be other-worldly—is not based on how much their status is affected in the afterlife but on the impact that ancestors exert on the lives and well-being, or lack thereof, of the living. As John Nelson explains regarding the purpose of butsudan shinkō practices, "If all goes well and the many variables of veneration are balanced appropriately, a family's ancestral spirits become allies in every endeavor undertaken by members of the household. Alternately, if neglected, ignored, or disrespected, spirits are believed to cause illness, barrenness, inclement weather, impotence, business or agricultural disasters, and untimely death (to name only a few possible afflictions)."[56] Using the term *worldly* is not intended to suggest a disbelief in superstition on the part of ritual participants. Ironically, Reader and Tanabe, who emphasize the pragmatism of practices, presume the viability, if not necessarily the validity, of supernatural beliefs among modern Japanese ritual participants. Certainly, ample evidence of the pervasive practice of divination, geomancy, exorcism, and other kinds of rites supports the idea that Japanese today remain committed to a premodern mythical worldview, which accepts the presence of spiritual forces functioning in the midst of a hi-tech society that otherwise embraces modernity.[57]

Regarding the issue of whether religious motivation is based primarily on practicality, despite citing the Nelson quote earlier, which seems to support this view by emphasizing the role of spirits in attaining health and wealth, my reaction to this question is "no" because rites for the supplication of or communion with spirits, including those of ancestors, are not performed strictly for pragmatic and materialistic reasons. Many Japanese respond to questions about the need to venerate ancestors by indicating that they would otherwise fear the repercussions, revenge, or retribution that the spirits would wreak if they failed to follow through with their petitions and ceremonies. This is also what motivates a carpenter to say a prayer to beseech the forest for forgiveness for the tree that was chopped down to provide wood for his craft or a mother to offer repentance at a Jizō temple for an aborted fetus in mizuko kuyō rites.

These practices are driven by many additional factors, including appropriating cultural and national legacies, endorsing various aspects of naturalism and spiritualism, and seeking pathways of nostalgia and escapism. It is important to recognize that, in Japan, the affirmation of life and well-being through ritual and its effects is not necessarily accompanied by a romantic negation or denial of death and vice versa, that is, the affirmation of death and the afterlife by means of ceremonies is not accompanied by the ascetic denial of life. Rather, a seamless web of interactions encompasses the practicality and impracticality of the continuum of living and dying.

Is There a Problematic Side of Practical Benefits?

Nevertheless, ritual participants have been referred to by numerous scholars in the field as religious "clients," "customers," or "consumers," whose "in order to attain benefits" motives increasingly take precedence over their "because of social obligations" sets of intentions.[58] Priests provide exorcism and purification rites for new houses and cars, while sumo wrestlers and restaurants use salt to get rid of ghosts, and all Japanese spend a great deal of money for food and gifts in beseeching the departed for aid. Practical gains are offered at various sacred sites for everything from warts and the ailments of those who have a disability or are elderly to exam taking and traveling. The ritual participants' focus on materiality is evident in their goals and aims, as well as their use of objects, such as amulets, talismans, charms, and icons, including holy water, incense, votive banners, ofuda, ema, hamaya, omamori, omikuji, and other forms of engimono.

Reinforcing the importance of practical benefits, H. Neill McFarland suggests the following in his discussion of Daruma, a Zen Buddhist icon that symbolizes the commitment to meditation by the sect's founding figure but is also used as a good luck charm for attaining success in business ventures:

> Despite the sophistication of modern Japan, the country's shrines and temples and sidewalk fortune-tellers constitute an enormous and profitable industry, supplying a great variety of amulets, charms, and oracles to millions of people unwilling to entrust their success to their own skills and mere chance...the use of Daruma Figures has been extended to an almost unlimited range of concerns, including most commonly marriage, easy childbirth, recovery from illness, passing a

school entrance examination, employment in a good company, safety in driving, safety in factory work, prosperity in business, and election to a political office.[59]

Furthermore, people follow customs for seeking practical benefits—whether from Daruma, Inari, or some other symbol or icon—at every stage of existence, from taking college entrance exams to finding a spouse, buying a new car, having a healthy baby, and preparing for one's own or for accepting a family member's death. In that sense, death-oriented rites, including prayers at temples known as *pokkuri-dera*, at which ritual participants seek a quick and painless demise for themselves, seem very practical.

One of the main concerns I have with the Reader/Tanabe approach, however, is that the authors acknowledge, yet dismiss, the implication that their emphasis on participation in religious rituals, which is based exclusively on the practicality and materiality of genze riyaku, indicates a degenerate quality in Japanese religiosity, as if the practices were deficient or misguided. The title of their book as wordplay in English suggests a lack of genuine spirituality as the driving force and excludes other elements. However, the authors argue that, although Japanese practices appear to constitute only a " 'casual religion' of popular shrine and temple visiting…it should be taken seriously" and is "not invalid" or to be "disregarded as a frivolous sideshow…rather than a reflection of serious religious values."[60]

A number of other prominent examples of research tend to reinforce the "decline, or corruption, thesis" (*daraku shugi*) regarding practical benefits. For example, in a famous and very influential book first published in 1963, Tamamura Taijō has remarked on widespread skepticism and disillusionment regarding the commercialization of mortuary practices, which often are cynically expressed as "funeral Buddhism" (*sōshiki bukkyō*).[61] From a parallel angle concerning life-oriented rites, Winston Davis apparently agrees with this in pointing out "the expansion of professional priesthoods which has tended to encourage the commercialism of festivals and has made possible the sale of amulets and blessings in the shrine throughout the whole week."[62]

In an independent article that further supports the notion of decline, George Tanabe, citing previous writings by Edwin Reischauer, has commented, "The two legs on which Japanese Buddhism stands ritually and economically are funeral services and the practices of worldly benefits (*genze riyaku*), the one serving the dead, the other the living. Take away funerals, memorial rites, good luck charms, talismans, and prayers for good things, and Buddhism will topple over."[63] Tanabe also remarks about Buddhism, "But it thrives nonetheless. In providing services for gaining practical benefit, Buddhism shares a large market with only one other religion, Shinto. In the sector of funerals and memorial rites, it commands a more than 90 percent monopoly. With death rates projected to continue to rise for another twenty years or so, the immediate outlook is good."[64] In other words, the idea that funerary rites are performed for practical benefits means that the benefit goes to the boundless greed of the clergy.

Mark Rowe adds to this skepticism when he suggests that the "problem of funerals" (*sōshiki mondai*) actually has two levels. One is the problem that many observers, both native and foreign, have with the high cost of excessively sumptuous funerals, which has led to the creation of laws and policies that hinder or prohibit extreme spending and to attacks on priests for benefiting from these rites. The other aspect refers to the problem that Buddhist temples are currently facing in that they must reckon with constant social changes that undermine their long-standing means of bringing in revenue through funerary rites, which sustain their existence.[65] From this perspective, the notion that temples and priests have a "financial problem" with what for many people is the basis for there being a "social problem" with Buddhism in the first place goes to the heart of how pervasive the deficient nature of funerary customs can appear to be. However, Rowe's own work is neutral and cogent in describing the situation and very insightful in showing the flexibility of some forms of Buddhism that are in the midst of undergoing adaptations and adjustments to the current social environment.

In response to these types of analysis, I suggest that the labeling of all religious practices as genze riyaku, which intimates that this constitutes a serious social problem, may go beyond legitimate criticism and lead to a cynical view based on an Orientalist judgment. In an odd way, this could represent a throwback to early theories by D. C. Buchanan and others, which suggest that Inari and various forms of folk worship are not really real religions.[66] That outlook is also evoked in recent statements from less reliable sources that may not be contradicted strongly enough by the genze riyaku scholars, such as, "Shinto is a primitive faith: it imparts no ethical doctrine and possesses no holy scriptures. It is at the heart a system of animistic belief in natural spirits (*kami*)—the religious system of an ancient nation of rice farmers that has survived into the modern age."[67]

Multifunctionality of Japanese Religiosity

The main problem with an exclusive emphasis on practical benefits is that this is by no means the full extent of the story of what motivates religious practices. In this section I cite a couple of counterexamples of the wider impact of funerary customs in order to argue for a multifunctional view of Japanese religiosity based on the impractical this-worldly benefits of anshin rather than the practical this-worldly benefits of genze riyaku. For instance, in *Shalom, Japan*, Shifra Horn comments ironically on her experience of her husband's buying a used butsudan without knowing its meaning while stubbornly refusing to get rid of it as a sign of his disdain for superstition. She was immediately informed by her Japanese friends that several odd experiences in the house were poltergeist events and that she needed to procure the services of a priest to exorcise the *obaka*, a generic term that refers to all sorts of ghouls, negative energies, dark forces, and haunted creatures said to delight in frightening the life out of the living.

Horn's friends told her that she was supposed to give food offerings to the spirit of the butsudan and that that is why the obaka was upset and doing strange things in her house.[68] As she comments, "Almost every Japanese"—to whom she refers in another context as "the sophisticated, modern-day Japanese"—"I approached on the subject supplied me with their version of their experiences with the obaka. I got the impression that the entire island of Japan is alive with devils, ghosts, and spirits."[69] Regardless of whose perception was more valid in this case—Horn's, which defers to the native consciousness, or her husband's sense of a foreigner's distance and skepticism—the anecdote shows the powerful legacy of premodern beliefs in tatari that are wrought by giving more priority to ancestors than to striving for practical goals.

In a very different vein regarding the issue of whether death is seen as a matter of gaining practical benefits or realizing peace of mind, like many other commentators on Japanese society, Horn notes the impressive experience of sakura viewing in a Japanese cemetery. She discusses how the typical view in Japan, where people take death naturally and are very comfortable walking around casually in a graveyard to see the cherry blossoms while drinking beer and eating sushi—"What could be more natural to life than death itself?" she asks—"is nearly opposite to the West, with our conservative, unenlightened, and deep-rooted prejudices."[70] "It was soon apparent to me," Horn remarks, "that outings of this kind—life among the dead—were not only something perfectly acceptable but also most desirable... Our Japanese friends, who had noticed the terror which gripped me at the sight of the gravestones, tried to reassure me, explaining that by holding our festivities in the cemetery we were including the dead in the joy of the living, and that I should free myself of all my previous beliefs and Western conceptions regarding cemeteries."[71]

The role of anshin as a decidedly impractical aspect of funerary practices is revealed from yet another perspective in films like Akira Kurosawa's postwar *Ikiru* and the more recent Academy Award-winning *Departures* (*Okuribito*, literally "Undertakers"). In contrast to *The Funeral*'s sensational social criticism of mortuary rites, both of these films bring to light the very positive spiritual and emotional effects of traditional customs such as the wake, in that *Ikiru*'s deceased hero is celebrated and the memory of his cancer-facing achievements in helping society transforms the cynical lives of his beleaguered colleagues. It is noteworthy that Kurosawa was influenced by American films like the retrospective and penitential *It's a Wonderful Life* and in turn affected Ingmar Bergman's *Wild Strawberries*, which features a similar story of an older man in a lifeless existence coming to terms with and fulfilling his psychological needs while confronting the inevitable endgame of death. Also, the corpse-preparation activity depicted in *Departures* shows how death rites help to form intimate psychological bonds and a broad sense of reconciliation between the living and the dead, as well as the past and the present, even while the narrative highlights that old taboos about dealing with deceased bodies—as opposed to their spirits—can cause a practitioner to be castigated by his family and friends.

These and related examples show that funerary rites are impractical in contributing to a close web of crossover relationships, as highlighted by Ama Toshimaro's remarks about Japanese religiosity:

> It is also believed that people who die do not go far away, but watch over their blood relatives from the grave and return to this world on New Year's Day and during the summer obon (ancestors) Festival period. To believe that the dead become ancestors after death, and interact with descendants through annual events, means that people are able to live without fearing what awaits them after death.... The idea of comforting the ancestral grave still continues; many Japanese people visit the ancestral grave during the spring and autumn equinox, and it has been said that this reverence of the grave practiced by Japanese people is quite rare around the world.[72]

Therefore, while everyday behavior may indeed embrace some of the intentions ascribed to the goal of accruing practical benefits through acquiring efficacious amulets and talismans, the Japanese visit shrines regularly and actively participate in funerary rites for a number of additional motives. An analysis of funeral practices reveals that there is a wide variety of factors at play that are not materialistic. These include obligatory factors, such as mitigating fear of retribution from tormented ancestors and fulfilling a sense of duty and obligation to the family and danka on the part of congregants who visit graves at temples that may have been run for generations by a priestly family. Priests seek to perpetuate tradition but also depend on income from rites, as well as benefits from certain tax breaks for religious institutions. Also included are more intangible factors like seeking a calm oasis and sanctuary amid the *sturm und drang* of daily stressful existence, conjuring the rewards of nostalgia and historical memory by preserving or clinging to the past of an all-too-rapidly changing cultural legacy, or exercising one's feelings of contrition and repentance in order to gain redemption by communing with the spirits. Additional impractical motives include seeking a contemporary venue for affirming premodern supernatural beliefs, appreciating the value of inheriting family legacies that pass on traditional skills and crafts related to ritual practices, and establishing cooperation with the larger community of the block or neighborhood.

Finally, an examination of the conundrum of religious motivation may at first seem to reinforce the view of the specialization of traditional institutions in that, for example, "Funerary rites in contemporary Japan are overwhelmingly Buddhist, and the performance of these ceremonies is the primary function of temples and their priests."[73] This is reinforced by the traditional saying, "For sickness, pray to Kōbō [Daishi, a Buddhist saint]; For desires, pray to Inari (Byo Kōbō, yoku Inari)."[74] However, a closer look at Tokyo sites and rites reinforces the conclusions expressed in chapter 3 to the effect that "it is impossible to divide religions like this precisely as there are deep connections between them. For example, the Buddhist funeral...could be described as merely putting religious Buddhist clothing onto a particular folk belief."[75]

From what has been seen, the funerary process in many respects is Buddhist in name only, just as life-oriented rites are Shinto in name only. In fact, rituals for both existence and nonexistence are part and parcel of Japanese folk religiosity, which generates endless examples of assimilation, amalgamation, and various and sundry combinatory or syncretistic movements that embrace the unity of living and dying. These practices are found—but not much talked about—in the multitude of shrines and temples, large and small, scattered throughout the High City and the Low City neighborhoods of modern Tokyo.

NOTES

1. Interestingly, the website got a significant facelift in March 2010 but still has no English version even though so many of the sites mentioned in this book, including butsudan shops located in other areas of Japan, do have this feature.

2. Ian Reader and George J. Tanabe Jr., *Practically Religious: Worldly Benefits and the Common Religion of Japan* (Honolulu: University of Hawaii Press, 1998).

3. Ian Reader, *Religion in Contemporary Japan* (Honolulu: University of Hawaii Press, 1991), p. 27.

4. Taitō Ward does not feature this as one of its four main tourist sites, which include Ueno, Yanaka, Asakusa, and Asakusabasi (the site of the old Asakusa-mitsuke gate built by the shogunate); see http://www.taitocity.com/kanko.

5. Paul Waley, *Tokyo: City of Stories* (New York: Weatherhill, 1991), p. 15.

6. Edward Seidensticker, *Low City, High City* (Rutland, Vt.: Tuttle, 1984), pp. 207–208. Furthermore, he says of Ueno Park and the Kan'eiji temple area, "In 1873, Ueno became one of the first five Tokyo parks and the largest of the original five. The others were the grounds of Asakusa Kannon, the Tokugawa cemetery at Shiba, some shrine grounds east of the river, and a hill in the northern suburbs long famous for cherry blossoms" (p. 116).

7. Paul Waley, *Tokyo Now & Then: An Explorer's Guide* (New York: Weatherhill, 1984), p. 146.

8. The term *Edokko*, which means "child of Edo," implying someone who demonstrates Shitamachi culture, first appeared in print in 1771. The Edokko was said to have been born in Shiba, outside the city, but raised in Kanda, or "Shiba de umarete, Kanda de sodate"; see Waley, *Tokyo: City of Stories*, p. 66. It is also often said that, in the folklore of the city Kanda came to stand for Shitamachi, almost as Shitamachi stood for the city itself.

9. Tora-san is honored by a statue near the statue, which is a perennial photo op for visitors to the temple. Interestingly, the temple abbot is a textual scholar of Mahayana sutras, including the *Lotus Sutra*, which is chanted daily in the main hall.

10. See the classic study by Amino Yoshihiko, *Muen kugai raku: Nihon chūsei no jiyū to heiwa*, 2nd ed. (Tokyo: Heibonsha, 1987).

11. Jean Pearce, *More Foot-Loose in Tokyo: The Curious Traveler's Guide to Shitamachi and Narita* (New York: Weatherhill, 1984), p. 82.

12. Waley, *Tokyo: City of Stories*, p. 127.

13. Ibid., p. 153.

14. An interesting wordplay involves Kotsukappara, in which *kotsu* means "slope," and Kotsu Avenue, in which the homophone means "bones."

15. Edward Fowler, *San'ya Blues: Laboring Life in Contemporary Tokyo* (Ithaca, N.Y.: Cornell University Press, 1996).

16. John H. Martin and Phyllis G. Martin, *Tokyo: A Cultural Guide to Japan's Capital City* (Rutland, Vt.: Tuttle, 1996), p. 176.

17. Pearce, *More Foot-Loose in Tokyo*, p. 46.

18. Waley, *Tokyo Now & Then*, p. 210; also, as cited by Stephen Mansfield, *Tokyo: A Cultural History* (New York: Oxford University Press, 2009), p. 217, from J. E. de Becker's 1899 study of the Yoshiwara, *The Nightless City*: "In this gloomy dismal

place lie the bones of the courtesan who only up to yesterday resembled a beautiful butterfly or lovely blossom when seen in all the glory of her gorgeous apparel, with her glossy black hair ornamented with gold and her snowy-white body clad in rich brocade robes now exchanged for the cerements of death."

19. Mark Schreiber, "A Ride on the Darker Side of Tokyo's History," *Japan Times* (Sept. 15, 2002); http://search.japantimes.co.jp/cgi-bin/fl20020915a3.html (accessed June 24, 2010).

20. Waley, *Tokyo: City of Stories*, p. 134. To cite the full passage:

Asakusa had something for everyone. And never more so than in the year 1920, when the novelist Tanizaki Jun'ichirō wrote of its "innumerable classes of visitor and types of entertainment, and its constant and peerless richness preserved even as it furiously changes in nature and in its ingredients, swelling and clashing in confusion and then fusing into harmony." Asakusa possessed a cornucopia of pleasure; it had "old theater, song theater, new theater, moving pictures, things Western, things Japanese, Douglas Fairbanks, Onoe Matsunosuke [Japan's first idol of the screen]; ball riding, equestrian acrobatics, Naniwa chanting, girlie theater music, merry-go-rounds, Hana Yashiki [a sort of garden-cum-zoo-cum-outdoor entertainment parlor]; the Twelve Stories tower; air-gun shooting; prostitution; Japanese food, Chinese food, Western food, Rairaiken [a Chinese restaurant], wonton, noodles, oysters, rice, horse meat, snapping turtles, and eels." (*Meiji Taishō zushi: Tōkyō* [An Illustrated History of Tokyo in the Meiji and Taishō Eras], 3 vols., ed. Ogi Shinzō and Maeda Ai [Tokyo: Chikuma Shobō, 1978], 2:40).21. Ibid., p. 21.

22. Pearce, *More Foot-Loose in Tokyo*, p. 56.

23. Ibid.; also noted, "Since then the goddess has maintained her enforced solitude in a box within boxes. She is a true goddess, unseen, existing on faith alone."

24. Ibid., p. 55.

25. While other religions in the world have many kinds of pilgrimages in which the intent is to make a spiritual journey as an ascetic to find oneself among divine forces in an individual quest, in Japan pilgrimage tends to be part of the meeting point of secular and sacred, whether on a grand scale, such as going through the 88 Buddhist temples of Shikoku, or a miniscale, such as visiting the Shichifukujin sites in a Tokyo neighborhood. Pilgrimage and leisurely travel have gone hand in hand in Japan throughout its history, and today's groups of people, often elderly, who venture together as "pilgrims" to various sacred spaces, seem much more like they are on a recreational tourist excursion to quaint or historical sites. In this sense, the secular neither overpowers nor succumbs to, nor is it disguised as, the sacred, but the realms seem to naturally blend together.

26. Pearce, *More Foot-Loose in Tokyo*, p. 54.

27. This was traditionally held on the eleventh month according to the lunar calendar, in which "rooster days" occur twelve days apart, so that the festival can take place three times in a single month; Japan uses the solar calendar to regularize

all traditional holidays that were originally based on the lunar calendar. One example is *Obon*, traditionally held on the full moon of the seventh month, but now it takes place on July 15 in many areas (or, in some cases, on August 15, even though this would be the eighth solar month, which is still a modernization because the midlunar month would not likely be the fifteenth day).

28. Waley, *Tokyo Now & Then*, p. 209.

29. Concerning the myths of how the name of the neighborhood was derived, one legend is that it was derived from the Kappa shrine mentioned later, and another refers to a man called Kappa Kawataro, who tried to stop flooding in the area, while yet another is that it is because vendors of *kappas* (raincoats, a word probably derived from a Portuguese variation on "gabardine") spread them out to dry on the bridge (hence, Kappabashi, or Kappa Bridge); see ibid., pp. 142–146.

30. See Theodore C. Bestor, *Tsukiji: The Fish Market at the Center of the World* (Berkeley: University of California Press, 2004).

31. Pearce, *More Foot-Loose in Tokyo*, pp. 95–96.

32. Karen A. Smyers, *The Fox and the Jewel: Shared and Private Meanings in Contemporary Japanese Inari Worship* (Honolulu: University of Hawaii Press, 1999), p. 189.

33. Andrew Bernstein, *Modern Passings: Death Rites, Politics, and Social Change in Imperial Japan* (Honolulu: University of Hawaii Press, 2006), p. 21. Mariko Namba Walter's research confirms this in "The Structure of Japanese Buddhist Funerals," in *Death and the Afterlife in Japanese Buddhism*, ed. Jacqueline Stone and Mariko Namba Walter (Honolulu: University of Hawaii Press, 2008), pp. 247–279; for example, "More than 65 percent of Japanese say they have no faith in a particular religion, and yet 94 percent of their funerals are conducted with Buddhist rites," p. 247.

34. John K. Nelson, "Household Altars in Contemporary Japan: Rectifying Buddhist 'Ancestor Worship' with Home Décor and Consumer Choice," *Journal of Religious Studies* 35(2) (2008), p. 308.

35. Ibid., p. 326. Also, George J. Tanabe Jr. notes, "In a national survey of its temples and members, the Sōtō Zen sect learned that most people do not want their priests to do anything other than perform funerals," in "The Orthodox Heresy of Buddhist Funerals," in *Death and the Afterlife in Japanese Buddhism*, ed. Stone and Walter, p. 326. For a historical perspective, Tamamura Fumio points out:

> In *Eihei Kōroku* 永平広録, the collected sayings of Zen Master Dōgen 道元 (1200–1253), the ratio between lectures on Zen meditation versus those on funerals is 99% (Zen meditation) to 1% (funerals). Dōgen focused on Zen meditation in the context of explicating monastic regulations. On the other hand, in *Entsū Shōdō zenji goroku* 円通松堂禅師語録, a collection of Zen Master Shōdō Kōsei's 松堂高盛 (1431–1505) sayings, the ratio between lecture topics focusing on Zen meditation to funeral is 8% (Zen meditation) to 92% (funerals). This text reveals a sharp increase in lectures on funerals and a significant decrease in those on Zen meditation. In short, by 1500, clerics in the Sōtō Zen school

found themselves performing funerals as a normal part of their daily ritual life, alongside the practice of Zen meditation." (in "The Development of the Temple-Parishioner System," *Japanese Journal of Religious Studies* 36[1] [2009]: 12–13).

36. Bernstein, *Modern Passings*, pp. 37–38. Bernstein also points out that funerals in North America, too, were sumptuous affairs, for which families threw huge feasts and those of high standing liberally distributed rings, scarves, and gloves to attendees. See also Kōkyō Murakami, who comments that during the Meiji era "(t)here was a saying that two funerals in two years would bankrupt a middle-income family," in "Changes in Japanese Urban Funeral Customs during the Twentieth Century," *Japanese Journal of Religious Studies* 27(3–4) (2000), pp. 340 and 346.

37. Bernstein, *Modern Passings*, p. 38.

38. On the controversies surrounding the issue of kaimyō, which can serve as a kind of indulgence granting salvation to those who lived a life lacking in moral rectitude and can also be used in a discriminatory way to stigmatize lower classes and out-casts, who cannot afford to buy a prestigious name, see Steven Heine, *Zen Skin, Zen Marrow: Will the Real Zen Buddhism Please Stand Up?* (New York: Oxford University Press, 2008), pp. 148–151.

39. Bernstein, *Modern Passings*, p. 29, notes the following:
    There is no scriptural injunction within the Buddhist canon requiring cremation. In fact, Buddhist texts commonly recognize four different ways to dispose of a corpse: earth burial (*dosō*), water burial (*suisō*), exposure in the wild (*fūsō*, literally, "wind burial"), cremation (*kasō*). Nevertheless, because it was believed that Shākyamuni Buddha had been cremated, aristocrats and then commoners came to regard the practice as particularly meritorious, a means to "becoming a Buddha" (*jōbutsu*). Just as the relics of Shākyamuni were enshrined, so too were the cremated remains of those aspiring toward buddhahood (or at least a Buddhist paradise). Some were transported long distances to locations considered particularly sacred, such as the temple complex on Mt. Kōya.

40. Hiroko Nakata, "Funeral: Japan's Funerals Deep-Rooted Mix of Ritual, Form," *Japan Times* (July 28, 2009); http://search.japantimes.co.jp/cgi-bin/nn20090728i1.html (accessed May 10, 2010). Also, in Japan the total revenue generated by funerals is currently around 1.5 trillion yen based on about one million deaths a year, but the number of deaths may double by the year 2040, with the revenue going up accordingly.

41. According to Nelson, "Household Altars in Contemporary Japan," p. 311, the *ihai* in Japan was a more permanent and meaningful item than the memorial tablet in Korea and China, where it was considered temporary and intermediary and in most cases was ceremonially burned after a couple of years.

42. Ibid., p. 312.

43. Ibid., p. 309. One of the earliest surviving shrine-altars is an exquisitely lacquered one dating from the seventh-century.

44. Ibid., p. 313.

45. http://www.ibpcosaka.or.jp/network/e_trade_japanesemarket/religion_goods/ buddhist_household97.html (accessed Apr. 12, 2010).
46. Shifra Horn, *Shalom, Japan* (New York: Kensington, 1996), p. 66.
47. Hikaru Suzuki, *The Price of Death: The Funeral Industry in Contemporary Japan* (Stanford, Calif.: Stanford University Press, 2000); and Murakami, "Changes in Japanese Urban Funeral Customs during the Twentieth Century."
48. Nelson, "Household Altars in Contemporary Japan," p. 320.
49. Ibid., p. 322.
50. http://www.yagiken.co.jp/shop/tokyo/index.html (accessed Mar. 25, 2010).
51. Corrie Pikul, "Ancestor-Worship Chic: Do Cramped New Yorkers Want the Spirits of Their Departed Forebears as Roommates?" *New York Magazine* (July 24, 2006).
52. Horn, *Shalom, Japan*, pp. 68–69; Horn comments that the reason that wakes are better attended than the actual funeral is that the nighttime schedule does not conflict with the workday.
53. http://www.crematory.jp/direct/english/direct_E.html (accessed Apr. 4, 2010).
54. Reader and Tanabe, *Practically Religious*, p. 25.
55. Ibid., p. 23.
56. Nelson, "Household Altars in Contemporary Japan," p. 312.
57. As one of countless examples that one could cite to demonstrate this point, the property of one of the main hotels in centrally located and very pricey Akasaka, the Hotel New Japan, located only minutes away from Sannō Hie Jinja and Toyokawa Inari and which housed numerous international celebrities before it burned down in 1981, was left vacant for many years despite obvious demands for the real estate, in large part because of a belief that it was contaminated by misguided geomancy. Another factor was a prolonged dispute over insurance claims.
58. Winston Davis, "Japanese Religious Affiliations: Motives and Obligations," *Sociological Analysis* 44(2) (1983): 138; and Winston Davis, *Japanese Religion and Society: Paradigms of Structure and Change* (Albany: State University of New York Press, 1992), p. 31.
59. H. Neill McFarland, *Daruma: The Founder of Zen in Japanese Art and Popular Culture* (New York: Kodansha International, 1987), pp. 62–63.
60. Reader and Tanabe, *Practically Religious*, p. 256; see also Fabio Rambelli, *Buddhist Materiality* (Stanford, Calif.: Stanford University Press, 2007).
61. Tamamura Taijō, *Sōshiki Bukkyō* (Tokyo: Daihōrinkaku, 1963); see also Mark R. Mullins, "The Place of Ancestors in Buddhism and Christianity," http://www. kosei-shuppan.co.jp/english/text/mag/2007/07_789_3.html (accessed May 12, 2010).
62. Davis, *Japanese Religion and Society*, p. 24.
63. Tanabe, "Orthodox Heresy of Buddhist Funerals," p. 325.
64. Ibid.

65. See Mark Rowe, "Sticker for Nails: The Ongoing Transformation of Roles, Rites, and Symbols in Japanese Funerals," *Japanese Journal of Religious Studies* 27(3–4) (2000): 353–378.

66. D. C. Buchanan, "Inari: Its Origins, Development, and Nature," *Transactions of the Asiatic Society of Japan*, 2nd ser., 12 (1935): i–191.

67. "Gotta Have Faith," in *Time Out Guide to Tokyo* (London: Time Out Guides, 2007), p. 80.

68. Horn, *Shalom Japan*, pp. 55–75.

69. Ibid., p. 58. She also comments that the bustudan went back to Israel with her and was given to a friend who was a Japanese-born Israeli. He renovated and filled it with Jewish talismans written in Japanese and other pieces of Judaica that had orig-inated in Japan. He promised to donate the butsudan, full of Jewish holy artifacts and a Japanese obaka, to the Diaspora Museum of Tel Aviv. At the time of writing, Horn was not sure whether the curators of the museum would agree to risk the obaka's mischief or whether the butsudan would find a permanent home there and serve the very respectable and responsible purpose of a Jewish-Japanese tabernacle.

70. Ibid., p. 64.

71. Ibid.

72. Toshimaro Ama, "Interview with Hisashi Kondo," *Japan Plus: Asia-Pacific Perspectives* 4(3) (2006): 36.

73. Bernstein, *Modern Passings*, p. 21.

74. Smyers, *Fox and the Jewel*, p. 22.

75. Ama, "Interview with Hisashi Kondo," p. 37.

JAPANESE GLOSSARY

Religious Sites with Locations (all in Tokyo City 東京都)

Asakusa Ōtori Jinja	浅草鷲神社	台東区千束 3–18–7
Ekōin	回向院	荒川区南千住 5–33–13
Enmeiji	延命寺	荒川区南千住 2–34–5
Entsūji	円通寺	荒川区南千住 1–59–11
Hikawa Jinja	氷川神社	港区赤坂 6–10–12
Iriya no Kishibōjin	入谷鬼子母神	台東区下谷 1–12–16
(aka Shingenji)	真源寺	
Jōkanji	浄閑寺	荒川区千住 2–1–12
Nogi Jinja	乃木神社	港区赤坂 8–11–27
Sannō Hie Jinja	山王日枝神社	千代田区永田町 2–10–5
Shitaya Jinja	下谷神社	台東区東上野 3–29–8
Sōgenji (or Kappadera)	曹源寺(かっぱ寺)	台東区松が谷 3–7–2
Tamahime Inari Jinja	玉姫神社	台東区清川 2–13–2
Toyokawa Inari	豊川稲荷	港区元赤坂 1–4–7
(aka Myōgonji)	妙厳寺	

Terms and Names

Akasaka	赤坂
Akasaka Fudōzon	赤坂不動尊
Akasaka Inari Jinja	赤坂稲荷神社
Akasake-mitsuke	赤坂見付
aku soku nehan	悪即涅槃
akubasho	悪場所
ame	雨
Amida	阿弥陀
anshin	安心
anshin dekita	安心できた

Aoyama-ichōme	青山一丁目
Aoyama Reien	青山霊園
Asakusa	浅草
Asakusa Kannon	浅草観音
Atago Jinja	愛宕神社
bakumatsu	幕末
Bashō	芭蕉
betsuin	別院
bon-odori	盆踊り
bunraku	文楽
burakumin	部落民
butsudan	仏壇
butsudan shinkō	仏壇信仰
Butsudō	仏道
Butsugu	仏具
butsuma	仏間
chinju	鎮守
Chōkokuji	長谷寺
chōme	丁目
Chōnai Iseya ni, inu no koso	町内伊勢屋に犬こそ
chōnin	町人
Daibutsu	大仏
Dai hannya kyō	大般若経
danka	檀家
danka seido	檀家制度
daraku shugi	堕落主義
dentō butsudan	傳統仏壇
deshi	弟子
dōgu	道具
dosō	土葬
Eiheiji	永平寺
Eikyūji	永久寺
ema	絵馬
en (relations)	縁
en (garden)	園
engi	縁起
engimono	縁起者
Enryakuji	延暦寺
ensō	円相
eta-hinin	穢多非人

feng shui	風水
fudai daimyō	譜代大名
Fudō Myōō	不動明王
Fujigaoka	富士が丘
Fukugawa	福川
furisode	振袖
furusato	ふるさと
fūsō	風葬
gaijin bochi	外人墓地
gemba	現場
gendai butsudan	現代仏壇
genze hi-riyaku	現世非利益
genze riyaku	現世利益
giri	義理
gofunai	御府内
goma	護摩
gongen	権現
gongen-zukuri	権現造
haibutsu kishaku	廃仏毀釈
haiden	拝殿
hakama	袴
hakamairi	墓参り
Hakusan Jinja	白山神社
hamaya	濱谷
hanko	はんこ
hatsumode	初詣
Hieizan	比叡山
Hie Jinja	日枝神社
Hie-no-kami	日枝の神
hijiri	聖
honden	本殿
honji-suijaku	本地垂迹
honne	本音
honzon	本尊
Hotei	布袋
Ikiru	生きる
ihai	位牌
Imado Jinja	今戸神社
Inari	稲荷
Inarichō	稲荷町

inari-zushi	稲荷寿司
Isshindō	一心堂
ittoki	一時
izakaya	居酒屋
jibutsudō	持仏堂
jichinsai	地鎮祭
jingu	神宮
jinja	神社
jōbutsu	成仏
jōkamachi	城下町
Jōmyōin	浄名院
junshi	殉死
kaguchō	家具調
kaimyō	戒名
Kameido Tenjin	亀戸天神社
kami	神
kamidana	神棚
Kaminarimon	雷門
kami no kuni	神の国
Kanda Myōjin	神田明
Kan'eiji	寛永寺
Kannon	観音
kanpei-taisha	官幣大社
Kappabashi	合羽橋
karaka	唐か
kasōba	花葬場
kimochi	気持ち
kimon	鬼門
kimono	着物
kitō jiin	祈祷寺院
kitsune-yomeiri	狐嫁入り
Kiyosumi	清澄
kōan	公案
kokka Shinto	国家神道
Kokoro	こころ
kokubetsu-shiki	告別式
Kokugaku	國學
Kokuritsu Gekijo	国立劇場
Kokusai Avenue	国際道理
komainu	狛犬

kotsu (bones)	骨
kotsu (slope)	塚
kōtsū anzen	交通安全
Kotsu Avenue	骨道理
Kotsukappara	小塚原
Kōyasan	高野山
Kubikiri Jizō	首切り地蔵
kumade	くまで
kuyō	供養
Kyū Furukawa Teien	旧古河庭園
mainichi no shinkō	毎日の信仰
mairi	参り
Maneki Neko	招き猫
matsuri	祭り
me	目
Meiji Jingu	明治神宮
meinichi	命日
meishi	名詞
meishinteki	迷信的
minami	南
Minami Senjū	南千住
minkan shinkō	民間信仰
Minowa	三ノ輪
minzoku	民族
minzoku Shintō	民俗神道
mitsuke	見付
miyamairi	宮参り
mizuko kuyō	水子供養
mokugyo	木魚
Mori Ōgai	森鷗外
muen	無縁
muenbotoke	無縁仏
Mumonkan	無門間
Myōgonji	妙厳寺
Nagekomidera	投込寺
naginata	なぎなた
namidabashi	泪橋
Naritasan	成田山
Natsume Sōseki	西田幾多郎
nembutsu	念仏

Nezu Jinja	根津神社
nigiyaka	にぎやか
Nihonbashi	日本橋
nihonjinron	日本人論
Nihon Shoki	日本書紀
nikujiki saitai	肉食妻帯
Ningyōchō	人形町
ninjō	人患
Nippori	日暮里
Nishi Arai Daishi	西荒い大師
nobe-okuri	野辺送り
Nogi Maresuke	乃木希典
Nogizaka	乃木坂
obaka	お馬鹿
obon	お盆
ofuda	お札
Ohaka ga nai!	お墓がない
oharai	お払い
ohigan	お彼岸
Ōji Inari Jinja	王子稲荷神社
oku	奥
Oku no hosomichi	奥の細道
Okuribito	おくりびと
omamori	お守り
omikoshi	御みこし
omikuji	御神籤
omiyage	おみやげ
omote	表
onmyōdō	陰陽道
Ōoka Tadasuke	大忠相
oshogatsu	お正月
Osōshiki	お葬式
Otafuku	お多福
Otoko wa tsurai yo	男はつらいよ
pokkuri-dera	ぽっくり寺
rakugo	落語
Rashōmon	羅生門
reiken	霊験
reikozaka	霊狐坂
renga	連歌

ribingu	リブング
Rikugien Garden	六義園
riyaku	利益
rōnin	浪人
Ryōbu Shinto	両部神道
sakoku	鎖国
sampuru	サンプル
sankin kōtai	参勤交代
Sannō Gongen	山王権現
Sannō Matsuri	山王祭
sanpo	散歩
San'ya	山谷
seken	世間
Sen to Chihiro no Kamikakushi	千と千尋の神隠し
Senjū	千住
sensei	先生
Sensōji	浅草寺
sentō	銭湯
senzo sūhai	先祖崇拝
seppuku	切腹
sezoku	世俗
shichidō garan	七堂伽藍
Shichifukujin	七福神
shichigosan	七五三
shinbutsu bunri	神仏分離
shinbutsu shugō	神仏習合
shinjū	心中
shinkō	信仰
Shinobazu	不忍池
shin shūkyō	新宗教
Shintō	神道
Shitamachi	下町
Shitaya	下谷神社
shizen sō	自然葬
shizuka na	静かな
Shōbōgenzō	正法眼蔵
shōtsuki saga	祥月佐賀
shugyō	修行
shūha	宗派

shūkyō	宗教
sōgi	葬儀
Soka Gakkai	創価学会
Sōtō Zen	曹鬼禅
sōshiki	葬式
sōshiki Bukkyō	葬式仏教
sōshiki mondai	葬式問題
suisō	水葬
Suitengu Jinja	水天狗神社
Taishakuten	帝釈天
Tanabata	七夕
ta no kami	田の紙
tatari	祟り
tatemae	建前
tengu	天狗
Tenka Matsuri	天下祭
Tennōji	天王寺
terauke seido	寺受け青銅
Tobi Fudōdera	飛び不動寺
Tōgō Heihachirō	東郷 平八郎
Tōgō Jinja	東郷神社
tokubetsu meishō	特別名勝
ton'ya-gai	問屋街
Toranomon	虎ノ門駅
torii	鳥居
Tori no Ichi	酉市
tozama daimyō	外様大名
tsukiyama	築山
Tzurezuregusa	つれずれ草
Ueno	上野
ukiyo-e	浮世絵
ura	裏
wabi-sabi	侘寂
waka	和歌
wakon yōsai	和魂洋才
Yagiken Company	八木研株式会社
yakuimon	薬医門
yamabushi	山伏
Yamanote	山手
Yanaka	谷中

Yanaka Reien	谷中霊園
Yasukuni Jinja	靖国神社
Yoshiwara	吉原
Yotsuya Sanchōme	四谷三丁目
yukan	湯灌
Yushima Seidō	湯島聖堂
Yushima Tenjin	湯島天神
zazen	座禅
zenshin	善神

BIBLIOGRAPHY

WORKS IN ENGLISH

Ama, Toshimaro. "Interview with Hisashi Kondo." *Japan Plus: Asia-Pacific Perspectives* 4(3) (2006): 35–39.

——. *Why Are the Japanese Non-Religious?: Japanese Spirituality: Being Non-Religious in a Religious Culture*. Lanham, MD.: University of America, 2005.

Ambros, Barbara. *Emplacing a Pilgrimage: The Ōyama Cult and Regional Religion in Early Modern Japan*. Cambridge, Mass.: Harvard University Asia Center, Harvard University Press, 2008.

Anderson, Benedict. *Imagined Communities: Reflections on the Origin and Spread of Nationalism*, 2nd ed. New York: Verso, 1991.

Antoni, Klaus, Hiroshi Kubota, Johann Nawrocki, and Michael Wachutka, eds. *Religion and National Identity in the Japanese Context*. Münster, Germany: LIT, 2002.

Ashihara, Yoshinobu. *The Hidden Order: Tokyo through the Twentieth Century*. Tokyo: Kodansha, 1989.

Bachnik, Jane M. "Orchestrated Reciprocity: Belief versus Practice in Japanese Funeral Ritual." In *Ceremony and Ritual in Japan: Religious Practices in Industrialized Society*, ed. Jan van Bremen and D. P. Martinez. New York: Routledge, 1995.

Bargen, Doris G. *Suicidal Honor: General Nogi and the Writings of Mori Ōgai and Natsume Sōseki*. Honolulu: University of Hawaii Press, 2006.

Barthes, Roland. *The Empire of Signs*. New York: Hill and Wang, 1983.

Bellah, Robert. *Tokugawa Religion: The Values of Pre-Industrial Japan*. Glencoe, Ill.: Free Press, 1957.

Bernstein, Andrew. *Modern Passings: Death Rites, Politics, and Social Change in Imperial Japan*. Honolulu: University of Hawaii Press, 2006.

Berry, Mary Elizabeth. "Public Life in Authoritarian Japan." *Daedalus* 127(3) (1998): 133–165.

Bestor, Theodore C. *Tsukiji: The Fish Market at the Center of the World*. Berkeley: University of California Press, 2004.

——. *Neighborhood Tokyo*. Tokyo: Kodansha International, 1989.

——, Patricia G. Steinhoff, and Victoria Lyon Bestor, eds. *Doing Fieldwork in Japan*. Honolulu: University of Hawaii Press, 2003.

Bocking, Brian. *A Popular Dictionary of Shinto*. Surrey, UK: Curzon, 1996.

Bodiford, William M. "Zen in the Art of Funerals: Ritual Salvation in Japanese Buddhism." *History of Religions* 32(2) (1992): 146–164.

Bolitho, Harold. *Bereavement and Consolation: Testimonies from Tokugawa Japan*. New Haven, Conn.: Yale University Press, 2003.

Booth, Alan. *Look for the Lost: Journeys through a Vanishing Japan*. New York: Kodansha America, 1995.

Borup, Jorn. *Japanese Rinzai Zen Buddhism: Myōshinji, a Living Religion*. Leiden: Brill, 2008.

Botsman, Daniel V. *Punishment and Power in the Making of Modern Japan*. Princeton, N.J.: Princeton University Press, 2005.

Brown, Peter. *The Cult of the Saints: Its Rise and Function in Latin Christianity*. Chicago: University of Chicago Press, 1982.

Brown, Phillip. *Central Authority and Local Autonomy in the Formation of Early Modern Japan*. Stanford: Stanford University Press, 1993.

Buchanan, D. C. "Inari: Its Origins, Development, and Nature." *Transactions of the Asiatic Society of Japan*, 2nd ser., 12 (1935): i–191.

Bureau of Religions. *Handbook of the Old Shrines and Temples and Their Treasures in Japan*. Tokyo: Bureau of Religions, Department of Education, 1920.

Buruma, Ian. *Inventing Japan: 1853–1964*. New York: Modern Library, 2003.

Campbell, Joseph. *The Power of Myth*. New York: Anchor, 1985.

Carver, Norman F. *Form and Space in Japanese Architecture*. Tokyo: Shokokusha, 1955.

Coaldrake, William H. *Architecture and Authority in Japan*. London: Routledge, 1996.

———. "Edo Architecture and Tokugawa Law." *Monumenta Nipponica* 36(3) (1981): 235–284.

Cooke, Gerald. "In Search of the Present State of Buddhism in Japan." *Journal of the American Academy of Religion* 42(1) (1974): 18–34.

———. "Traditional Buddhist Sects and Modernization in Japan." *Japanese Journal of Religious Studies* 1(4) (1975): 267–330.

Cotter, Holland. "Urban Uplift: Sanctuaries for the Spirit." *New York Times* (December 25, 2009).

Covell, Stephen G. *Japanese Temple Buddhism: Worldliness in a Religion of Renunciation*. Honolulu: University of Hawaii Press, 2005.

———. "The Temple/Juridical Person: Law and Religion in Japan." *Asian Cultural Studies* 26 (2000): 7–23.

Cybriwsky, Roman. "Shibuya Center, Tokyo." *Geographical Review* 78(1) (1988): 48–61.

———. *Tokyo: The Changing Profile of an Urban Giant*. Boston: Hall, 1991.

———. *Tokyo: The Shogun's City at the Twenty-First Century*. Chichester, UK: Wiley, 1998.

Dale, Peter N. *The Myth of Japanese Uniqueness*. New York: Routledge, 1986.

Davis, Winston. *Dōjō: Magic and Exorcism in Modern Japan.* Stanford: Stanford University Press, 1980.

———. *Japanese Religion and Society: Paradigms of Structure and Change.* Albany: State University of New York Press, 1992.

———. "Japanese Religious Affiliations: Motives and Obligations." *Sociological Analysis* 4(2) (1983): 131–146.

Dorai, Francis, ed. *Insight City Guide Tokyo.* Singapore: Apa, 2007.

Dore, R. P. *City Life in Japan: A Study of a Tokyo Ward.* Berkeley: University of California Press, 1958.

Dunn, Charles. *Everyday Life in Traditional Japan.* Tokyo: Tuttle, 1969.

——— *DK Eyewitness Travel Guides: Japan.* New York: DK Publishing, 2008.

Ebersole, Gary L. *Ritual Poetry and the Politics of Death in Early Japan.* Princeton, N.J.: Princeton University Press, 1989.

Egginton, June, and Nick O'Donnell. *New York Walks.* London: Petersen, 2006.

Enbutsu, Sumiko. *Tokyo: Exploring the City of the Shogun.* Tokyo: Kodansha International, 2007.

Engel, Heino. *Measure and Construction of the Japanese House.* Boston: Tuttle, 1985.

Figal, Gerald. *Civilization and Monsters: Spirits of Modernity in Meiji Japan.* Durham, N.C.: Duke University Press, 1999.

Fowler, Edward. *San'ya Blues: Laboring Life in Contemporary Tokyo.* Ithaca, N.Y.: Cornell University Press, 1996.

Fridell, Wilbur. *Japanese Shrine Mergers, 1906–1912.* Tokyo: Sophia University Press, 1973.

Wei-hsun Fu, Charles, and Steven Heine, eds. *Japan in Traditional and Postmodern Perspectives.* Albany: State University of New York Press, 1995.

Garon, Sheldon. "State and Religion in Imperial Japan, 1912–1945." *Journal of Japanese Studies* 12(2 (1985): 273–302.

Gilday, Edmund. "Bodies of Evidence: Imperial Funeral Rites and the Meiji Restoration." *Japanese Journal of Religious Studies* 27(3–4) (2000): 273–296.

Gill, Tom. *Men of Uncertainty: The Social Organization of Day Laborers in Contemporary Japan.* Albany: State University of New York Press, 2001.

———. "Whose Problems? Japan's Homeless People as an Issue of Local and Central Governance." In *Contested Governance in Japan: Sites and Issues,* ed. Glenn D. Hook. London: RoutledgeCurzon, 2005.

Gluck, Carol. *Japan's Modern Myths: Ideology in the Late Meiji Period.* Princeton, N.J.: Princeton University Press, 1985.

Gordon, Andrew. *A Modern History of Japan: From Tokugawa Times to the Present.* New York: Oxford University Press, 2003.

Graburn, Nelson H. H., John Ertl, and R. Kenji Tierney, eds. *Multiculturalism in the New Japan: Crossing the Boundaries Within.* New York: Berghahn, 2008.

Grapard, Allan G. *The Protocol of the Gods: A Study of the Kasuga Cult in Japanese History.* Berkeley: University of California Press, 1993.

Greenblatt, Stephen. *Will in the World: How Shakespeare Became Shakespeare*. New York: Norton, 2005.

Groemer, Gerald. "The Creation of the Edo Outcaste Order." *Journal of Japanese Studies* 27(2) (2001): 263–293.

Grossman, Cathy Lynn. "Survey: 72% of Millennials 'more spiritual than religious.'" *USA Today* (April 26, 2010).

Gunji, Masakatsu. "Kabuki and Its Social Background." In *Tokugawa Japan: The Social and Economic Antecedents of Modern Japan*, ed. Chie Nakane and Shinzaburō Ōishi. Berkeley: University of California Press, 1995, pp. 192–212.

Haley, John. *Authority without Power: Law and the Japanese Paradox*. New York: Oxford University Press, 1991.

Hall, Peter. *Cities of Tomorrow: An Intellectual History of Urban Planning and Design in the Twentieth Century*. Malden, Mass.: Wiley-Blackwell, 2002.

Hardacre, Helen. *Religion and Society in Nineteenth-Century Japan: A Study of the Southern Kantō Region, Using Late Edo and Early Meiji Gazetteers*. Ann Arbor: Center for Japanese Studies, University of Michigan, 2002.

——. *Shintō and the State: 1868–1988*. Princeton, N.J.: Princeton University Press, 1989.

Harootunian, H. D. *Things Seen and Unseen: Discourse and Ideology in Tokugawa Nativism*. Chicago: University of Chicago Press, 1988.

Hane, Mikiso. *Peasants, Rebels, and Outcastes: The Underside of Japan*. Lanham, MD.: Rowman and Littlefield, 2003.

Hanley, Susan B. *Everyday Things in Premodern Japan: The Hidden Legacy of Material Culture*. Berkeley: University of California Press, 1999.

Heine, Steven. "Abbreviation or Aberration: The Role of the *Shushōgi* in Modern Sōtō Zen Buddhism," in *Buddhism in the Modern World*, ed. Steven Heine and Charles S. Prebish. New York: Oxford University Press, 2003, pp. 169–192.

——. *Did Dōgen Go to China? What He Wrote and When He Wrote It*. New York: Oxford University Press, 2006.

——. *Shifting Shape, Shaping Text: Philosophy and Folklore in the Fox Kōan*. Honolulu: University of Hawaii Press, 1999.

——. *The Zen Poetry of Dōgen: Verses from the Mountain of Eternal Peace*. Mount Tremper, N.Y.: Dharma Communications, 2005.

——. *Zen Skin, Zen Marrow: Will the Real Zen Buddhism Please Stand Up?* New York: Oxford University Press, 2008.

Hitoshi, Miyake. *Shugendō: Essays on the Structure of Japanese Folk Religion*, ed. H. Byron Earhart. Ann Arbor: Center for Japanese Studies, University of Michigan, 2001.

Hobsbawm, Eric, and Terence Younger, eds. *The Invention of Tradition*. New York: Cambridge University Press, 1992.

Hori, Ichirō. *Folk Religion in Japan: Continuity and Change*, ed. Joseph M. Kitigawa and Alan L. Miller. Chicago: University of Chicago Press, 1994.

————, Ikado Fujio, Wakimoto Tsuneya, and Yanagawa Keiichi, eds. *Japanese Religion: A Survey by the Agency for Cultural Affairs*. Tokyo: Kodansha International, 1972.

Horn, Shifra. *Shalom, Japan*. New York: Kensington, 1996.

http://www.cnngo.com/tokyo/play/tokyo-map-terror-143802.

http://www.crematory.jp/direct/english/direct_E.html.

http://www.hiejinja.net/jinja/kouza/bunka/hiyosi/index.html.

http://www.ibpcosaka.or.jp/network/e_trade_japanesemarket/religion_goods/bud-dhist_household 97.html.

http://www.taitocity.com/kanko.

http://www.vg.no/nyheter/innenriks/artikkel.php?artid=10003532.

Hubbard, Jamie. "Premodern, Modern, and Postmodern: Doctrine and the Study of Japanese Religion." *Japanese Journal of Religious Studies* 19(1) (1992): 3–27.

Humphrey, Caroline, and Piers Vitebsky. *Sacred Architecture: Symbolic Form and Ornament Traditions of East and West Models of the Cosmos*. London: Baird, 2003.

Hur, Nam-lin. *Death and Social Order in Tokugawa Japan: Buddhism, Anti-Christianity, and the Danka System*. Cambridge, Mass.: Harvard University Asia Center, Harvard University Press, 2007.

————. *Prayer and Play in Late Tokugawa Japan: Asakusa Sensōji and Edo Society*. Cambridge, Mass.: Harvard University Asia Center, Harvard University Press, 2000.

———— *Ikiru*. Dir. Kurosawa Akira. 1952.

Ishii, Kenji. "The Secularization of Religion in the City." *Japanese Journal of Religious Studies* 13(2–3) (1986): 193–209.

Ivy, Marilyn. *Discourses of the Vanishing: Modernity Phantasm Japan*. Chicago: University of Chicago Press, 1995.

Jaffe, Richard Mark. *Neither Monk nor Layman: Clerical Marriage in Modern Japanese Buddhism*. Princeton, N.J.: Princeton University Press, 2001.

"Japanese Lifestyle." http://www.japaneselifestyle.com.au/tokyo/akasaka.htm.

Jeffery, Richard. "Aoyama Cemetery: Gaienmae." http://tokyoq.com/weekly_updates/tqoole/cemetery.html

Jinnai, Hidenobu. "The Spatial Structure of Edo." *Tokugawa Japan: The Social and Economic Antecedents of Modern Japan*, ed. Chie Nakane and Shinzaburō Ōishi. Berkeley: University of California Press, 1995, pp. 121–146.

————. *Tokyo: A Spatial Anthropology*. Trans. Kimiko Nishimura. Berkeley: University of California Press, 1995.

Joas, Hans, and Laus Wiegandt, eds. *Secularization and the World Religions*. Trans. Alex Skinner. Liverpool: Liverpool University Press, 2009.

Katō, Takahashi. "Governing Edo." In *Edo and Paris*, ed. James L. McClain, John M. Merriman, and Ugawa Kaoru. Ithaca, N.Y.: Cornell University Press, 1994, pp. 41–67.

Kawabata, Yasunari. *The Scarlet Gang of Asakusa*. Berkeley: University of California Press, 2005.

Kawano, Satsuki. *Ritual Practice in Modern Japan: Ordering Place, People, and Action*. Honolulu: University of Hawaii Press, 2005.

Kavanagh, Chris. "Household Altars in Contemporary Japan." *God Knows What: An Irreverent Look through the Worlds of Religion, Anthropology, and Skepticism*. http://godknowswhat.wordpress.com/2009/04/07/review-household-altars-in-contemporary-japan.

Kenny, Elizabeth. "Shinto Funerals in the Edo Period." *Japanese Journal of Religious Studies* 27(3–4) (2000): 239–271.

Kerr, Alex. *Lost Japan*. Melbourne: Lonely Planet, 1996.

Ketelaar, James Edward. *Of Heretics and Martyrs in Meiji Japan: Buddhism and Its Persecution*. Princeton, N.J.: Princeton University Press, 1990.

Kira, Moriko, and Mariko Terada, eds. *Japan towards Totalscape: Contemporary Japanese Architecture, Urban Design, and Landscape*. Rotterdam: Nai, 2001.

Koizumi, Kazuko. *Traditional Japanese Furniture*. Tokyo: Kodansha International, 1986.

LaFleur, William R. *Liquid Life: Abortion and Buddhism in Japan*. Princeton, N.J.: Princeton University Press, 1992.

Lay, Arthur Hyde. "Japanese Funeral Rites." *Transactions of the Asiatic Society of Japan* 19 (1891): 507–544.

Lifton, Robert Jay, Shūichi Katō, and Michael R. Reich. *Six Lives, Six Deaths: Portraits from Modern Japan*. New Haven, Conn.: Yale University Press, 1979.

Lippit, Seiji M. *Topographies of Japanese Modernism*. New York: Columbia University Press, 2002.

Maeda, Ai. *Text and the City: Essays on Japanese Modernity*. Durham, N.C.: Duke University Press, 2004.

Mann, Nicholas R. *The Sacred Geometry of Washington, D.C: The Integrity and Power of the Original Design*. New York: Barnes and Noble, 2006.

Mansfield, Stephen. *Tokyo: A Cultural History*. New York: Oxford University Press, 2009.

Markus, Andrew L. "The Carnival of Edo: Misemono Spectacles from Contemporary Accounts." *Harvard Journal of Asiatic Studies* 45(2) (1985): 499–541.

Martin, John H., and Phyllis G. Martin. *Tokyo: A Cultural Guide to Japan's Capital City*. Tokyo: Tuttle, 1996.

Mason, J. W. T. *The Meaning of Shinto*. Victoria, Canada: Trafford, 2006.

McCarthy, Terry. "Japan Bids Sayonara to Geisha Politics." *Independent* (November 28, 1993).

McClain, James L., John M. Merriman, and Ugawa Kaoru. *Edo and Paris: Urban Life and the State in the Early Modern Era*. Ithaca, N.Y.: Cornell University Press, 1994.

McFarland, H. Neill. *Daruma: The Founder of Zen in Japanese Art and Popular Culture*. New York: Konansha International, 1987.

Miller, Alan S. "Why Japanese Religions Look Different: The Social Role of Religious Organizations in Japan." *Review of Religious Research* 39(4) (1998): 360–370.

Milton, Giles. *Samurai William: The Englishman Who Opened Japan*. New York: Penguin, 2002.

Mitsuru, Hashimoto. "*Chihō*: Yanagita Kunio's 'Japan.'" In *Mirror of Modernity: Invented Traditions of Modern Japan*, ed. Stephen Vlastos. Berkeley: University of California Press, 1998, pp. 133–143.

Miyake, Hitoshi. *Shugendō: Essays on the Structure of Japanese Folk Religion*. Ann Arbor: University of Michigan Press, 2001.

Mizoguchi, Koji. *Archaeology, Society, and Identity in Modern Japan*. New York: Cambridge University Press, 2006.

Mori, Kōichi. "Yanagita Kunio: An Interpretive Study." *Japanese Journal of Religious Studies* 7(2–3) (1980): 83–115.

Morioka, Kiyomi. *Religion in Changing Japanese Society*. Tokyo: University of Tokyo Press, 1975.

Morris-Suzuki, Tessa. *Re-Inventing Japan: Time, Space, Nation*. New York: Sharpe, 1998.

Mullins, Mark R. "The Place of Ancestors in Buddhism and Christianity." http://www.kosei-shuppan.co.jp/english/text/mag/2007/07_789_3.html (accessed May 12, 2010).

———, Shimazono Susumu, and Paul L. Swanson, eds. *Religion and Society in Modern Japan*. Berkeley: Asian Humanities Press, 1993.

Murakami, Kōkyō. "Changes in Japanese Urban Funeral Customs during the Twentieth Century." *Japanese Journal of Religious Studies* 27(3–4) (2000): 335–352.

Nagahara, Keiji. "The Medieval Origins of the *Eta-Hinin*." *Journal of Japanese Studies* 5(2) (1979): 385–403.

Naito, Akira. *Edo, the City That Became Tokyo: An Illustrated History*. Tokyo: Kodansha International, 2003.

Nakamichi, Hirochika. "Memorial Monuments and Memorial Services of Japanese Companies: Focusing on Mount Kōya." Trans. Scott Schnell. In *Ceremony and Ritual in Japan*, ed. Jan Van Breman and D. P. Martinez. New York: Routledge, 1995.

Nakata, Hiroko. "Funeral: Japan's Funerals Deep-Rooted Mix of Ritual, Form," *Japan Times* (July 28, 2009). http://search.japantimes.co.jp/cgi-bin/nn20090728i1.html.

Nelson, John K. "Household Altars in Contemporary Japan: Rectifying Buddhist 'Ancestor Worship' with Home Décor and Consumer Choice." *Japanese Journal of Religious Studies* 35(2) (2008): 305–330.

———. *A Year in the Life of a Shinto Shrine*. Seattle: University of Washington Press, 1996.

Newman, J. P. *The Flowery Orient: Temples and Shrines in Heathen Lands*. Whitefish, Mont.: Kessinger, 2004.

Nishiyama, Matsunosuke. *Edo Culture: Daily Life and Diversions in Urban Japan, 1600–1868*. Honolulu: University of Hawaii Press, 1997.

Nozaki, Kiyoshi. *Kitsune: Japan's Fox of Mystery, Romance, and Humor*. Tokyo: Hokuseido, 1961.

Ohaka ga nai! Dir. Hara Takahito. 1998.

Okuribito. Dir. Takita Yōjirō. 2008.

Ono, Sokyo. *Shinto: The Kami Way.* Boston: Tuttle, 2004.

Ooms, Herman. "A Structural Analysis of Japanese Ancestral Rites and Beliefs." In *Ancestors*, ed. William H. Newell. The Hague: Mouton, 1976, pp. 61–90.

Osōshiki. Dir. Itami Jūzō. 1984.

Ota, Carol. *The Relay of Gazes: Representations of Culture in the Japanese Televisual and Cinematic Experience.* Lanham, MD.: Lexington, 2007.

Packard, Keiko Imai. *Images of Asia: Old Tokyo.* New York: Oxford University Press, 2002.

Pearce, Jean. *Foot-Loose in Tokyo: The Curious Traveler's Guide to the 29 Stages of the Yamanote Line.* New York: Weatherhill, 1976.

———. *More Foot-Loose in Tokyo: The Curious Traveler's Guide to Shitamachi and Narita.* New York: Weatherhill, 1984.

Pikul, Corrie. "Ancestor-Worship Chic: Do Cramped New Yorkers Want the Spirits of Their Departed Forebears as Roommates?" *New York Magazine* (July 24, 2006).

Plutschow, Herbert. *A Reader in Edo Period Travel.* Kent, UK: Global Oriental, 2006.

Pye, Michael. "Rationality, Ritual, and Life-Shaping Decisions in Modern Japan." In *Japan and Asian Modernities*, ed. Rein Raud. London: Kegan Paul, 2007, pp. 1–27.

Rambelli, Fabio. *Buddhist Materiality.* Stanford: Stanford University Press, 2007.

Raud, Rein. *Japan and Asian Modernities.* London: Kegan Paul, 2007.

Reader, Ian. "Back to the Future: Images of Nostalgia and Renewal in a Japanese Religious Context." *Japanese Journal of Religious Studies* 14(4) (1987): 287–303.

———. *Making Pilgrimages: Meaning and Practice in Shikoku.* Honolulu: University of Hawaii Press, 2006.

———. *Religion in Contemporary Japan.* Honolulu: University of Hawaii Press, 1991.

———, and George J. Tanabe Jr. *Practically Religious: Worldly Benefits and the Common Religion of Japan.* Honolulu: University of Hawaii Press, 1998.

Rogers, Lawrence, ed. and trans. *Tokyo Stories: A Literary Stroll.* Berkeley: University of California Press, 2002.

Rowe, Mark. "Grave Changes: Scattering Ashes in Contemporary Japan." *Japanese Journal of Religious Studies* 30(1–2) (2003): 85–118.

———. "Sticker for Nails: The Ongoing Transformation of Roles, Rites, and Symbols in Japanese Funerals." *Japanese Journal of Religious Studies* 27(3–4) (2000): 353–378.

———. "Where the Action Is: Sites of Contemporary Soto Buddhism." *Japanese Journal of Religious Studies* 31(2) (2004): 357–388.

Rowe, Peter. *East Asia Modern: Shaping the Contemporary City.* London: Reaktion, 2005.

Rozman, Gilbert. "Edo's Importance in the Changing Tokugawa Society." *Journal of Japanese Studies* 1(1) (1974): 91–112.

Saburo, Ienaga. "Japan's Modernization and Buddhism." *Contemporary Religions in Japan* 6 (1965): 1–41.

Sadler, A. W. "The Shrine: Notes toward a Study of Neighborhood Festivals in Modern Tokyo." *Asian Folklore Studies* 34(2) (1975): 1–38.

———. "The Tokyo Shrine Revisited." *Asian Folklore Studies* 51(1) (1992): 7–23.

Sakurai, Joji. "Afterlife Names Are Worth a Bundle to Buddhist Priests." *San Diego Union-Tribune* (April 4, 1999): A-31.

Sand, Jordan. *House and Home in Modern Japan: Architecture, Domestic Space, and Bourgeois Culture, 1880–1930.* Cambridge, Mass.: Harvard University Asia Center, 2005.

Schmidt, Petra. *Capital Punishment in Japan.* Leiden: Brill, 2002.

Schneede, Uwe M. *Edvard Munch: The Early Masterpieces.* London: Schirmer Art Books, 1988.

Schreiber, Mark. "A Ride on the Darker Side of Tokyo's History." *Japan Times* (September 15, 2002). http://search.japantimes.co.jp/cgi-bin/fl20020915a3.html.

Screech, Timon. "The Strangest Place in Edo: The Temple of the Five Hundred Arhats." *Monumenta Nipponica* 4(4) (1993): 407–428.

Seidensticker, Edward. *Low City, High City.* Rutland, Vt.: Tuttle, 1984.

———. *Tokyo Rising: The City since the Great Earthquake.* Cambridge, Mass.: Harvard University Press, 1990.

Seigle, Cecelia Segawa. *Yoshiwara: The Glittering World of the Japanese Courtesan.* Honolulu: University of Hawaii Press, 1993.

Shimazono, Susumu. "The Commercialization of the Sacred: The Structural Evolution of Religious Communities in Japan." *Social Science Japan Journal* 1(2) (1998): 181–98.

———. "Religious Influences on Japan's Modernization." *Japanese Journal of Religious Studies* 8(3–4) (1981): 207–222.

Shinno, Toshikazu. "From *Minkan-shinkō* to *Minzoku-shūkyō*: Reflections on the Study of Folk Buddhism." *Japanese Journal of Religious Studies* 20(2–3) (1993): 187–206.

Shioda, Michio. *Ueno-eki monogatari: Ueno to Asakusa o sodateta furusato eki.* Tokyo: Kossai Shuppansha, 1982.

Shively, Donald H. "Sumptuary Regulation and Status in Early Tokugawa Japan." *Harvard Journal of Asiatic Studies* 25 (1965): 123–164.

Shoji, Kaori. *Seeing Tokyo.* Tokyo: Kodansha International, 2006.

Silverberg, Miriam. "Constructing the Japanese Ethnography of Modernity." *Journal of Asian Studies* 51(1) (1992): 30–54.

Sizemore, Russell F., and Donald K. Swearer, eds. *Ethics, Wealth, and Salvation: A Study in Buddhist Social Ethics.* Columbia: University of South Carolina Press, 1990.

Smith, Robert J. *Ancestor Worship in Contemporary Japan.* Stanford: Stanford University Press, 1974.

Smyers, Karen A. *The Fox and the Jewel: Shared and Private Meanings in Contemporary Japanese Inari Worship*. Honolulu: University of Hawaii Press, 1999.

———. "Of Foxes, Buddhas, and Shinto Kami: The Syncretic Nature of Inari Beliefs." *Japanese Religions* 16(3) (1991): 62–64.

Sorensen, André. *Land Readjustment and Metropolitan Growth: An Examination of Suburban Land Development and Urban Sprawl in the Tokyo Metropolitan Area*. New York: Pergamon, 2000.

———. *The Making of Urban Japan: Cities and Planning of Edo to the Twenty-First Century*. New York: Routledge, 2002.

Suzuki, Hikaru. *The Price of Death: The Funeral Industry in Contemporary Japan*. Stanford: Stanford University Press, 2000.

Swanson, Paul L., and Clark Chilson, eds. *Nanzan Guide to Japanese Religions*. Honolulu: University of Hawaii Press, 2006.

Swyngedouw, Jan. "Religion in Contemporary Japanese Society." In *Religion and Society in Modern Japan*, ed. Mark R. Mullins, Shimazono Susumu, and Paul Swanson. Berkeley: Asian Humanities Press, 1993.

———. "Secularization in a Japanese Context." *Japanese Journal of Religious Studies* 3(4) (1976): 283–306.

Tamamuro, Fumio. "The Development of the Temple-Parishioner System." *Japanese Journal of Religious Studies* 36(1) (2009): 11–26.

———. "Local Society and the Temple-Parishioner Relationship within the Bakufu's Governance Structure." *Japanese Journal of Religious Studies* 28(3–4) (2001): 261–292.

Tanabe, George J., Jr. "The Orthodox Heresy of Buddhist Funerals." In *Death and the Afterlife in Japanese Buddhism*, ed. Jacqueline Stone and Mariko Namba Walter. Honolulu: University of Hawaii Press, 2008, pp. 325–345.

Tanigawa, Akio. "Excavating Edo's Cemeteries: Graves as Indicators of Status and Class." *Japanese Journal of Religious Studies* 19(2–3) (1992): 271–297.

Teeuwen, Mark, and Fabio Rambelli, eds. *Buddhas and Kami in Japan: Honji Suijaku as a Combinatory Paradigm*. London: RoutledgeCurzon, 2003.

Thompson, Christopher S., and John W. Traphagan, eds. *Wearing Cultural Styles in Japan: Concepts of Tradition and Modernity in Practice*. Albany: State University of New York Press, 2006.

Time Out Guide to Tokyo. London: Time Out Guides, 2007.

Time Out Shortlist Tokyo. London: Time Out Guides, 2008.

Tokyo: Shitamachi, Yamanote Wokkingu. Tokyo: JTB, 2008.

Tsurumi, E. Patricia, ed. *The Other Japan: Postwar Realities*. Armonk, N.Y.: Sharpe, 1988.

Umeda, Astushi. *Japan: A Bilingual Atlas*. Tokyo: Kodansha International, 1991.

Van Bremen, Jan, and D. P. Martinez, eds. *Ceremony and Ritual in Japan: Religious Practices in an Industrialized Society*. London: Routledge, 1995.

Vlastos, Stephen, ed. *Mirror of Modernity: Invented Traditions of Modern Japan.* Berkeley: University of California Press, 1998.

Waley, Paul. *Tokyo: City of Stories.* New York: Weatherhill, 1991.

———. *Tokyo Now & Then: An Explorer's Guide.* New York: Weatherhill, 1984.

Walters, Gary D'A. *Day Walks near Tokyo.* Tokyo: Kodansha International, 1992.

White, Merry Isaacs. *Perfectly Japanese: Making Families in an Era of Upheaval.* Berkeley: University of California Press, 2002.

Wicker, Christine. "How Spiritual Are We?" *Parade* (October 4, 2009): 4–5.

Wolferen, Karel Van. *The Enigma of Power.* New York: Vintage, 1989.

Worrall, Julian, Erez Golani Solomdon, and Joshua Lieberman. *21st-Century Tokyo: A Guide to Contemporary Architecture.* New York: Kodansha, 2010.

Wöss, Fleur. "Pokkuri-Temples and Aging: Rituals for Approaching Death." In *Religion and Society in Modern Japan*, ed. Mark R. Mullins, Shimazono Susumu, and Paul L. Swanson. Berkeley: Asian Humanities Press, 1993.

WORKS IN JAPANESE

Amino Yoshihiko. *Muen kugai raku: Nihon chūsei no jiyū to heiwa*, 2nd ed. Tokyo: Heibonsha, 1987.

Arakawa Genki. *Jiin handobukku: Bochi hen.* 1978. Rev. ed. Tokyo: Sansei shobō, 1988.

Ariga Kizaemon. *Mura no seikatsu sōshiki.* Tokyo: Miraisha, 1968.

Arikawa Ichihō. *Shitai wa shōhin! Warui sōgiya.* Tokyo: Deita hausu, 1992.

Asaka Katsusuke. "Kasōba no rekishi to henyō." In *Sōsō bunkaron*, ed. Sōsō bunka kenkyūkai. Tokyo: Kokon shoin, 1993.

———, and Yagisawa Sōichi. *Kasōba.* Tokyo: Daimeidō, 1983.

Asoya Masahiko and Tanuma Mayumi, eds. *Shinōsai shiryō shūsei.* Tokyo: Perikan, 1995.

Bokhoven, Jeroen. *Sōgi to Butsudan.* Tokyo: Iwata shoin, 2005.

Bunkachō. *Shūkyō nenkan, Heisei nana nen ban.* Tokyo: Gyōsei, 1996.

Chikazu Keishi. "Genze riyaku hitei no ronri." In *Nihon shūkuō no genze riyaku*, ed. Nihon Bukkyō kenkyūkai. Tokyo: Daizo shuppan, 1970, pp. 324–341.

Daitō Satoshi. *Otera no kane wa naranakatta.* Tokyo: Kyōikushirio shuppankai, 1994.

Edo Tokyo sanpo. Tokyo: Ninbunsha, 2003.

Fujii Masao, ed. *Sōgu daijiten.* Tokyo: Kamakura shinsho, 1995.

Gamō Masao. "Edo no machi zukuri." In *Dai-Edo mangekyō*, ed. Nō-san-gyo-son bunka kyōkai. Tokyo: Kumimotosha, 1991, pp. 58–65.

Gorai Shigeru. *Inari shinkō no kenkyū.* Okayama: Sanyō shimbunsha, 1985.

Haga Noburu. *Sōgi no rekishi.* Tokyo: Yūzankaku shuppan, 1991.

Hashimoto Mineo. *Ukiyo no shisō.* Tokyo: Kōdansha, 1975.

Hiramatsu Yoshirō. *Edo no tsumi to batsu.* Tokyo: Heibonsha, 1988.

Hiro Sachiya. *Bukkyō to Shintō*. Tokyo: Shinchō sensho, 1987.

Hiroata Masaki. *Sabetsu no shisō*. Vol. 22, Nihon kindai shisō taikei. Tokyo: Iwanami shoten, 1990.

Iijima Yoshiharu. "Genze riyaku no kami to wa nani ka." In *Nihon no kami*, vol. 2, ed. Yamaori Tetsuo. Tokyo: Heibonsha, 1995.

Inada Tsutomu and Ōta Tenrei. *Sōshiki muyōron*. Tokyo: Sōshiki o kaikakusurukai, 1968.

Inoue Haruo. *Ima sōgi, ohaka ga kawaru*. Tokyo: Sanseidō, 1993.

Inoue Yasumoto. *Bochi keiei*. Tokyo: Kokon shoin, 1941.

Kashiwara Yūsen. "Kinsei Shinshū to genze riyaku." In *Nihon shūkyō no genze riyaku*, ed. Nihon Bukkyō kenkyūkai. Tokyo: Daizō shuppan, 1970, pp. 238–252.

Kato Takahisa, ed. *Shinsōsai daijiten*. Tokyo: Ebisu kōshō shuppan, 1997.

Kida Minoru. *Kichigai buraku shūyū kikō*. Tokyo: Fusanbō, 1981.

Kimura Kiyotaka. "Dōgen to Inari." *Fushimi Inari Taisha "Aka"* 38 (1995): 41–45.

Kishino Seiryū. *Tokyo no otera/jinja: Nozo toki sanpo*. Tokyo: Koseidō, 2008.

Kobayashi Daiji. *Sabetsu kaimyō no rekishi*. Tokyo: Yūzankaku shuppan, 1987.

Kōseihō Seikatsu and Eiseikyoku Kikakuka, eds. *Chikujō kaisetsu: Bochi, maisō nado ni kan suru hōritsu*. Tokyo: Daiichi hōki shuppan, 1991.

Kotani Midori. *Senzō saishi no genjō to ohaka no kongo*. Tokyo: Raifu dezainu kenkyūjo, 1997.

Matsumae Takeshi, ed. *Inari myōjin: shōichii no jitsuzō*. Tokyo: Chikuma shobō, 1988.

Matsumura Kiyoshi. *Nihonjin wa Naze Kitsune wo Shinkōsurunoka?* Tokyo: Daishindō, 2006.

Miyamoto Kesayo. "Inari kami to bukkyō." *Daihorin* 51(10) (1984): 170–173.

Miyata Noboru. "Edo chōnin no shinkō." In *Edo chōnin no kenkyū*, vol. 2, ed. Nishiyama Matsunosuke. Tokyo: Yoshikawa kōbunkan, 1973, pp. 227–271.

———. *Yōkai no minzokugaku: Nihon no mienai kūkan*. Tokyo: Iwanami shoten, 1985.

Mizumoto Kunihiko. "Kōgi no saiban to shūdan no okite." In *Saiban to kihan: Nihon no shakaishi* 6, ed. Yamaguchi Keiji. Tokyo: Iwanami shoten, 1987, pp. 283–316.

Mog Mumon. *Sōshiki, hōji no shikata*. Tokyo: Yoyogi shoten, 1941.

Mori Kenji. *Haka to sōso no shakaishi*. Tokyo: Kōdansha, 1993.

Murakoshi Tomoyo. *Tama reien*. Tokyo: Tōkyōto kōen kyōkai, 1994.

Nakamura Naokatsu, ed. *OInari-san*. Tokyo: Asunarosha, 1976.

Nakamura Teiri. *Nihonjin no dōbutsukan: henshintan no rekishi*. Tokyo: Kameisha, 1984.

Namihira Emiko. *Kegare*. Tokyo: Tōkyōdō, 1985.

Naoe Hiroji, ed. *Inari shinkō*. Tokyo: Yūzankaku shuppan, 1983.

Natsume Soseki. *Kokoro*. Tokyo: 1914.

Nishio Ujizō, ed. *Bochi kokoroe*. Osaka: Nishio, 1985.

———. *Inari shinkō to shūkyō minzoku. Nihon shūkyō minzokugaku sōsho*, vol. 1. Tokyo: Iwata shoin, 1994.

Sakurai Tokutarō. *Nihon no shamanizumu: Minkan miko no denshō to seitai.* 2 vols. Tokyo: Yoshikawakō bunkan, 1974–1977.

Shibuya Kishū. *Anata no sōshiki, anata no ohaka.* Tokyo: San'ichi shobō, 1993.

Shigematsu Kazuyoshi. *Nihon keibatsu shiseki kō.* Tokyo: Seibundō, 1985.

Shimada Hiromi. *Kaimyō: naze shigo ni namae wo kaeru no ka.* Kyoto: Hōzōkan, 1994.

Sōgi Kaimyō: Koko Ga Shiritai. Tokyo: Daihōrinkaku, 1994.

Sōsai gojūnen: Kabushiki Kaisha Kōeskisha no ayumi. Osaka: Hōkōsha, 1982.

Takatori Masao. *Bukkyō dochaku.* Tokyo: Nihon hōsō shuppan kyōkai, 1973.

Takayanagi Kaneyoshi. *Hinin no seikatsu.* Tokyo: Oyamakaku, 1981.

Tamamuro Taijō. *Sōshiki Bukkyō.* Tokyo: Daihōrinkaku, 1963.

Tanaka Kiyoshi. *Aoyama Reien.* Tokyo: Tōyōto kōen kyōkai, 1994.

Toyokawa Kaku Myōgonji. *Reiba Toyokawa Inari.* Toyokawa shi, 1961.

———. *Toyokawa Inari shinkō annai*, ed. Fujii Toshimichi. Tokyo: Toyokawa Inari betsuin, 1978.

Ueda Noriyuki. *Ganbare Bukkyō! Otera runesansu no jidai.* Tokyo: NHK Books (Nihon hōsō shuppan kyōkai), 1994.

Watanabe Hiroshi. *The Architecture of Tokyo.* London: Menges, 2001.

Watanabe Masahito, ed. *Aruku, Tokyo: Chiyoda sen* [*Let's Walk Tokyo: Chiyoda ku*]. Tokyo: Kenji sumi, 2009.

Yanagawa Keiichi. *Matsuri to girei no shūkyōgaku.* Tokyo: Chikuma shobō, 1987.

Yasui Shirō. *Jitsuroku "Toyokawa Inari Monogatari."* Tokyo: Keizai, 1986.

Yoshida Hisashi. *Bochi shoyūkenron to bochi shiyōkenron.* Tokyo: Shinseisha, 1962.

Yoshino Hiroko. *Kitsune: Inyō gogyō to Inari shinko. Mono to ningen no bunka shi*, vol. 39. Tokyo: Hōsei daigaku shuppankyoku, 1980.

INDEX